C000068525

John Fulton, Paul Van Dyke

Ten Epochs of Church History

Vol. 7

John Fulton, Paul Van Dyke

Ten Epochs of Church History
Vol. 7

ISBN/EAN: 9783337865054

Printed in Europe, USA, Canada, Australia, Japan

Cover: Foto ©Lupo / pixelio.de

More available books at **www.hansebooks.com**

LIBRARY OF THE
UNIVERSITY OF VIRGINIA

PRESENTED BY

HENRY T. LOUTHAN

Ten Epochs of Church History

✱

Edited by

John Fulton, D.D., LL.D.

✱

Vol. VII.

Ten Epochs of Church History

THE

AGE OF THE RENASCENCE

AN OUTLINE SKETCH OF THE HISTORY OF THE PAPACY FROM THE RETURN FROM AVIGNON TO THE SACK OF ROME (1377–1527)

BY

PAUL VAN DYKE

WITH AN INTRODUCTION BY

HENRY VAN DYKE

New York
The Christian Literature Co.
MDCCCXCVII

CONTENTS.

PERIOD I.

From the Return from Avignon to the Accession of Nicholas V. (1377-1447).

INTRODUCTORY RETROSPECT.

v

PERIOD II.

From the Accession of the First Humanist Pope to the French Invasion of Italy (1447-1494).

AN INTRODUCTION

BY
HENRY VAN DYKE

AN INTRODUCTION.

HEN the writing of this book was proposed to me, some years ago, I undertook it with alacrity, on account of the interest in the subject which I had long cherished, and yet with some grave misgivings lest the pressure of other work, already promised, but not performed, should rob me of the time needed to accomplish this task with thoroughness and precision. For I knew the Age of the Renascence well enough, through previous studies from the literary, artistic, and philosophic points of view, to see that a man could not hope to make even an outline sketch of the Church in this complex period without much labor and steady thought.

The very brevity of the book proposed was an added difficulty. It is hard to be concise without becoming inaccurate. To make the results of study clear when the lack of space compels the omission of its processes; to justify conclusions without giving authorities; to condense volumes of reading into a chapter of writing, and that chapter again into a paragraph, and that paragraph into a single sentence; to select the characters of men who really embody

the tendencies of their age; and to find adjectives
which shall be equivalent to biographies, distinct and
vivid, without being unjust or violent;—in short, to
draw a convincing picture, not of a single generation
only, but of a movement which pervaded many generations and races, and to do this within the compass
of a few hundred pages, is an enterprise not to be
effected without serious toil.

Facing such a task as this, realizing its difficulties
more and more sharply as the plan of the book took
shape, and feeling at the same time the ever-increasing demands of other duties and literary engagements, I sought and gratefully welcomed the consent
of my brother to make this volume a joint labor of
fraternal authorship. Together we surveyed the
field, marked out its limitations, rejoiced in the rich-
ness of its promise, and groaned a little, yet not de-
spondently, at the prospect of the many hard places
and obstacles.

On this preliminary journey of exploration we
found ourselves in the full harmony of intellectual
comradeship. The purpose, the method, the guiding
principles of such a book as we wished to write
seemed to us plain and self-evident. Abstract theories of the nature of the Church troubled us little.
Special pleading for or against the Papacy disturbed
us even less. The question of absorbing interest was
not, What ought the Church to be in a correct scheme
of doctrine? but, What was the Church in the actual
unfolding of human life? What part did the ecclesiastical institution play in the conflicts of the Renascence? What did the idea of the Papacy mean as a

positive force, coöperating or conflicting with the other forces of the age? How far did it affect, and how far was it affected by, the influences which produced the great awakening of the fourteenth and fifteenth centuries? What was the real relation of the Church as an organization to Christianity as a spiritual life? How potently did that spiritual life make itself felt in the progress of the world?

The answer to these questions was not a matter of theory, but of fact.

We felt sure that it was not to be found in the books of dogmatic theology or ecclesiastical history, nor in the decrees of councils, nor in the bulls of Popes, nor in the theses of reformers—except in so far as all of these were veritable details in the great panorama of life. Their value lay, not in what they professed or claimed, but in what they actually represented. They were worth precisely what they expressed, reduced to the terms of reality.

The answer to our questions must be sought chiefly in the character of men and the history of nations. The type of ecclesiastical society produced by the contests between Pope and Antipope, the fashion of moral amelioration effected by the Reforming Councils, the style of humanity in which the spreading tree of Humanism bore its fruit—these were the things which we were drawn to study, and from which we hoped to derive some real and definite knowledge, to clarify our conception of the past, to broaden our judgment of the present, and to enlighten our vision of the future.

But as the work proceeded it became evident that

the lion's share of it must fall to my brother.   And
of this, for several reasons, I was very glad; chiefly
because I was sure that his leisure, his industry, and
his long previous studies in the special department of
ecclesiastical history fitted him for the more careful
and complete accomplishment of our design.   More-
over, there was a mortgage of other engagements,
particularly in connection with the Lectures on
Preaching at Yale University, in 1896, which more
than covered all my time and strength.

To his hands, therefore, the final execution of our
plan was committed. The collection of materials, the
workmanship, the filling in of the outline, are all his.
Such consultations as we have held in regard to the
work are not to be considered as in any sense edi-
torial or executive.   The book as it stands belongs
altogether to him.   Whatever credit it deserves for
scholarship, for clearness, for candor (and I hope that
is not small), must be given entirely to him.

For myself, it remains only to add this brief introduction, which I gladly do at his request, in order
that the formative ideas of the work may not be mis-
understood, nor its limitations overlooked.

It is a serious misfortune for a book when people
come to the reading of it without a perception of what
it offers to them. But it is a still greater misfortune
when they come with an expectation of finding what
it was never meant to offer; for in the latter case
they are inclined to lay upon the author the blame
of a disappointment which belongs more properly to
the reader, and to criticise as defects those necessary
omissions which belong to a consistent plan.

Let it be understood, then, at the outset, that this was not intended to be a small church history in the technical sense, nor even a fragment of a larger church history. The plan of the book was of a different nature. It was to give as graphic a view as possible of a single act in the great life-drama of humanity.

This act was the crisis of the Papal Church in that period of intellectual and social reconstruction called the Age of the Renascence, which transformed the mediæval into the modern world.

The scene opens with the return of the Pope from Avignon to Rome in 1377. It closes with the sack of Rome by the Spanish-German army, under the Duc de Bourbon, in 1527. Between these two points lies the dramatic story of a corrupt ecclesiastical body stubbornly resisting all attempts at reform from within and without, and at last succumbing to the pressure of great social and moral world-forces, which it was too prejudiced to comprehend, too proud to acknowledge, except for brief intervals, and too impotent to withstand, save with the fatal obstinacy of inherent weakness.

In sketching this story it was not intended to give full details of the various events and the manifold conflicts between nations and dynasties and parties and schools which entered into it. The exigencies of space would not permit this, even if the nature of the plan demanded it. Nor was it intended that the book should present references and lists of authorities to support its conclusions. Much as this might have been desired, it would be manifestly impossible

in such a brief compass.   Not even all of the great
features of the Age of the Renascence could be included.   The development of university life has been
barely touched; the artistic revival has been altogether passed over—to my own regret, but doubtless
for good reasons.

This wholesale process of omission was necessary
in order to make room on the small canvas for the
picture which we had in mind.   Details which were
not essential must be left out, lest they should obscure the vital features.   A process of negative ex-
aggeration must be used to arrive at a clear view of
the positive truth.

It would be better, for example, to omit the articles of many treaties, and the chronicles of many
dynastic wars, and the records of many synods and
councils, than to fail to give a vivid presentment of
such men as Petrarch, Boccaccio, Poggio, and Filelfo,
in Italy; Pierre d'Ailly, John of Gerson, and Faber
Stapulensis, in France; Wiclif, Colet, More, and
Tyndale, in England; Reuchlin and Ulrich von Hutten, in Germany; and Erasmus, that great intellectual cosmopolite.   These men, and others like them,
were, in fact, the makers of a new world in letters, in
morals, in manners.   It is impossible to know anything about the Age of the Renascence without getting at least a glimpse of these men as they lived and
moved and had their intellectual being.

Nor can the varying and tragic fortunes of the
Papacy during that eventful period be understood
without a clear, though swift, glance into the interior
life and personality of such popes as Nicholas V., the

first Humanist Pontiff; Pius II., the clever litterateur and diplomatist; Sixtus IV., the terrible man with many nephews; Alexander VI., the *Pontifex Maximus* of gallantry, whose patron goddess was Venus; Julius II., who ruled and fought under the sign of Mars; and Leo X., whose tutelary deity was Pallas Athene. From the first conception of this book it was intended to give more space to the graphic depiction of these and other like typical figures than to the formal narration of what is ordinarily called ecclesiastical history.

But it was foreseen at the outset that the actors in the drama would be found divided, by the crisis of events, into two classes, antagonistic, irreconcilable, and often apparently incapable of understanding each other. And so, in fact, it has proved to be in the writing of the book.

Here they stand, distinctly marked—the two great parties that have always contended for the guidance of mankind: the men of institutions, and the men of ideas; the men whose supreme allegiance binds them to an organization, and the men whose ultimate loyalty is to the truth; Wiclif and Huss and Savonarola and Hutten and Luther and Zwingli, against the Roman Curia and its defenders. Many of the men whose intellectual sympathies drew them to the party of ideas were bound by the deeper links of character to the party of institutions. To this class belong Reuchlin and Erasmus, Colet and More, Gerson and d'Ailly, and most of the elder Humanists. They were too fond of ancient order, too timid of change and confusion and possible misrule, ever to break with the Church, which obstinately resisted the reforming influence of ideas. But their personal hesitations were impotent to prevent the inevitable results of their work. Reuchlin might plead with his nephew Melancthon to beware of friendship with the heretical Martin Luther, but the affectionate solicitation went for nothing against the irresistible impulses of an awakened reason, a new-born scholarship, and a liberated conscience.

The younger Humanists, almost to a man, deserted the party of institutions for the party of ideas. The Bible was set free from the bondage of tradition and given to the common people—in German by Luther (1522), in French by Faber Stapulensis (1523), and in English by William Tyndale (1525). Thus the issue was clearly defined: Must a man believe what the Church teaches, no matter what the Bible says? or must the Church teach what men really believe, reading the Bible anew in the light of reason and the moral sense? Around this point the warfare of the Reformation was waged. It was the chief service of the Renascence as an intellectual and social movement that it brought this point of irrepressible conflict into distinct view, made it plain and distinct, and produced, in the service of literature and philosophy, the weapons which were at last used for the emancipation of faith.

In tracing the preliminary skirmishes of this mighty conflict, and describing the preparation of the armament with which it was to be fought, it was intended that this book should be impartial without being invertebrate. Our intention was to lay aside prejudices, but not to conceal convictions; to do justice to the character of men like Hadrian of Corneto, and the Cardinal Ximenes, and Adrian VI., without justifying their position. For, both in its conception and in its execution, this book proceeds from the standpoint that ideas are above institutions, and that liberty of reason and conscience is more precious than orthodoxy of doctrine.

Glancing forward over the contents of the volume as my brother has written it, I see that the composition of the picture, under his hands, has taken such a simple and natural form that it may be easily described in a few paragraphs.

First we have a brief review of the three forces which had changed the face of the world when the Pope came back to Rome from the Babylonian Captivity in France. The new patriotism, the new democracy, and the new learning—these were the equipollent and inseparable factors of the Renascence, now fully in action; and with these the Catholic Church had to reckon, if she would maintain her supremacy, or even her existence.

Then we have an account of the earnest efforts which were made to reform the Church from within. These efforts proceeded from four chief springs:

1. The revivals of religion in Italy, under the leadership of such enthusiasts as St. Catherine of Siena and Savonarola.

2. The national movement for reform in England, inspired by the teaching and influence of Wiclif and the Lollards.

3. The powerful after-echo of this movement in

Bohemia, under the guidance of John Huss and Jerome of Prague.

4. The party of Conciliar Supremacy in the Catholic Church, resisting the encroachments of Papal absolution, and demanding, through men like Gerson and d'Ailly, "the reform of the Church in head and members."

At the Council of Constance we see the last two of these forces falling foul of each other; and in the stories of Huss and Savonarola and the followers of Wiclif we read the fate of the men who dreamed that the Papacy could be reformed without the shedding of blood.

The four movements for the purification of the Church from within failed because they were essentially ecclesiastical. The tremendous momentum of the corrupt machine was too great to be checked by any resistance, save one which should have a firm foothold outside of the body to be checked, and abundant sources of independent strength. The ground for such a resistance was being prepared in Germany, in France, and in England during all the years of turmoil and shame and despair while the Papacy was punishing the passionate endeavors of the best members of the Church to reform it, and rewarding the successful conspiracies of its worst members to disgrace it.

The instrument of this preparation was the Renascence. It was not so much a mechanical alteration of the structure of human thought and society as it was a chemical change in the very elements of their composition. It transformed the scattered fragments of knowledge into the solid rock of scholarship. It metamorphosed the thoughts and feelings of men with the ardent heat of the love of learning, and crystallized their imaginations by the introduction of the historic spirit. It loosened, at least for a time, the solidarity of European Christendom; but it substituted for the treacherous débris of the failing sentiment of universal brotherhood, which no longer afforded a trustworthy footing, new points of coherence and support, in the sentiments of nationality and the patriotic enthusiasms which were begotten and intensified by the spread of historic knowledge and by the increase of once barbarous countries in wisdom, wealth, and power.

The book traces this process—hastily, of course, and in mere outline, and yet, it seems to me, with a true comprehension of its deep significance and far-reaching results. The endeavor of the writer is not to show what the Reformation added to the Renascence; that is another story, and belongs to a later volume. But this book is an attempt to exhibit what the Renascence did for the Reformation.

There can be no question whatever, and I think it can be seen from this book, that the two movements which were actually crowned with some measure of success in the purification of Christian faith and life —namely, the Protestant Reformation under Luther and Zwingli and Calvin, and the Catholic Reaction in the latter half of the sixteenth century—were both the legitimate offspring of the Renascence. If there had been no liberty of scholarship there never would have been an open Bible. If there had been no revival of patriotism the Germans never would have backed Luther against the world to defend his right of interpreting the Scriptures.

And so if the book is to have a lesson drawn from it, it must be this: The fortunes of the Church as an institution depend upon the same laws which God has implanted in all human society, and through which He continually manifests His presence and power. There is no ecclesiastical history apart from secular history. The Church which rests upon authority alone must take its chances with the other dynasties. No appeal to the supernatural can shield its pretensions from the searching tests of reason and conscience. The Christianity which is to survive and maintain its claims in the face of the world must be in harmony with the primal moral forces, love of liberty, love of truth, love of real goodness.

HENRY VAN DYKE.

NEW YORK, July 22, 1897.

PERIOD I.

FROM THE RETURN FROM AVIGNON TO THE ACCESSION OF NICHOLAS V. (1377–1447).

INTRODUCTORY RETROSPECT.

(CHAPTERS I., II., III.)

THE FORCES THAT HAD CHANGED THE CONDITIONS OF POWER DURING THE SEVENTY YEARS OF THE PAPAL ABSENCE FROM ROME.

CHAPTER I.

THE GROWTH OF PATRIOTISM OR THE SENSE OF NATIONALITY.

ON the 17th of January, 1377, all Rome was early afoot, and a great crowd streamed across the fields of Mount Aventinus to the gate of St. Paul, opening toward the sea. There the clergy of the city were gathered in festal array to receive the Pope. Landing from his galley, which had ascended the river from Ostia and lain at anchor all night just below the great Basilica of St. Paul without the Walls, Gregory XI. heard mass, and the festal procession started to enter the gate. Two thousand men-at-arms, commanded by his nephew, Raymond, Vicomte of Turenne, guarded the gorgeous train.   Behind the great banner of the Church, borne by the gray-haired Grand Master of the Knights of Rhodes, came the Pope, riding on a splendidly caparisoned palfrey beneath a baldachin carried by Roman nobles.   Around him moved a glittering cavalcade of cardinals and bishops, and a company of white-robed clowns and tumblers, the usual companions of all stately processions, heralded his approach.   In the gate stood the Senator of Rome in full armor, with the councillors and captains, waiting to put into Gregory's hands the keys of the city.   As he passed on his long journey through the fields and streets to the other side of the circle of walls, the entire population greeted him with shouts of joy.   Every bell was ringing, and from the crowded roofs and windows of the houses wreaths and flowers were showered into streets hung with tapestry and banners.   It was evening before the slow procession reached St. Peter's, brilliant with eighteen thousand lamps, and the exhausted Pope could at last kneel by the tomb of the apostles to give thanks to God for his return to the city of the Church.   So after a willing exile of seventy years the successor of St. Peter came back from the huge new palace on the banks of the Rhone to the ancient Vatican on the banks of the Tiber.

It was the end of the alliance of the Papacy with the house of France, called by all but those who caused and profited by it the " Babylonian Captivity of the Church."   Five successive Popes, each bishop of the bishops because he was Bishop of Rome, had never entered their cathedral of the Lateran, and

Christendom rejoiced when Gregory had returned to his first duty.

But while the Popes had been neglecting their own city to become the allies and then the vassals of the kings of France, three generations had made a new world, and the opportunities and conditions of power were changed. Old institutions were decayed, and new social, political, and religious forces were finding expression.

The first of these great forces limiting the power of the Papacy was the newly developed *sense of nationality*. In order to appreciate the bearing of this new force on problems of the government of the Church we must recall by suggestion the past relations of the Papacy to the political organization of Europe. When Christianity was made the religion of the Roman Empire under Constantine it became part of an ideal in which all nations were to form a single social organism holding one faith and obeying one government. And even when the barbarian invasion had broken the wall of Trajan and overrun Gaul, Spain, Italy, and Africa, men still mistook memories for hopes and looked to see order brought out of chaos by the reëstablishment of the law of the empire. The very conquerors gazed with awe upon the mighty social organization they had overthrown. Able to destroy, but not to create, they respected the Roman law and the Roman Church, and permitted their subjects to be judged by the one and consoled by the other. And as successive waves of invasion poured in till it seemed as if the richest and most civilized lands of the ancient world were to become the desolate possessions of predatory tribes, the thoughts of men turned with increasing desire toward the unity and peace which had been the ideal of the empire. So when the Franks had beaten back the Saracens from the plain of Tours, saving Europe, like the Greeks before them, from slavery to Asia, they aspired to the yet greater task of reëstablishing the Empire of the West to give peace and justice from the Mediterranean to the Baltic and from the ocean to the Danube. Charles the Great, perhaps the one most necessary and indispensable man in the history of the Western races, gathered together all the forms of law and religion in which there seemed a possibility of life, and on Christmas day of the year 800 was crowned by Pope Leo III. Emperor of the West. The ideal which this ceremony expressed is clearly shown in a mosaic designed by order of the Pope. Christ appears in it twice : above, as Saviour, surrounded by the apostles, whom he is sending forth to preach ; below, seated as ruler of the world. On his right kneels Pope Sylvester, on his left the Emperor Constantine ; to the one he is handing the keys of heaven and hell, to the other the banner of the Cross. In the opposite arch the Apostle Peter sits, with Leo and Charles kneeling on either hand to receive the pallium of an archbishop and the banner of the Church militant. The circumscription is, " Glory to God in the highest, and on earth peace to all men of good will." The makers of that mosaic hoped they had founded a divine institution with two heads, one supreme in spiritual, the other in temporal things, and both holding their power of God.

But the double eagle of Russia is not more impossible in the animal kingdom than the realization of this ideal in the realm of practical politics. The mediæval Church was so much of an empire, and the mediæval empire so much of a church, that neither seems to have been able to maintain its power for any long period without the aid of the other. But in spite of this common need it is difficult to find any pair of a great Pope and a great emperor who could dwell together in peace.

When the empire was weak the undefended Papacy became the prey of the fierce factions of the Roman nobility, and Popes who disgraced the throne of St. Peter sank to every conceivable depth of infamy. When a strong emperor defended by Teutonic soldiers the purity of elections and placed upon the throne a man worthy the office, he or his successor began a desperate struggle to secure those rights of appointing or investing bishops and abbots which the Emperor claimed for himself. In this struggle the Papacy had two favorite weapons: first, to stir up rebellion in the empire by means of the interdict and excommunication; and second, to create outside of the bounds of the empire a system of states whose rulers were willing to acknowledge, what the successors of Charles always denied, that the Popes not only consecrated, but conferred their authority and crowns. This policy, begun under Sylvester II. (999–1003), created, by direct gift of the crown through the Pope as the Vicar of Christ and ruler of rulers, a tier of kingdoms between the borders of the Eastern and Western empires: Hungary, 1000, Poland soon after, Croatia, 1076, Servia and Bulgaria in the thirteenth century. Then the Popes turned to the south and west to create the kingdoms of Naples, Aragon, Portugal, the Island of Man, the kingdoms of Scotland, Norway, the double kingdom of Corsica-Sardinia, and the kingdom of Trinacria. The English King became a feudal vassal of the Pope, and some of his successors paid tribute in a subjection considered so complete that a legate who took off his cap in the presence of the King was much blamed at the Papal court. Clement VI., going out into the unknown, even created (1344) for Louis of Castile a kingdom of the yet undiscovered Fortunate Isles. The swords of the vassals of the Papacy and the power to give the sanctions of religion to every rebellious vassal of the empire made the Popes too strong for the emperors. The last members of the imperial house of Hohenstaufen died in a vain attempt to maintain their power over the kingdom of Sicily, which the Popes had given to Charles of Anjou to be held as a fief of the Church. For sixty years there was no emperor, and when Henry VII., half by force and half by entreaty, received the crown at the Lateran from the hands of a cardinal in a ceremony shorn of many of its ancient rites, his rebellious Italian subjects held St. Peter's, and the bolts of their crossbows fell among the guests at the imperial banquet.

The end and aim of the Papal policy was clearly shown when Boniface VIII. changed the ancient mitre for the modern triple Papal crown and appeared before the pilgrims of the jubilee of 1300 one day in the Papal, the next in the imperial robes, shouting aloud, " I am Cæsar—I am Emperor!" [1]

But in destroying the empire and trusting their defence to the system of Papal States they had created, the Popes had prepared a weapon that could be turned against themselves. Kings, once grown strong, were as unwilling as emperors to submit to Papal control. France, from whom came the blow which revealed the hollowness of this Papal politics, was not, indeed, a member of the system of Papal States. Her kings had grown great without becoming vassals of the throne of St. Peter. But as against the empire she had always been closely allied to it, and the brother of King Louis had done homage to Clement IV. (1265) for the kingdom of Sicily, and become the protagonist in the fight against the empire which extinguished the race of Hohenstaufen. Philip the Hardy, however, cared little for past alliances, and his final answer to the pretensions of Boniface was to assault him in his own palace at Anagni (1303) by a band of mercenaries—a degradation so bitter to the proud old man that he died in a few weeks. His successor ruled a little more than a year, and after a conclave of nine months, the lobbying of Philip elected a Pope who transferred the chair of St. Peter to the banks of the Rhone. During the seventy years it remained there the preponderance of French

[1] There is some doubt as to the exactness of this anecdote, but none about the bull Unam Sanctam, which in 1302 asserted: "There are two swords, the temporal and the spiritual; both are in the power of the Church, but one is held by the Church herself, the other by kings only with the assent and by sufferance of the Sovereign Pontiff. Every human being is subject to the Roman Pontiff, and to believe this is necessary for salvation."

influence became steadily more evident. The proportion of Frenchmen in the College of Cardinals increased. Now it was thirteen out of eighteen, now it rose to twenty-five out of twenty-eight, and again to nineteen out of twenty-one. In one short space of a few years the Papacy and the Pope's brother lent 3,500,000 florins (probably equal in purchasing power to $40,000,000) to the French court.

From a Vicar of Christ who had abandoned the ancient capital of the world to become the tool of a French king men turned instinctively to the eternal King he represented, and the victorious English soldiers at Poictiers showed the error of the Papacy and the drift of events when they sang:

> " If the Pope is French,
> Christ is English."

In England this Papal subservience to the interests of France strengthened the ancient opposition to the interference of the Pope in English affairs. And in particular Englishmen resented the sale of ecclesiastical offices to foreign incumbents, who without ever visiting their charges drew the rents and incomes by proxies and spent them in the luxurious Papal court at Avignon. England had thrilled at the letter of good old Robert of Lincoln protesting against the order of the Pope bestowing a canonry in his cathedral upon an Italian, Frederick of Lavagna (1253). He declined to obey it as unapostolic, declaring it to be, " not a cure, but a murder of souls," " when those who are appointed to a pastoral charge only use the milk and the wool of the sheep to satisfy their own bodily necessities." And one hundred years later the Parliament (1351–53) forbade by statute the introduction into England of provisors or Papal bulls which interfered with the filling of English ecclesiastical offices by Englishmen, and forbade appeals to Rome by which causes involving the persons or property of ecclesiastics could be freed from the law of England. It was that revolt of patriotism against ecclesiastical encroachment, often felt by those entirely faithful to the spiritual teaching of the Catholic Church, which found its classic expression, eight generations later, in the words which Shakespeare put into the mouth of King John :

> " No Italian priest
> Shall tithe or toll in our dominions ;
> But as we under Heaven are supreme head,
> So under him, that great supremacy,
> Where we do reign we will alone uphold,
> Without the assistance of a mortal hand.
> So tell the Pope ; all reverence set apart,
> To him and his usurped authority."

Even in Germany, a prey to the greed of rapacious princelings whose people were to wait five hundred years for national unity, the assumptions of a Pope who seemed to use temporal control as a tool of the French King called out the spirit of patriotism without the form thereof. Pope John XXII. (1316–34) longed to free Italy from foreign influence and unite the entire peninsula under the political headship of the Papacy. He endeavored to accomplish this by diplomacy, and as a move in his deep and dangerous game of politics it became needful to depose Lewis of Bavaria from the kingship of Germany. Taking advantage of the party strifes of the German princes, the Pope drove him by ban and interdict to the utmost straits.   But when Lewis, in despair, was on the point of surrendering his claim to the crown, the publication of a single fact put all Germany for the moment behind him.   His rival had secretly agreed to pledge the ancient kingdom of Arelat to France as security for costs incurred by the King in acting as mediator between the empire and the Pope.   A storm of wrath denounced the bargain.   Then the Pope issued a bull separating the Italian lands of the empire from all connection with the kingdom of Germany.   All Germany rose at the insult, and for the first time in generations almost every German city and prince and bishop joined in common action.   By the vote of six of the great princes, confirmed by a Reichstag at Frankfort, disordered and disunited Germany declared that "the imperial dignity and power proceeded from of old directly through the Son of God. . . . Because, nevertheless, some, led by ambition and without understanding of Scripture, . . . falsely assert that the imperial dignity comes from the Pope, . . . and by such pestiferous dogmas the ancient enemy moves discord . . . and brings about seditions, therefore we declare that by the old right and custom of the empire, after any one is chosen emperor . . . he is in consequence of the election alone to be called true king and emperor of the Romans, and ought to be obeyed by all subjects of the empire."

CHAPTER II.

NEW THEORIES OF THE SEAT OF SOVEREIGNTY AND THE RISING TIDE OF DEMOCRACY.

HIS political change, by which during the thirteenth century the peoples became conscious of their national aspirations, found expression in theories concerning the seat of authority and the nature of power. Literature, which in the hands of the school-men had become the advocate of Papal claims, began to express the strongest and most searching criticism of them. About the court of the Emperor gathered a little knot of men of different nations, whose brilliant polemic writings attracted attention by the boldness and skill with which they attacked the whole logical edifice of the scholastic theory of Papal Supremacy. The English Franciscan, William of Occam, the most distinguished philosopher of his day; the Fleming, Jean of Jandun, celebrated dialectician of the Paris schools; the Italian, Michael of Cesena, General of the Franciscans; Brother Bonagratia, the distinguished theologian and jurist; the German, Henry of Thalheim, and others, formed the strongest literary coterie of the age, with Marsilius

11

of Padua, a well-known lawyer and physician, as
their brightest star.   His book, " The Defender of
Peace against the Usurped Jurisdiction of the Roman
Pontiff," was a daring arraignment and reversal of
traditional judgments about the source of authority
in Church and State.   For instance, he asserts that
" church " in its apostolic use means the entire body
of Christian men, and that all Christians, be they
clergy or laymen, are churchmen.   Temporal pains
and penalties do not belong to the law of the Gospel,
which is not a law at all, but a doctrine.   " Bishop"
and " priest " are used interchangeably in the New
Testament.   The popedom, a useful symbol of the
unity of the Church, is an institution begun later
than the apostolic age, whose historical growth is
clearly traceable.   The bishops of Rome gained pre-
eminence, not as St. Peter's successors, but from
the connection of their see with the ancient capital of
the Roman Empire.   The sovereignty of the State
rests with the people.   By them the laws are properly
made, and their validity comes from the people's
sovereignty.   The community of the citizens, or their
majority, expressing its will by representatives, is
supreme.   Government requires a unity of office, not
necessarily of number.   But if, as is usually wisest,
a king be chosen, he must be supported by enough
force to overpower the riotous few, but not the mass
of the nation.   In the ecclesiastical organization, also,
the authority rests not with the hierarchy, but is
derived from the whole Church, and the priestly class
are only their executives, responsible to a General
Council formed of clergy and laity alike.   The clergy

are the executives of the Church only in spiritual affairs. Their property and incomes are as much subject to the civil law as those of their lay brethren. His office does not change the responsibility of a clergyman to the civil law, for if he should steal or murder, who would say that these were to be regarded as spiritual acts? These opinions were formally condemned by the ecclesiastical authorities, and Marsilius was denounced as a radical innovator who would destroy Church and State.

Such bold denials of the theories which had been formed to support the social and ecclesiastical institutions of the middle ages had but little direct effect outside of the circle of clerks and theologians to whom they were addressed, but they were dimly felt and half-unconsciously formulated during the fourteenth century in political changes by which the feudal power and privileges of civil and ecclesiastical lords were in some places checked, in others destroyed, by the efforts of a middle class of burgher merchants or manufacturers and small landed freeholders. And behind and beneath these political changes there could be heard the half-articulate murmur of the rising tide of democracy, with its claim that men are equal before God and the laws, and its hope of a society so organized and governed that none should ever want but the idle and vicious.

It has been well said that mediæval man was chiefly occupied with the acquisition or defence of privileges. Feudal society was divided into very strictly separated classes, and the unwritten principle at its foundation was that all rights not expressly granted to a lower class were reserved for the higher.   Time had been when the enjoyment of these privileges meant the performance of certain necessary duties.   The castle of the lord, around which the wattled mud huts of the peasants clung like swallows' nests, may have been the abode of tyranny, but it was also a refuge from robbery.   To be unbound to any community, large or small, which thus possessed a leader and the means of self-protection, was to be exposed to unlimited outrage in a time when every man did that which was right in his own eyes to all who did not belong to his own community.   And it came to pass that to be a landless man was to be thought an outlaw, and to be a lordless man a thief. But as society became more orderly and private war less incessant, these privileges became oppressive to a people no longer bound to their superiors by perils shared, or grateful for defence against danger.   And peasant and burgher, chafing under the bondage of those to whom they were compelled to render services without service in return, began everywhere to long passionately for legal equality or freedom. A single circumstance gave force to this long-cherished desire.   Misery alone is sterile, and the dead weight of injustice will either crush a people to a servile temper or provoke a despair that perishes by its own ferocity.   The consciousness of power is needed to animate a useful revolution.   And during the fourteenth century this consciousness was diffused among the common people in some parts of western Europe by the demonstration of the irresistible force on the battle-field of a properly drilled and handled infantry. So long as the knight, with a couple of esquires and a score of professional men-at-arms cased in steel, mounted on heavy horses, and trained to ride and fence, was more than a match for the men of a dozen villages who had never learned how to march or to hold the simplest formation, revolt among the lower classes meant only the treacherous and useless murder of some isolated oppressors.

It was just at the turn of the thirteenth century (1302) when the shock of Courtrai sounded through the world. Twenty thousand Flemish artisans were brought to bay in a great plain by the much larger army of France. The few dispossessed nobles who were their military leaders killed their horses and knighted thirty merchants as a sign of fellowship, and shouting their war-cry of " Shield and friend!" the solid mass of men stood stoutly with boar-spears and iron-shod clubs against the French charge. In two hours fifteen thousand fallen men-at-arms choked the ditch which guarded their front, or were scattered over the plain. They covered the walls of the cathedral of Courtrai with the gilded spurs of the knights, and the roll of the dead sounds like a muster of the nobility of France—" fallen," as the chronicler laments, " by the hands of villeins." This consciousness of power gave hope, and from hope came effort. Therefore the fourteenth century is marked in many parts of the world by desperate struggles for liberty on the part of the peasant and artisan classes rising out of a half-servile condition.

The relation of this struggle to religion, and to the social and moral conditions with which religion is concerned, may best be illustrated by the English peasant revolt of 1381, which, long misjudged through the reports of its enemies, apparently a failure, is now recognized as one of the most remarkable and successful of revolutions.   In the middle of the century the power of the English peasant was suddenly increased by a singular cause.   The black death, starting in those crowded cities of Asia which have always been the homes of pestilence, spread slowly but steadily over Europe.   It is difficult to appreciate the horror of its visit in an age when the simplest rules of sanitary science were unknown and medical practice little more than superstition.   Cautious judges concede that twenty-five millions of people perished.   In England alone a conservative estimate allows that eight hundred thousand people, one third of the total population, died by a " foul death," which smote the children of the king and the children of the slave, so that there was not a house where there was not one dead.   As a consequence labor became so scarce that the price of it rose at once.   The noble whose crop cost to harvest £3 13s. 9d. the year before the plague had to pay £12 19s. 10d. the year after.   This situation hastened the process of freeing the *nativi*, or serfs, which had begun years before.   For those personal services, such as ploughing one day every week in the year, gathering the lord's nuts, making the lord's park walls over against his land, carrying the lord's corn home every fortnight on the Saturday, which reminded the tenants of their descent from bondsmen and thralls, were then quite largely commuted by the impoverished lords for money payments.

But the landowners who farmed by bailiffs were

not disposed to see their profits impaired and their rents lowered without a struggle. And as soon as the cessation of the plague enabled Parliament to meet, they passed the Statute of Laborers, which stood on the books for two hundred and fifty years. It provided that every able-bodied man or woman under sixty must work for any employer who sought him for suitable service at the wages of the year 1347, prohibited him from leaving his employer before the end of his term of service, forbade his employer to pay him higher wages, and provided penalties of fine or imprisonment for disobedience. It even forbade the employer to fulfil contracts for higher wages made before the passing of the act.

This law was met by the establishment of a vast secret combination of artisans and peasants,—the first trade-union,—which was so successful that twenty years after the plague the price of harvest labor was double that enforced by the statute. Then the lords, in despair, attempted to reverse the commutations to their ancient equivalents in forced labor. The result was to them a tremendous astonishment. The villeins of all England rose in revolt. For this they had been partly prepared by preaching, which gave the sanction of religion to their demand for justice. Men like John Ball, a priest of Kent, out of whose sermons were made such popular rhymes as:

> " When Adam delved and Eve span,
> Who was then the gentleman? "

had for years been denouncing the wickedness of the rich and the injustice of social and political conditions. They were now reinforced by priests armed

B

with the new knowledge of the Bible which was spreading rapidly from the teaching of the friends and pupils of Wiclif.   And many a hamlet heard the stern appeals of the prophets from tyranny to God applied to their own times.   So it was that when the southern force of the insurgents, entering London by the help of their sympathizers among the citizens, fired the palace of the Duke of Lancaster, they flung a plunderer caught with a silver cup back into the flames saying " they were seekers of truth and justice, not thieves."   It was this moral and religious basis of the rising which made the northern army of insurgents, when London lay at their mercy, receive the simple promise of their boy King to " free them and their lands forever, that they should be no more called serfs," with shouts of joy, and to quietly disperse to their homes with charters which, before the ink was dry, their King was secretly promising his councillors to wash out in blood.   But though the insurrection was conquered by treachery, and its leaders died by hundreds on the gallows, it did not fail.   Parliament revoked the concessions of the King and professed a willingness to perish all together in one day rather than grant " liberties and manumissions to their villeins and bond-tenants," but the peril had been too great for a second risk.   From that day to this many English-speaking men have ground the face of the poor; but since 1381, when the peasants were taught by the Poor Priests[1] to use

---

[1] It is not established that Wiclif gave any personal encouragement to the rising, but rather the contrary.   There is, however, an unmistakable spiritual resemblance between it and his teaching.

their power in the demand for the rights of humanity in the name of God and justice, no one has attempted to make serfs of the English laborers. And this spirit of democracy, the desire for freedom or equal rights before God and the laws, appealing against every caste and privilege in Church or State to conscience and the Bible, had during the seventy years of the Papal absence from Rome become a force which had everywhere to be reckoned with.

CHAPTER III.

THE NEW LEARNING.

PETRARCH, THE PROTOTYPE OF THE HUMANISTS.

THE general movement of the human spirit during the fourteenth century, producing patriotism, new theories of the seat of authority, and the desire for freedom, found a special expression for itself in Italy in the beginnings of the New Learning or the movement of the Humanists. This used, by a narrowness of thought and diction, to be called the Renascence, but is now rightly regarded as only the intellectual centre of that broad movement which affected every side of life.

To define so complex a movement as the New Learning is impossible. It can best be made clear in a sketch of the work and character of Petrarch, the prophet and prototype of Humanism, who died at Arqua, near Padua, three years before the return of the Papacy from Avignon.

His father was a Florentine notary, banished by the same decree with Dante, who finally settled at Avignon to practise his profession in the neighbor-

hood of the Papal court. In the jurists' library
were some manuscripts of Cicero, and as soon as
Petrarch could read he loved them. Doubtless his
father, who destined the lad for the law, smiled
approval at such appropriate tastes. But he soon
found out his mistake. This youngster with a voice
of extraordinary power and sweetness, who loved to
play his lute and listen to the song of the birds, was
not seeking in the works of the great Roman lawyer
legal information. It was the majestic swing, the
noble music, of the Ciceronian Latin which charmed
him, and as the years went on he suffered the pangs
which have been common in all ages to the lovers of
the Muses held by parental worldly wisdom to the
study of the law. Bad reports came back from the
tutors of Montpellier and Bologna. Reproaches and
excuses ended in a parental raid, which discovered
under the bed a hidden treasure of tempting manuscripts. They were promptly condemned to the
flames, and only the tears of the lad saved a Virgil
and one speech of Cicero, to be, as the father said,
smiling in spite of himself at the desperate dismay of
the convicted sinner, one for an occasional leisure
hour, the other a help in legal studies. And Virgil
and Cicero became to Petrarch lifelong companions.
The copy of the Æneid thus saved from the flames
had been made by his own hand, and he wrote
in it the date of the death of his son, his friends,
and the woman he loved. It was stolen from him
once, and returned after ten years, and he wrote
in it the day of its loss and the day of its return.
To Petrarch Virgil was "lord of language," a char-

acter noble as his genius, half poet and half saint, a divine master. But to say this was only to repeat Dante, and Petrarch did little for the influence of the Mantuan—could not, indeed, escape from that habit of allegorical interpretation which thought of a poet as a riddle-maker whose object was not to make truth clear and beautiful, but obscure.

But Petrarch may with truth be called the modern discoverer of Cicero. Not, indeed, that Cicero's name was before unknown, but that Cicero's works were little read and still less understood. Many of his finest pieces had not been seen for generations. And from his youth up Petrarch followed like a sleuth-hound every possible trace of a lost manuscript. When, riding along the roads, he caught sight of an old cloister, his first thought was, " Is there a Cicero manuscript in the library?" In the midst of a journey he suddenly determined to stop at Liege, because he heard there were many old books in the city, and his reward was two unknown speeches of Cicero. He not only hunted himself, but as his circle of friends and his means increased, he spread his efforts to Germany, Greece, France, Spain, and Britain—wherever any chance of a find was suggested. Of course he had his disappointments. Once he imagined he had secured the lost " Praise of Philosophy "; but though the style was Cicero's, he could read nothing in it to account for Augustine's enthusiasm, which had first put him on the track. At last the doubt was ended, for he found a quotation in another writing of Augustine's which was not in his manuscript. He was the victim of a false title. And when he discovered that what he had was an extract of the "Academica," he always afterward rated it as one of the least valuable of Cicero's works. Then he thought that he had found the treatise on "Fame." He loaned the volume which contained it, and neither he nor the world has ever seen it since —surely the costliest book loan on record.[1]

But no disappointment damped his enthusiasm. When the manuscript of Homer was sent to him as a present from Constantinople, though he could read no word of Greek, nor find any one who could, he knew that this was the book beloved of Horace and Cicero. He took it in his arms and kissed it. How great must have been his joy when, in the cathedral library of Verona, he unexpectedly stumbled on an old half-decayed manuscript of some of Cicero's letters! He was sick and tired, but he would trust his frail treasure to no copyist. He announced his find to Italy in an epistle to Cicero himself, and henceforth he enriched literature by a stream of citations whose source, warned by experience, he never trusted out of his own hands. Why he never allowed it to be copied during his lifetime can best be explained by those collectors who dislike to have replicas made of their pictures. Nor was he content with the writings of antiquity. The portraits of Roman emperors on coins excited his imagination. Others had collected coins and medals as rarities, but he was the first modern to understand their value as historical monuments.

---

[1] Voigt says there is no proof that it really was the treatise on "Fame." But his doubt seems based only on the general principle that a lost fish increases in size—which is not always true.

From the great men of the past he learned to exercise a common-sense criticism on the methods and results of the traditional learning of his time. In scorn and enthusiasm he flung himself with all his powers on the scholastic system of instruction, and denounced the universities as nests of ignorance, adorning fools with pompous degrees of master and doctor. In particular he objected to the division of disciplines. If he were asked what art he professed he would answer that there was but one art, of which he was a humble disciple: the art of truth and virtue, which made the wisdom of life. But he was not content with vague denunciation. The professors of every discipline—history, arithmetic, music, astronomy, philosophy, theology, and eloquence—heard his voice accusing them of an empty sophistry without real relation to life.

The objects of his first and bitterest attacks were astrology and alchemy, whose pretensions then flattered the ear of princes and dazzled the hopes of peasants. He denounced astrology, stamped with the authority of a teacher's chair at Bologna and Padua, as a baseless superstition, and, in the very spirit of Cicero toward the augurs, related with glee how a court astrologer of Milan had told him that, though he made a living out of it, the whole science was a fraud. He accused the physicians also of being charlatans. When Pope Clement VI. was ill, Petrarch wrote a letter warning him against them. He was wont to say that no physician should cross his threshold, and when custom compelled him to receive them in his old age, wrote with humor of his persistence in neglecting all their orders and his consequent return to health. But he made far more effective attacks than any mere witty expression of a personal mood. To his friend the distinguished physician Giovanni Dondi he gave strong reasons for his scorn of the ordinary practitioner. He did not deny that there might be a science of medicine. He suggested that the Arabs had made the beginnings of it. But he denied to the empirics and pretenders who were imposing on the people by wise looks and long words every title of real learning. And he pointed out as the path to a science of health and disease the entirely different method of modern medicine. The lawyers so hated in his youth felt the lash of his invective. He called them mere casuists, splitting hairs in a noble art once adorned by the learning and eloquence of Cicero, but sunk to a mere way of earning bread by clever trickery in the hands of men ignorant and careless of the origin, history, and relations of the principles of law. And he took a keen delight in pointing out the blunders in history and literature made by the greatest jurist of his time. But it was in philosophy that he came into sharpest conflict with the scholastic method, which hung like a millstone around the neck of learning. To make dialectics an end instead of a means he called putting the practice of boys into the place of the finished wisdom of men. Logic was only an aid to rhetoric and poetry, and ideas worth far more than the words which the schoolmen put in their place. When they hid behind the shield of Aristotle, Petrarch was not dismayed. In the pamphlet " Concerning his Own Ignorance and that of Many Others " he dared to say that Aristotle was a man and there was much that even he did not know.   And he finally asserted that, while no one could doubt the greatness of Aristotle's mind, there was in all his writings no trace of eloquence—a word which took as much courage to cast as the stone from the shepherd's sling that freed Israel.

It was the word of an independent.   And this independence, this assertion of his personal individual judgment, marks the second service of Petrarch. He was not only a critic of scholastic methods and an instaurator of learning, but he threw a high light on the value of the individual.

We have seen why the mediæval man instinctively regarded himself as one of a class.   The serf or burgher, noble or ecclesiastic,was a member of a great corporation, and his chances and duties were limited not only by circumstances and abilities, but by obligations joining him to his fellows in every direction.   The necessities of a half-barbarous condition had made the social unit, not the man or his family, but the community.   And the ideal of the feudal system was a single great organization, ruled in ascending stages by a civil hierarchy of overlords, with every detail of life guided and directed by the spiritual hierarchy of the clergy, who bound or loosed the oaths that held society together, directed consciences by the confessional, and, by denying the means of grace in the sacrament, could cast any man out from the fellowship of God and man in this world and the next.   Hence mediæval society lacked the mobility and freedom needed to develop individuality. In those days travelling was difficult. For the most part a man expected to die where he was born, and do his duty in that rank of life to which God had called him, unless, indeed, his relation to the social corporation drew him from his home on war or pilgrimage. As against the overwhelming pressure of this corporate sense there was little to develop the consciousness of the ego. Even if the man of the middle ages went to the university, travelled, and mingled with his fellows, his mind was still confined. He found there no chance or impulse to measure the heights and depths of his own nature, or to investigate freely the world without. The authority of tradition defined the objects and methods of study, and in every university of the middle of the thirteenth century the " freedom of academic teaching " was limited with a strictness from which even the narrowest denominational institutions of learning would shrink to-day. The organized discipline of study had largely sunk into a base mechanic exercise, a mere gymnastic of the mind. In this social and intellectual atmosphere it was difficult for man to know himself.

The literary instinct of Petrarch has presented in dramatic form the moment when he first broke these bonds and realized the value of self. That love of nature which appears in his sonnets in such close connection with his power of self-analysis gave the occasion. So far as we know, Petrarch was the first modern man to climb a mountain for the sake of looking at the view. About the year 1336, when he was thirty-two years old, he and his brother

Gerard set out from Vaucluse to climb Mount Ventoux. Gerard was evidently very much bored, and remained all day in that state of subacute irritation common to men who have been seduced by the enthusiasm of a friend into a tiresome expedition for which they have no taste. But Petrarch wrote: "I stood astonished on the top. Under my feet floated the clouds; before my eyes the snow-covered heads of the Alps towered over the beloved plains of Italy. I knew them, alas! far from me, and yet they seemed so near that I could almost touch them. Then I remembered the past. I ran over in thought my student years in Bologna, and saw how wishes and tastes had indeed changed, but vices and faults remained unchanged or were grown worse. Again I turned my gaze on the wonderful spectacle of nature that had drawn me to the top of the mountain, saw round about me mountains and valleys, land and sea, and rejoiced at the view. Thus gazing, now singling out some single object, now letting my sight range far into the distance, now raising eyes and soul to heaven, I unconsciously drew out of my pocket Augustine's 'Confessions,' a book I always carry with me, and it opened at this passage: 'Men go to wonder at the peaks of the mountains, the huge waves of the sea, the broad rivers, the great ocean, the circles of the stars, and for these things forget themselves.' I trembled at these words, shut the book, and fell into a rage with myself for gaping at earthly things when I ought to have learned long ago, even from heathen philosophers, that the soul is the only great and astonishing thing. Silent I left the mountain and turned my view from the things without me to that within."

And this dramatic announcement marks the beginning of the modern habit of introspection. Naturally he developed the defects of his qualities, and complains constantly of a spiritual malady he calls acedia. Melancholy, the mood of heavy indifference to all objects of thought and feeling,—the malaria of the soul,—had long been known. The early fathers denounced it, and the mediæval theologians, who saw much of it in the cloisters, ranked it among the deadly sins. But a single trait of Petrarch's character developed this old-fashioned melancholy into the modern *Weltschmerz*. He was the victim of a ceaseless appetite for fame which no praise could satisfy—a passion which tormented most of the early Humanists and spread from them to the whole society of Italy during the fifteenth century. This passion led him constantly to do things he despised and made such a gulf between his knowledge of what he was and his ideal of what he ought to be that he despaired at times of himself and the world.

For no sketch of Petrarch is complete which fails to show him not only as an instaurator of learning and an asserter of individuality, but also as a humbug. Even Napoleon, with the resources of France to help him, could not pose with the ceaseless subtlety and variety of Petrarch. Every strong and true passion of his soul was mingled with self-seeking and self-consciousness. He was a lover of nature and of solitude; but he always took care to select an accessible hermitage and to let all the

world know where it was.   When he dwelt in his
house by the fountain of Vaucluse, with an old housekeeper and two servants to look after him, and an old
dog to lie at his feet, he describes his life among the
simple peasants as that of one busily content with
watching the beauties of nature and reading the
words of the mighty dead, who was willing to let the
striving world wag on as it will.   But in reality it
was that of a scholar listening eagerly to every echo
of his fame which reached him from the outer world,
and counting the pilgrims drawn to his solitude by
his growing reputation.   He was fond of beginning
his letters, " In the stillness of dusky night," or, " At
the first flush of sunrise," and perfectly conscious of
the interest aroused by the suggested figure of the
pale student bent over his books in mysterious and
noble loneliness.   With that curious weakness which
leads inveterate vanity to find pleasure in betraying
itself, Petrarch has written that when he fled from
cities and society to his quiet houses at Vaucluse or
Arqua, he had done it to impress the imaginations of
men and to increase his fame ; which, like all the acts
and words of a *poseur*, was probably about half true
and half false.

One who thus enthroned and adored his own
genius demanded, of course, tribute from his friends.
And in all the letters he exchanges with his intimates we find that the topic is never their concerns,
but always the concerns of Petrarch.   He is fond
of decorating his epistles to them with Ciceronian
phrases on the nobility of friendship.   All the great
men of antiquity had friends.   But he who stepped

aside from the part of playing chorus to Petrarch's rôle of hero did so at his peril.   To criticise his writing even in the smallest was to risk a transference to the ranks of his enemies.

His love for Laura was undoubtedly genuine. There is a breath of real pain in his answer to a teasing friend: "Oh, would that it were hypocrisy, and not madness!"   But Petrarch was not unaware that all the world loves a lover.   No one felt more acutely than he did the patient dignity conferred by a hopeless passion for an unattainable woman.   As his fountain of Vaucluse became more beautiful to him because he had made it famous, so he loved Laura more because he had sung his love for all the world to hear.

Petrarch was religious, and in spite of his admiration for Plato and Cicero, wrote that he counted the least in the kingdom of heaven as greater than they. He is continually denouncing the profligacy of the Papal court at Avignon, whose members deserted their duties at home to live in luxury on the income of benefices they never visited.   But Petrarch himself was priest, canon, and archdeacon without ever preaching a sermon or saying a mass, residing near his cathedral, or caring for the poor.   And no man of his time was more persistent in the attempt to increase his income by adding new benefices to the ones whose duties he already neglected.· He who runs may read this in a mass of begging letters, where pride and literary skill ill conceal the eagerness of the request and the wrath and bitterness of disappointment.   He was a lover of freedom, whose praises he

sang with all his skill.   But he shocked even his most
faithful friends by accepting the hospitality and making gain of the favor of the Visconti, whose unscrupu-
lous power was threatening every free city of North
Italy.

His devouring ambition, the appetite for success
as symbolized by fame or wealth, appears perhaps
most plainly in his attitude to the memory of Dante.
This became so notorious that it was openly ascribed
to envy, and his friend Boccaccio bravely wrote to tell
him of the slander, expressing in the letter his own
boundless admiration for the great dead.   Petrarch's
reply is cold.   He does not use Dante's name.   It is
the charge of envy which troubles him.   How could
he be charged with envy of one who had written
nòbly, indeed, but in the common speech and for
the common people, while he had only used it in his
youth and half in play?   How could he who did not
envy even Virgil envy Dante?

This egotism was fed by such a banquet of admiration as has been spread for few men.   The cities
of Italy did not wait for his death to rival each other
in honoring him.   A decree of the Venetian Senate
said that no Christian philosopher or poet could be
compared to him.   The city of Arezzo greeted him
with a triumphal procession and a decree that the
house of his birth might never be altered.   Florence
bought the confiscated estates of his father and presented them to the man " who for centuries had no
equal and could scarcely find one in the ages to
come," "in whom Virgil's spirit and Cicero's eloquence had again clothed themselves in flesh."

Wherever he went men strove who should do him most honor. An old schoolmaster made a long journey to Naples to see him, and, arriving too late, followed over the Apennines to Parma, where he kissed his head and hands. Letters and verses in basketfuls brought admiration from every part of Italy, from France, Germany, England, and even from Greece. Perhaps the most prized of all these symbols of admiration was the bestowal of the poet's crown—a revival of a traditional and seldom-practised rite. At the age of thirty-six two invitations to receive it reached him on the same day: one from the University of Paris, and one from the Roman Senate. He chose Rome as the inheritor of imperial dignity, the true centre of Christendom. Led by a stately procession through the city to the Capitol, he received the crown from the hand of a Senator, delivered a festal speech, and went in procession to St. Peter's, where he knelt before the altar of the apostles and laid his wreath upon it. The day closed with a great banquet in the house of the chief of the Roman nobles. And these distinctions, sentimental as was their form, exaggerated as was the rhetoric in which they were phrased, were the tributes for great service to humanity. Not that Petrarch discovered anew classic literature, the rights of criticism, or the value of the individual. He accomplished little that was definite in criticism or history. Roger Bacon was a more original reformer of the methods of science, and there were *men* before Petrarch. But he came in the fulness of time, and by the force of genius gathered together and ex-

c

pressed the tendencies of his own age in a work
and a personality strong enough to break the road
which was to be followed by four generations of
the New Learning.   And they were to be the spiritual centre of the great social movement of the
Renascence, and the strongest of those forces which
were to limit the new opportunities and duties of
the Papacy, returned to the dignity of its ancient
seat in the Eternal City.

CHAPTER IV.

THE CONDITION IN WHICH THE RETURNING POPE
FOUND ITALY AND THE PATRIMONY OF ST.
PETER—THE BEGINNING OF THE GREAT
SCHISM—TWO VICARS OF CHRIST FIGHT FOR
THE TIARA.

HE Pope had come back to Rome not simply out of veneration for the ancient seat of the Papacy, but because he was forced to defend to the utmost his temporal authority in Italy.

During his absence the cities of Italy had been exposed to two dangers. The first was the presence of great bands of mercenary soldiers with just discipline enough to hold together and fight. The loosely ruled kingdom of Naples, swarming with brigands, was the regular school of leaders for these bands, and their ranks were recruited by adventurers from France, Germany, and England. When unemployed they plundered, and when hired for war they were equally dangerous to friend and foe. Werner of Urslingen, one of the earliest of their commanders (1348), had this inscription on his sword: "I am Duke Werner, leader of the Great

Company, the enemy of God, of mercy, and of pity."

The second danger which threatened the Italian cities was the power of tyrants, who, with the help of mercenaries, absorbed or seized the rights of many municipalities and turned them into personal posses-sions.   These men everywhere refused to pay their tributes to the Pope as their feudal overlord.   And to defend its own rights and answer the cry of the suffering cities the Papacy had, in 1353, sent the Spaniard Gil d'Albornoz as legate to Italy.   The situation taxed even his abilities, for the Free Com-panies roamed like human locusts, devouring what the tyrants spared.   Bernabo Visconti, the greatest of these tyrants, serves as their type.   He was the nephew of that Giovanni Visconti who, as Arch-bishop of Milan, completed the long process of usur-pation by which his family had become lords of the city and a great tributary territory.   Bernabo's power was unlimited, his wealth enormous, and he used both in a way which suggests the worst of the old Roman emperors.   The central object of the administration of home affairs was the Prince's hunt-ing, and his people were compelled to keep five thousand boar hounds and be responsible for their health.   To interfere with the savage brutes meant death by torture ; and the unfortunates upon whose hands one of these unwelcome guests died ran no small danger of being fed to the rest of the pack. He it was who gave a Papal messenger carrying a bull of excommunication the choice of being thrown off the bridge into the river or swallowing his own parchment; and answered the Archbishop of Milan, who 'refused his commands: " Know you not that I am Pope, emperor, and king in my country, and that God himself can't do anything in it against my will? "

Against this big tyrant Albornoz could do little, even with the help of Florence, the type and ideal of those cities that were struggling to maintain their ancient privileges as chartered municipalities of the Holy Roman Emp're. But the horde of little tyrants felt his hand, and at his death in 1367 a large number of the cities of the Papal States, defended by new citadels filled with Papal garrisons, enjoyed some measure of local privilege as vassals of the Pope. But he found no successor. And his death let loose on Italy a horde of hungry legates who used his citadels for oppression and plunder. For the most part Frenchmen, they trampled not only on the chartered liberties, but also on the feelings, of their cities and provinces.

Gerard von Puy, for instance, Abbot of Montmajeur and Legate of Perugia, held the city by the terror of his mercenaries as with a hand of iron. He himself banished and killed and extorted money. His nephew and favorite openly carried off two noblewomen of the city. The Governor answered the protests of the burghers in the first case with an indecent jest, and in the second by condemning his nephew to death unless he returned the woman in fifty days. And the facts would seem to justify the words of that ardent lover of the Church, St. Catherine of Siena, who, in a letter to Gregory XI., called his legates " incarnate demons."

The year before Gregory started to return to Rome, the city of Florence, which through the long strife with the empire had been a faithful ally of the Popes, raised a blood-red banner with the word *Libertas* in silver letters, and united eighty cities of Tuscany in a League of Freedom against " the barbarians who have been sent to Italy by the Papacy to grow fat on our goods and blood."

City after city rose at the call of the League. Città di Castello, Montefiascone, and Narni were up in November. Viterbo threw open her gates to the Florentine Prefect, and the burghers joined his troops in storming the citadel. The first week in December the streets of Perugia rang with shouts: "The people! the people! Death to the abbot and the pastors!" In quick succession, Spoleto, Assisi, Ascoli, Forli, Ravenna, all the cities of the Mark, the Romagna, and the Campagna caught the flame of enthusiasm, drove the garrisons from their citadels, and raised the red banner of the League. And finally in March, Bologna, mightiest of the Papal vassals, rose, crying, "Death to the Church!" Almost all Italy, except the great maritime states of Genoa and Venice, stood united against the Pope in a league whose watchwords were " Freedom " and " Italy for the Italians." From Avignon the alarmed Gregory struck with all his power at the head of the League. He thundered at Florence the sternest anathema on the Papal records. It declared every single burgher of Florence outlawed in goods and person, bade every Christian country banish all Florentines, and gave the right to any one who wished to seize their property and make slaves of them and their families. But Florence would not give way. When the bull was read in full conclave to their ambassador, he fell on his knees before a crucifix in the audience-room, and appealed to Jesus Christ, the Judge of the world, against this sentence of his Vicar. It was this spirit that had brought Gregory back to Italy to save the patrimony of St. Peter. And he found himself at once plunged in a miserable and desperate game of war and diplomacy. For he could put no dependence except on brutal mercenaries whose plundering and massacres under his banners foretold the miseries which Italy was to suffer from their kind for a hundred and fifty years. Gregory sickened under the anxieties and horrors of his position, and on the 27th of March, 1378, he died, longing for France and regretting his return.

The dangerous position of the Papacy at once became apparent when the cardinals met to elect his successor. The lack of any true political basis for its governmental authority over Rome exposed it constantly to the danger of mob violence; and the house thus shaken by storm from without was divided against itself. For the Papacy was not even in theory a despotism, but an oligarchy of ecclesiastical princes. And the Pope was supposed to seek constantly the advice and assistance of those whom Urban V. (1362–70), in a letter to the Roman people, called "our brothers the cardinals." The cardinals were the leaders of the Roman clergy, and bore the titles of the principal bishoprics, parish churches, and deaconries in and around Rome. In the election of the Bishop of Rome, as in that of every other bishop, there had been originally, according to the ancient phrase, three elements: the will of God, the choice of the people, the vote of the clergy. The choice of the turbulent Roman populace had no weight for centuries; but now they were determined to exert their power at least far enough to prevent the choice of any one born out of Italy. Sixteen cardinals went into the palace of the Vatican to hold the election. Four were Italians, one a Spaniard, and the rest Frenchmen. Already an embassy from the city magistrates had represented to the College their need of a Roman, at least of an Italian, Pope, that the city might not be again sunk into poverty and dishonor by the withdrawal of the Papacy. They had promised a quiet election, but they either could or would not keep their promises. The great square in front of St. Peter's was filled with a mob, and as the cardinals entered the Vatican the Roman populace entered with them. For there was a report that the cardinals were bringing in French troops, and suspicious eyes searched every room from garret to cellar, and even poked halberds and swords under the beds to make sure that no soldiers were hidden there. At last they left, but only to pass the night in the square drinking, sounding trumpets, and calling for a Pope.

The next morning, after mass, the cardinals began to vote. Instantly the bells of the city rang storm; and again the whole populace, in arms, flooded the square and surged against the very doors of the palace. Under these auspices twelve votes were cast for the Archbishop of Bari, a good canonist, who had for a time served as vice-chancellor at Avignon. Ten days later, for the first time in ninety years, a Pope was crowned in Rome.

The new Pope, who took the name of Urban VI., was a man of strict personal morals and stern ideas of the duty of ecclesiastical princes, and he had his work cut out for him. St. Bridget, a highly honored ascetic reformer, in a letter to his predecessor, Gregory XI., thus concisely expressed the prevalent opinion of the Papal court: "To be sent to the court of Avignon is like being sent to hell. There rules the greatest pride, an insatiable greed, the most horrible voluptuousness. It is a dreadful sink of awful simony. A house of ill fame is already more honored than the Church of God."

And making due allowance for the exaggerations usual both in the compliments and invectives of the time, the statement is probably a fair one. But, after all, the men of the Papal court were only the results of a system of abuses so inveterate that they regarded its wrongs as rightful privileges. The administration of the Church, steadily centralized by the great Popes from Hildebrand to Boniface for purposes of reform and to humble the empire, had during the Babylonian Captivity grown into a great ecclesiastical bureau, the profits of whose patronage were enormous and its corruption notorious. The Papal court was to a great extent flooded by the scions of noble houses spending the incomes of accumulated benefices in luxury, and finding in the purple of a prince of the Church only the opportunity to advance the fortunes of their friends by ecclesiastical politics. The reformer Urban was forced without supporters upon this corrupt old machine by an uprising of the people, and the stout, red-faced little man, with his rash temper and his unforgiving mood, honest and brave as he was, possessed neither the breadth nor the self-control for his task.

Within a week of the day when he set the crown on his head Urban publicly called the Cardinal Orsini a "ninny." He fell upon the Cardinal La Grange in full conclave, accusing him of having betrayed France for gold and of trying to betray the Church. Finally La Grange rose. "You are Pope now," he said, "and I cannot answer you. But if you still were what you were a few days ago, a little Archbishop of Bari, I would say to you, 'Little Archbishop,' you are a shameless liar.'" And turning on his heel, he left the room. "Holy Father," said Robert of Geneva, "you show little honor to the cardinals, which is against the customs of your predecessors. Perhaps our turn will come to show little honor to you."

It seemed an evil hour for dissension, when Urban had to guide the ship of St. Peter through so great a storm. The war with the League of Freedom still dragged along its fruitless horrors. And yet this outward danger seemed greater than it was. For the centre of the revolt was broken when the Pope came back to Rome. The power of the splendid ideal of the Papacy over the minds of men could only be obscured by the most pressing abuses, and the return from Avignon had changed the Dominium Temporale itself from a symbol of French tyranny into a centre and visible expression of that moral and religious headship of Rome which was a pride to every Italian. The people of the Italian cities had neither the patience nor the self-control to be worthy of freedom. They would not accept military discipline and could do nothing but street fighting; and their local hatreds were so strong that nothing but the pressure of unbearable suffering could unite them. When the chief cause of their revolt was thus removed, religious feeling, jealousy, and diplomacy began to break the League. Urban did not play his part badly, and three months after his coronation he made peace with Florence, the last antagonist of the Church.

But civil war was breaking out in the Curia. By the end of June all but the four Italian cardinals were assembled in Anagni, and the Papal treasurer joined them with the tiara and the crown jewels. Negotiations were in vain. On the 9th of August the thirteen non-Italian cardinals announced that the election of Urban was forced and uncanonical. And on the 31st of October, 1378, having been joined by three of the Italians, they elected and crowned a new Pope, who took the name of Clement VII. He was the Cardinal Robert of Geneva, a little pale-faced man of distinguished manners and a defect in gait which he strove sedulously to hide. The second son of the Duke of Savoy, he was connected by blood or marriage with many of the greatest houses of Europe, understood four languages, spoke eloquently, and dressed magnificently.

The impending schism had everywhere horrified

the faithful churchmen, who hoped for better days. St. Catherine of Siena wrote beseeching Cardinal Pedro de Luna to avert the danger of a quarrel between "the Christ on earth and his disciples." "Everything else, war, shame, sorrows of all kinds, were only a straw and a shadow compared to this misfortune."

But the schism once made, in spite of its horror, the world promptly chose sides. Flanders, England, the greater number of the states of the German Empire, and all North Italy renewed their allegiance to Urban. But France, Savoy, Scotland, Spain, and Naples received the legates of the Antipope. And two Vicars of Christ waged pitiless war with mercenary troops around the walls of Rome.

To sustain his falling cause, Urban, deserted by all the Princes of the Church, appointed twenty-nine cardinals at one creation, of whom twenty-two were Italians. But five refused the dignity; and the rest could hardly bear the harsh temper of the Pope who made them. In the winter of 1385 Urban was in the strong castle of Lucera,[1] perched among the great chestnuts of the hills between Salerno and Naples. Seven cardinals suspected of conspiracy languished half clad and fed in the cold dungeons. One of them, broken by disease and age, was brought into the great arched hall and tortured until the Papal secretary who has left the description, unable to bear the sight, begged permission to leave the castle because of a pretended headache. But Urban, walking up and down on the terrace below, read

---

[1] Now Nocera.

aloud the office for the day, that the executioners, reminded of his presence by the sound of his
voice, might not be slack in their work. When a
Neapolitan army camped among the vineyards
around the castle, the besiegers might see how the
fierce old Pope, his face flaming with impotent rage,
hurled out every day another anathema that devoted
them to perdition, even as the lights borne at his
side were hurled into darkness at the end of the
curse.

Freed by a sudden attack of mercenaries collected
by his allies, Urban sought refuge in Genoa. One
of his wretched captives, unable to bear the rapid
journey, was put out of the way on the road. An
Englishman among them owed his freedom to the
intercession of his King. Five others were carried
into the gates of the building of the Knights of St.
John, assigned by the city for Urban's residence.
One tradition says they were sewn up alive in sacks
and cast into the harbor by night; another that they
were starved or strangled and buried in the cellar.
It is only certain that men never saw them come
out of those gates into the light of day.

PERIOD I.

CHAPTER V.

HE scandal of open war for the Papal crown, between a ruthless tyrant and a jaded man of the world who loved the game of ecclesiastical politics, aroused indignant protest in the hearts of all lovers of religion. And one great churchman was driven by the shock of it to change his lifelong demand for reform into an attack on the organization of the Church and the theory of the Papacy.

John Wiclif, a doctor of Oxford, was acknowledged to be the most learned man of England, and his fame abroad would probably have ranked him in the international guild of scholars as the most distinguished university teacher of his day. In addition to this fame as a scholar he possessed great popular influence as a bold and powerful preacher in the mother tongue. In each of these two characters he had protested against the abuses of the Papacy at Avignon. As a scholastic he expressed his protest in the treatises "De Dominio Civili" and "De Dominio Divino," which were probably intended,

46

under the single title "De Dominio," to form
the introduction to his great work, "Summa in
Theologia."

The prologue to the treatise "De Dominio Divino"
announces his intention of beginning a course of di-
vinity by an exposition of the doctrine of Lordship
based upon Scripture proofs; and the author at once
proceeds, with unlimited learning, to seek a base for
his doctrine in scholastic metaphysics. He discusses,
in passing, the nature of being; the relation of universals to sensible objects; the different stages of
being, such as *essentia* and *esse, pro se esse, esse intel-
ligibile*, and *esse actuale*, and their mutual relations;
the possibility of demonstrating faith, and the right
of free inquiry; the eternity of the world, with a
criticism of various opinions on the subject; the
question of necessity and free will, and the relation of
the persons of the Trinity; and the demonstration
of such ideas as "The process by which the primary
ens is specificated is substantiation, rendering it capable of acquiring accidents" makes it rather difficult
reading for these degenerate days. It is only in the
last chapter that he becomes practical and to us
readable. For he then develops the idea that God
being the immediate Lord of all things, human property and authority are always held as vassals of God
by a tenure tested by due service to him. When this
conclusion was again fed into the mill of scholastic
logic there was ground out the conclusion that property and authority were forfeited by sin—a conclusion
which, when applied, not as a practical judgment to
any given unendurable wrong, but held as an abstract

principle, was fatal to the existence of every institution of human society.

But when Wiclif stepped out of his study he showed the man behind the great scholastic. The traditional logic of his class bore him at times, with the clumsy gallop of an animated hobby-horse, whither he would not. But when he dismounted he could give effect to the keen common sense of his practical judgment in phrases which spoke to the noble and the ploughboy —phrases which smote spiritual wickedness in high places like winged arrows of the wrath of God. What gave point to these weapons was the knowledge of the Bible which he was spreading among the common people of England. The art of preaching had sunk very low. Large numbers of the parish priests had given it up altogether, and those who practised it were apt to inflict upon their hearers the linked dulness, long drawn out, by which syllogism gave birth to syllogism in the endless genealogies of scholastic discussion. The popular begging friars, on the other hand, amused and demoralized their hearers by coarse jests and old wives' fables, drawn from the legends of the saints, from the Gesta Romanorum, or even from the distorted stories of Greek and Roman mythology. These abuses were flagrant, and known of all men; and Wiclif, the most celebrated teacher in England, ex-member of Parliament and royal ambassador, voluminous author and faithful parish priest, who had voiced, amid the applause of a people, the nation's protest against Papal aggression, set himself to the task of showing a better way. He was too much a child of his age to be free in the pulpit from some of the very faults he condemned. But beneath the rhetorical ornaments and cumbrous construction of the celebrated scholastic, his parishioners and the chapels of Oxford heard a new tone of manly directness denouncing sin and calling them to the life of faith. And from chapel and lecture-room went an organized band of " Poor Priests," clad in coarse red garments, barefoot, and staff in hand, to carry the sacred fire now into a town market-place, now to the village church of a friendly rector, and, when that was closed, standing upon some convenient tomb to preach to the living among the graves of the dead.

Selecting the best of these friends and pupils, Wiclif began and, by their help, finished a translation of the Latin Bible. The noble who read Norman French had long known the Bible in that tongue; so long as the churl had spoken Anglo-Saxon he could read much of it; but now for generations there had been no version intended for the men and women of England who worked with their hands. And Wiclif, laying aside the hindrance of a Latinized style formed in the practice of the subtle hair-splitting of his traditional metaphysics, made or inspired one which, together with the poems of Chaucer, exerted on Middle English the same creative power that Shakespeare and the King James version had on Modern English.

To the man who was thus passing from the discussion of the Church to the truth she symbolized, behind the official to the idea of his duty, through worship and theology to religion as a new life, the fires of war blazing between two cursing Popes

D

seemed the very blast of hell. He had hailed with joy the election of Urban as a " Catholic head, an evangelical man, a man who, in the work of reforming the Church, follows the due order by beginning with himself and the members of his own household. From his works, therefore, it behooves us to believe that he is the head of our Church." But when Urban, going from bad to worse, called England to arms for his cause, and the Bishop of Norwich used the authority of the Vicar of Christ to urge all Christians to bring fire and sword among the meadows and cities of Flanders, Wiclif poured out pamphlets of protest in Latin and English. And his wrath, slowly gathering head and finding ever sterner and clearer expression, bore him where his logic had never carried him, through indignant appeal to the Pope to obey Christ, to the total rejection of the whole system which made such a perversion possible, and, finally, to a denunciation of the Papacy as Antichrist.

For this revolt made by Wiclif the man, Wiclif the scholar had been slowly preparing by progressive changes in theology. Not that these changes ever carried him entirely outside the limits of mediæval thought in regard to the teaching of the Bible. The great system of Catholic theology had come into being, to use the mixed metaphor of Paul, as a growth and a building, owing much to the unconscious logical development which led the thoughts of men from age to age, as the novelty of one generation became the orthodoxy of another, and much to the labor of the great thinkers who served the Church.

Wiclif was led to criticise parts of this edifice, but he never rejected the chief corner-stone—the idea that Christ was a second Moses, a divine Lawgiver, and the Gospel a new law.   Of the three elements of the relation of the soul to God, knowledge, trust, and obedience, he emphasizes the first and last, but scarcely touches the second.   He does not image salvation as a gift of God's love, coming to whosoever will receive it in the childlike confidence which gives to all life a filial character, but is fain to regard it as given by God in some sort as an exchange for the effects wrought in a man's thought, feeling, and deeds by faith.   He ought not, therefore, to be ranked according to our modern nomenclature among " Protestants."   For, disregarding the isolated heresies ultimately condemned by the Church, his theological system as a whole is to be classified as " Catholic."

His most important attack upon the theology of his time was in that point where the doctrines of God as the Author, man as the object, Christ as the Mediator, of salvation, and the Church as his visible representative, meet—the sacrament of the Lord's Supper.   Stripped of technical language, the process which led him to this may be briefly indicated as follows.   So far as that department of theology which discussed the Church was concerned, the Catholic theory had its logical base in the idea that clergy were a distinct order of men.   They might differ among themselves in honor through all the ascending scale of a complex hierarchy, but between all of them and the laity there was a great gulf fixed. The impulse which developed this idea, and defended it by the practice of celibacy and the doctrine of the sacrament of ordination, was the desire to give to the clergy a superior sanctity because they were priests ministering at the altar of God in the sacrifice of the eucharist, in which they made sacrifice for the sins of the people and were the mediators of the grace needed for daily living.   Upon the clergy the Church rested, not, indeed, in the fully and clearly developed doctrines of Catholic theology, but in those phrases and conceptions which were popularly taught and accepted as representing that theology.   In opposition Wiclif taught that the centre of gravity of the Church was not in earth, but in heaven, in the counsel of God; for the Church consisted of " the whole body of the elect."   So, while he nowhere uses the Pauline phrase, " the universal priesthood of believers," he asserts the duty of believers to rebuke an unworthy priest, nay, if need be, to judge and depose him; and he defended this assertion by such precedents from the canon law as the order of Gregory VII. that congregations should not hear mass from married priests.   He even asserts, " Nor do I see but that the ship of Peter may be filled for a time with laity alone."   It is easy to understand that one who wrote thus for the early chapters of his " Summary of Theology " should be led, just before the end of his life, to criticise the doctrine of the sacraments.

In the sacrament of the Lord's Supper, as Wiclif received it from the Church, were involved a practice and two ideas not found in the New Testament:[1] the

---

[1] This is, of course, denied by Roman Catholic apologists.

withholding of the cup from the laity, transubstantiation, and the sacrifice of the mass. And he was the first of three successive protesters, each of whom rejected one of these things. John Huss (burned 1415) was to bequeath to his followers a protest against the withholding of the cup. Martin Luther (protested 1517), passing for the first time entirely outside of mediæval theology, was to attack the fundamental conception of the mass, as a repetition of the death of Christ—to deny that the sacrament was a sacrifice offered to God to make continually renewed propitiation for those sins by which the people break the law of salvation. Wiclif attacked the doctrine of transubstantiation. This doctrine was formed by the schoolmen, and can only be stated in the technical terms of their logic. It asserts that after the words of consecration the bread and wine are changed, not in their accidents, but in their substance, into the body and blood of Christ. The accidents of a thing are the phenomena by which it is perceived, such as taste, smell, hardness. The substance is a non-sensible something, only to be laid hold of by the mind; which is behind all accidents. And the doctrine of transubstantiation asserts that, while the bread and wine of the Lord's Supper taste and look like bread and wine, they are actually and substantially the flesh and blood of Christ. Before the Papal schism Wiclif certainly accepted this teaching, as when, for instance, he wrote of Christ, " He was a priest when in the supper he made his own body." But the mood induced by what seemed to him a flagrant *reductio ad absurdum* of the Papal

theory, led him to reëxamine and reject the doctrine
of transubstantiation on threefold grounds: of Scripture, which never suggests the idea and by implica-
tion several times denies it; of tradition, because it
originated in the later and corrupt ages of the Church
and was unknown to Jerome and Augustine; of reason, because it assumes ideas which, tested by the
very logic it employs, are false and self-contradictory.
And he drew his argument to a point in a stern
denunciation of the "idolatry of the priests of Baal,
who worship gods they have made," and the presumption of attributing to "synners the power to
make God."

Members of the Church were, as in the Roman
communion they still are, trained by the whole
drift of the usual discipline and by every act of
their public worship to centre the expression of
belief and religious feeling in this sacrament. And
her apologists instinctively feel that it is the means
by which the mediæval theology summarized by
Thomas Aquinas passes over into the religious life
of the people. It is easy to understand, therefore, that all who reverenced the ancient and accepted forms of learning and piety felt a shock of
horror at this attack and the words in which it was
expressed. And all the hirelings and greedy place-
men who had fought Wiclif so long were quick to
take advantage of this revulsion of honest religious
feeling. When he had been summoned before the
Bishop of London for resisting Papal aggression
upon the rights of England, he had walked into court
between the Grand Marshal of the realm and the

King's uncle, and they could do nothing against him, because the people held him for a prophet. When a bull from Rome had summoned him to trial on a charge of heresy based on nineteen theses drawn from his writings, the organized scholarship of England, as represented by Oxford University, rose in his defence, the burghers of London filled the court-room with menacing murmurs, and Sir Henry Clifford, in the name of the Princess of Wales, peremptorily demanded a suspension of judgment. But from the time when he passed beyond demands for the reform of abuses to an attack upon the organization of the Church, his enemies and her defenders began to gain upon him. Groan as men might under ecclesiastical abuses, peremptory as were the demands for reform from every quarter of Europe, the love of the ancient mother was still strong and tender, and the power of the great ideal of a visible Vicar of Christ still unbroken over the human heart. There was as yet no social institution whose ruling powers were willing to defend any one whose protest involved a clear denial of any essential or fundamental element of Church doctrine or organization. William Courtenay, Bishop of London, fourth son of the Earl of Devonshire, and on his mother's side a great-grandson of Edward I., had been made Primate of England after the murder of the mild Sudbury by the insurgent peasants. He was an able, stern, and zealous ecclesiastic, and a court under his presidency, in the spring of 1382, condemned ten theses as heretical. One, " that God ought to obey the devil," was probably only Wiclif's statement, in the form of one of those paradoxes loved by the schoolmen, that God permitted evil and Christ suffered himself to be tempted.   The rest related, directly or indirectly, to the sacrament of the altar.   Armed with this general condemnation, which mentioned no names, the Archbishop silenced first Wiclif's scholars.   By the help of the young King he repressed the itinerant preaching, and with the aid of the conservative minority of Oxford, frightened, arrested, or silenced the ablest of Wiclif's friends.   He was too cautious to attack Wiclif himself, who, defended by the gratitude of the people, the power of a skilful appeal to Parliament, and their jealousy of the abuse of the royal prerogative in the proceedings, remained untouched in his rural parish of Lutterworth.   The net was drawing round him, and he lectured no more at Oxford.   But in the English speech, to which he had given form, he spoke by sermon and tract to the people of England.   And then he passed suddenly from strife to peace.   His assistant has told how a stroke of paralysis, falling on him at the moment of the elevation of the host, while he was hearing mass in his own church, lamed that powerful tongue and, three days later, stilled the brain and heart.

It is impossible to say how numerous his followers, who came to be called Lollards, were.   At all events, though spared for nearly twenty years by most of the bishops, and protected by a party in Parliament, they never gained cohesion and power enough to make any effective move for the reforms demanded by their teacher.   The accession of the house of Lancaster to the throne seems to have been accom-

panied by an ecclesiastical reaction, strengthening
the conservative hierarchy. In 1401 Parliament
passed the statute De Hæretico Comburendo, which
for the first time made all heretics guilty of death by
the law of England. And under its pressure Lollardy
rapidly sank out of sight, emerging dimly behind the
abortive revolt for which Sir John Oldcastle suffered
death in 1414. After that its doctrines, practices,
and protests may have lived secretly among the
peasants, but it never appears again as a recognized
force in life or an effective power in Church or State.

It was Wiclif the scholar whose work lived on most
clearly from age to age. His English Bible was a
lasting appeal from all tradition back to the earliest
records of the source of Christianity, an assertion that
the knowledge of religion belongs to the common
people, and that its plainest and most direct appeals
must always be submitted to the common judgment
and conscience of mankind. His other writings also
lived when he was dead. Adalbert Ranconis, a great
teacher of the recently founded University of Prague,
bequeathed a foundation for travelling scholarships,
to enable Bohemian students to visit Oxford and
Paris. Their transcriptions of Wiclif's later manuscripts are still in existence, and through them his
ideas became the source of the first truly national
reform, the first demand for the abolition of ecclesiastical abuses which united a whole people in willingness to resist the authority of Rome to determine
doctrine and rule the conscience.

Five years later Urban died, fighting to the last
for the possessions of the Church and his own au-

thority.   Theodoric of Niem, the vivid chronicler of the schism, says, "He had a hard heart," and quotes upon him the proverb, "*Sudden honor always makes a poor man over-proud.*"   He took up with rash and obstinate self-confidence the tremendous burden of the Papacy, before which the good have always shrunk and the strong and wise trembled.   And he died hated even by those who obeyed him.   The proud puritan, with narrow sympathies and intolerant temper, was not large enough for his opportunity. Because he could not distinguish between his personal animosity and zeal in the cause he fought for, he brought upon the Church evils greater than those from which he tried, with the sternest honesty of intent, to save her.

CHAPTER VI.

POPE AND ANTIPOPE—THE WHITE PENITENTS AT ROME—THE SIEGE OF AVIGNON—THE FOLLOWERS OF PETRARCH, THE HUMANISTS, OR MEN OF THE NEW LEARNING.

HE death of Urban did not check in the least the struggle for the Papal tiara, which was to drag its slow length along amid treachery, bloodshed, and bribery for forty years. The Popes on either side are distinguished by nothing but their names and the varying degrees of skill with which they avoided yielding to the growing demand of Christendom for a General Council to allay the schism. The record of their intrigues is dull and unprofitable, and even the steady discharge of their mutual anathemas has a stereotyped and unreal tone, like stage thunder. About the only things in the story of the Papacy during these years which the muse of history can record without yawning are, perhaps, the scattered evidences of the deep religious feeling of Europe, and the firm attachment of men to the institutions and customs of the Church, which remained unshaken through all confessed abuse, and unrebuffed by the steady refusals of the demand for reform.

Boniface IX. proclaimed, in 1390, a jubilee pilgrimage to Rome, and the gifts of the pilgrims from Germany, Hungary, Bohemia, Poland, and England filled up the empty treasury. In advance his agents had sold all over the world vast numbers of indulgences, which secured to the purchasers all the spiritual benefits of the pilgrimage for the price the journey would have cost. Ten years later the century jubilee brought crowds of pilgrims, some even from France, which obeyed the other Pope.

More remarkable evidences of attachment to religion were the processions of the White Companies of Flagellants. The habit of flagellation grew up in the cloisters as a means of keeping the flesh under, an expression of penitence for sin, and a method of prepaying the penalties of purgatory. It was strongly defended as a useful discipline and a pious exercise by the celebrated Peter Damiani in the eleventh century. Mutual public flagellation by companies of laity had, however, been discountenanced by Church and State. But when the black death desolated Europe in the middle of the fourteenth century such companies had appeared, journeying through the cities of Germany, beating one another in the market-places, and reading a letter from Christ, which they said had dropped from heaven. Nine thousand of them passed through the city of Strassburg in three months. At first the clergy were powerless to stop the custom, but in six months the hysteric excitement was repressed by the civil and ecclesiastical authorities, and before the end

of the year a Papal bull forbade it as schismatic.   It
thus became a method of expression for heretic and
anti-hierarchical spirits, and a number of its secret
practisers perished at the stake.   But in the year
1397 there suddenly appeared in Genoa companies
of people clothed in white and wearing great masks
with holes cut for the eyes.   They marched in procession, singing hymns, and beating each other in
pairs with scourges.   The habit spread over all Italy.
The Flagellants of Florence were reckoned at forty
thousand.   Some cities forbade their entrance, and
when they approached Rome the Pope sent four
hundred lancers to turn them back.   But the Captain
and all his men joined the procession, which included
also many priests and bishops, and as they marched
forward the inhabitants of Orvieto, ten thousand in
number, joined them.   The day after their entry
into Rome most of the inhabitants put on the white
robe.   All the prisons were opened and the prisoners
set free.   The most precious relics of the city were
exposed in special services, and the Pope gave the
apostolic benediction to an immense multitude crying
out, " Mercy! Mercy!" while he was moved to tears.
Two contemporaries wrote that all Italy prayed and
took the sacrament, while everywhere injuries were
forgiven and deadly feuds healed.   But these effects
passed as swiftly as they had come.   The opening
of the prisons, the enormous crowd of strangers in
the city, the intense excitement, brought their natural
evils.   The Pope forbade the flagellation processions.
The leader of a new train of pilgrims was arrested
and afterward executed for frauds, and the move-

ment dissipated itself, leaving behind a bad outbreak of the plague.

The Antipope, Benedict XIII., was facing a different sort of pilgrimage. Marshal Boucicault led the royal army against the castle of Avignon in the summer of 1398. But the huge pile that still towers on its rock above the Rhone was not easy to take, and the obstinate Spaniard, apparently giving way in straits, and breaking his convention as soon as he was reprovisioned, maintained his position until 1403, when, in disguise, and carrying only the consecrated host, " the prisoner of Avignon " escaped.

But meanwhile, in all stillness, the new intellectual force whose first exponent was Petrarch was finding broader expression. Its development may be briefly indicated in the slow increase of the numbers and influence of the Humanists, or followers of the New Learning. Among the thousands of these men who for several generations loved letters or sought the glory of them there was every variation in character, but marked common traits betray a secret law by which they must have drawn their being from the spirit of the age. They can be arranged, without too much forcing, around groups of three in successive generations.

Boccaccio was a contemporary of Petrarch's, for he was only nine years younger and died only one year later; but he took toward his friend so entirely the attitude of a disciple that he is always looked upon as a follower and successor. He had neither the greatness nor the meanness of his master. He did not, because he could not, do as much, but he did nothing for effect. He longed for fame, but he scorned riches, not in words alone, but with the pride which several times refused to change the independence of a scholar and a citizen of free Florence to become the favorite of a court. Once only he tried to sit at the table of Mæcenas. When the rich Florentine, Niccola Acciaijuoli, became Grand Seneschal of Naples, Boccaccio accepted a pressing invitation " to share his luck " and become his biographer. But when he was given in the splendid palace of his patron a room and service far below that of his own simple house, the proud poet resented the insult by leaving at once, and answered a sarcastic letter from the Seneschal's steward by the only invective which, in an age of quarrels, ever came from his pen. The plump little man, with his merry round face, and twinkling eyes never dimmed by envy, and a clear wit untinged with malice, lived all his life among the bitterest party and personal strifes, he became a distinguished citizen, and conducted with success three important embassies, but he died without an enemy. His enthusiasms were deep and self-forgetful. When he spoke of Dante, whose poem, by a vote of the City Council, he expounded in the cathedral every Sunday and holy day, his eyes moistened and his voice trembled with wonder and love. He writes to Petrarch with a humble and touching joy in his friendship to one so unworthy, which asks for no return. Petrarch used this feeling, which he accepted as if it were a homage due to him, as incense to burn on the altar of his insatiable egotism; but, after all, he loved the faithful Florentine, and left him by will fifty gold florins to buy a fur-lined coat to wear cold nights when he read late.

Boccaccio is known to the untechnical reader only as the author of the Decameron. The book is the beginning and still a model of Tuscan prose, and ranks him forever among the rarest masters of the art men love best—the art of story-telling. He took his material wherever he could, and it is difficult to believe that to offer some of the tender and pure stories of the collection to those who were willing to enjoy some of the others was not casting pearls before swine. But we must remember that it was written for a princess by a man of the world, who gives no sign that he is offending against good manners. For there existed in that and for succeeding generations an incredible freedom of speech. Whether this of itself indicates a larger license in living than that which prevails among the idle and luxurious of this age, in which vice is spoken of chiefly by *double entendre*, is hard to decide—at least for those who know the vast distinction between essential morality and soc'al custom. But whatever may be the truth of this comparison, it is certain that Boccaccio had lived openly, after the fashion of the age, the life of a libertine, and it is difficult to see how any moral defense of the Decameron as a whole can be accepted by a serious-minded person. The only consolation under the brand-mark of a Philistine which is certain to follow the confession of such a judgment is that Boccaccio himself thought so; for he begged an old friend not to give the book to his wife, who would certainly judge him unfairly by it; or, if he insisted on doing it, at least to explain that he wrote that sort of thing only in his youth. In his vulgarity, and also to some extent in his repentance, he is a representative of the Humanists. In every generation, from Petrarch down, many of their leaders were willing to use the utmost skill of their pens in promoting the worship of the goddess of lubricity amid the laughter and applause of Italy.

Nothing could have astonished Boccaccio more than to know that fame would come to him as the writer of the Decameron, and not through his great service to scholarship. Not, indeed, that his work marks any real advance in scholarship. Although he offered hints valuable to the future, like the idea of correcting texts by collating manuscripts, he lacked strength to cut out the paths to which he pointed. He never shook himself free from reverence for tradition and awe before all that was written. When, for instance, he finds in Vincentius Bellovacensis that the Franks were descended from Franko, a son of Hector, he does not believe it, but he is unwilling to denounce it as a fable, because "nothing is impossible with God." His service was to give the inspiration of an example and to spread by the contagious influence of personality the enthusiasm for letters. Petrarch, when he left his dying gift, knew the real Boccaccio, the man who showed Italy the image of the student happy in the companionship of his books, a living picture of scholarship powerful to hold and fire the imagination, like Dürer's beauti-

E

ful little etching of St. Jerome in his cell.   When the
first teacher of Greek came to Italy Boccaccio hastened to meet him at Venice, took him to Florence,
and kept the dirty old cynic in his house, learning
from him the Greek letters and the elements of
grammar.   He never seemed to get farther, and
knew Homer only in the stiff translation of the
master which he copied with his own hand, buried
under the extraordinary comments of the old man
as he read it.

Enthusiasm like this could not fail of a strong
impression among the Florentines, and soon after
his death we find his friends organized into a
learned club for stated discussion.   The place of
meeting was in the convent of the Augustins, San
Spirito, to which Boccaccio had left all his books and
in whose church he wished to be buried.   The soul
and leader of the association was Luigi de' Marsigli,
an Augustinian monk, son of a noble Florentine
family.   At first a student of the University of Pavia,
he took his master's degree in theology at Paris.
But the meetings under his guidance used no scholastic methods of discussion.   It was more a free conversation between the finest spirits of Florence on
Livy and Ovid, Augustine, or some question of
archæology as to the origin of Florence, or a historical personage like Ezzelin or Frederick II.   We do
not know much about this club, except that in it for
the first time men could get the elements of education and the tone of scholarship outside of the Church
and the university, still in bondage to the ghost of a
mediæval Aristotle and a mediæval theology.

The most striking of these younger men who formed the centre of learning in Florence for their generation was Coluccio Salutato. Trained in the University of Bologna as a notary, he spent two years as an under-secretary of the Curia, and carried from the service a lasting hatred for the corruptions of the Papal court. Afterward he led for several years the wandering life of a knight-errant of the pen seeking for fortune, and finally settled in Florence as a clerk in the service of the government. At the age of forty-five he rose to be Chancellor of State, having charge of the records and correspondence of the Republic. And during all his life there streamed out from the government house of Florence upon the eyes of a weak and restless generation the light of a steadfast soul that loved liberty and feared only God. It was his ideal for Florence that she should be a city not only " hating and cursing tyranny within her own walls, but always ready to defend with all her strength the privileges of the other cities of Italy." He put this eloquence of sincere and bold conviction into the letters and proclamations of the Republic, clothed in swinging rhetoric and ornamented by the phrases of Seneca and Petrarch. They were copied and circulated even beyond the Alps, while men wondered to find life and beauty in State documents. Gian Galeazzo Visconti, the most dangerous enemy of the Republic, who hid like a spider in the palace at Milan, strove to draw all the cities of Italy into the meshes of his crafty tyranny, said, " One letter of Salutato's can do me more harm than a thousand Florentine men-at-arms."

Salutato died in the harness at the age of seventy-six, honored by all his neighbors; for he had brought up ten sons to be honest and honorable, and, except forty-five florins and his collection of manuscripts, this man, who had for thirty years dealt with the rich tyrants of Italy and known all the secrets of the State, left neither house nor property outside his paternal inheritance.   He has one lasting claim to the enduring gratitude of posterity: he was the first man to make an index to a book.   Over his head as it lay on the bier, wreathed by public order with the laurel of the scholar and poet, the banners of the city and all its guilds were dipped, and a marble monument told to coming generations the gratitude of the Republic to the honest chancellor who had brought the power of the New Learning into the service of the State.   He had to defend his love of letters against ascetics, to whom all beauty was a snare, he was accused of being a heathen philosopher by those who could not reconcile piety with the continual quotations of Seneca and Cicero, but his letters show the spirit of one who loved religion.   And therefore some of the strongest of them denounce the party strife and personal ambition which was degrading the ideal of the Papacy, devastating Italy with wild mercenaries, and threatening to destroy the liberties of Florence and her allies.

PERIOD I.

CHAPTER VII.

ORTHODOX DEMANDS FOR UNION AND REFORM:
(1) CATHERINE OF SIENA AND THE ASCETIC
PROPHETS OF RIGHTEOUSNESS; (2) THE
PARTY OF CONCILIAR SUPREMACY.

HE corruption of the Curia, now so apparent in the schism it caused,—this war between two factions of the Princes of the Church fiercely contending for wealth and power, while the hungry sheep looked up and were not fed,—aroused not only the root and branch dissent of Wiclif, but also created two distinct classes of protesters loyal to the Church and of an orthodoxy never seriously questioned.

The prototype of the first class is Catherine of Siena, canonized soon after her death. She was the daughter of a dyer, and from her earliest youth began to scorn delights and live days of prayer and praise, visiting the prisoners, clothing the poor, and tending the sick. Visions and dreams came to her. She had seizures in which she lay without speech or feeling, to awake and tell of conversations with Mary and the angels, whether in the body or out of it she knew not. At an early age she gained the privilege of wearing the robe of the order of St. Dominic as an associate sister without a vow. She became an ambassador of the Florentine Republic and a correspondent of princes. When Gregory, largely at her intercession, came back from Avignon and at once began to answer the revolt of his misgoverned cities by war, she poured out a flood of letters throbbing with righteous wrath and grief. "Peace, peace, peace, my sweet father," she wrote; "no more war; war against the enemies of the cross by the sword of the holy Word of God, full of love." In two things she never wavered: her loyalty to the Pope as the visible Vicar of Christ, and her readiness to rebuke the sins and follies of Papal policy; as when she told Gregory to his face that she found in Rome "the stench of intolerable sins." The holiness of her life and the earnest piety of her intent, symbolized in that extreme asceticism which, comparatively uninfluential upon the mind and heart of Teutonic peoples, has always appealed forcibly to the more intense and artistic temperament of the South, gave her enormous power. All Italy held her for a prophet; and a vigorous intellect and a strong common sense woven through all the mystic web of her visions enabled her to use her influence well. She died a few years before Urban, at the age of thirty-three (1380), worn out by privations, labors, and the griefs and ecstasies of a fervent spirit, exclaiming with her last breath, "I come not because of my merits, but through thy mercy—only through the power of thy blood." And Italy did not lack in any generation faithful witnesses in her likeness—

ascetic, mystical, given to visions, mingling patriotism with religion, denouncing sin with a fervid
eloquence that swayed the people like leaves in
the wind, or reasoning of righteousness, temperance, and judgment to come with a courage before
which the most reckless tyrant or the greediest
ecclesiastical politician secretly quailed. Lack of
space compels the omission of the portraits of these
prophets fallen on evil days until we come to Savonarola, the most splendid of their line.

From the earliest days of the schism voices had
been heard calling for a General Council of the
Church to heal the schism and check the corruption
and demoralization which had followed in its train.
This demand created an unorganized party, and
the party formulated a theory of the church reject-
ing the Papal Supremacy, and maintaining that the
source of ecclesiastical and dogmatic authority was in
a General Council. They were, of course, at liberty
to do this without transgressing the bounds of orthodoxy, for, however strenuously the Infallibility and
Supremacy of the Pope were maintained by argument
and force, they were not dogmatically defined as a
portion of the Catholic faith until our own generation.

The party of Conciliar Supremacy can best be seen
in the centre where it found a voice, the University
of Paris. And its best spirit is incarnate in two
Rectors of that famous school, which had been the
alma mater of so many Popes and owed its income
and most of its privileges to the Curia. Pierre d'Ailly
was the son of an artisan, born in 1350. When he
came up to the University of Paris at twenty-two he

was a pious and able youth, much given to the study
of the Bible.   His ability was soon noted.   The
students elected him a procurator, and the authorities
appointed him preacher to open a Synod at Amiens.
He chose as his theme the corruptions of the clergy,
and laid on the lash well.   But the zeal of the youth
for reform went hand in hand with a zeal for orthodoxy, and the same year he published his " Letter to
the New Jews."   It sternly rebukes those who dared
to question the finality of the Vulgate, the translation
of a holy man used by the infallible Church ; and
concludes that if we question this translation we
might question any other and the Catholic would be
set afloat on a devil's sea of doubt.

It was in 1380 that he came up for his doctor's
degree, and his thesis discussed the Church.   He
defended the whole hierarchical organization, but
claimed that the power of the Church was not material, but spiritual.   Christ answered before Pilate and
bade us give to Cæsar the things that are Cæsar's.
The foundation of the Church was Christ, and Peter
was a pillar of the great building, which consisted of
the fellowship of believers in Christ.   These conclusions he based on the Scriptures, which pointed to
Christ as the only foundation, and plainly taught in
Galatians ii. that Peter had erred.   The new law of
Christ was therefore the law of God's kingdom.
But that new law of Christ recorded in the Holy
Scriptures was not to be understood by the human
intellect and accepted by the human will.   The Kingdom of God could only enter into a man by the
supernatural gift of faith.   To give this God had

founded his visible Church, and without her none
could hear or obey the law of Christ. Outside the
Church, therefore, none could be saved. When he
came to define how the Church expressed the final
authority given her for salvation he fell into embarrassment. He mentions several opinions: that the
Universal Church cannot err, nor a General Council,
nor the Roman Diocese, nor its representative, the
College of Cardinals, nor a canonically elected Pope.
Of these he expresses approval only of the first. In
regard to the second he seems to be in doubt, and
the general impression of his thesis is that the infallible Church has no infallible organ of expression.
But he rather indicates this conclusion as the abstract
result of a scholastic discussion than as a distinct
practical judgment. On the burning question of the
day, how to get rid of the schism, he showed himself
a man of compromise, standing half way between
the Papalists, who thought the Pope independent of
the Council, and the Conciliarists, who thought that
a General Council would be independent of the
Pope.

The demoralization of the schism was complete,
and the condition of the French Church was now
unbearable. The churches were empty, the hospitals closed, parish priests begging in the streets,
while the hungry cardinals at Avignon consumed
the ecclesiastical funds. In 1381 an assembly of
the University voted unanimously to demand a
Council. The Regent of France was enraged, and
imprisoned the delegates who presented the request.
The University protested, and appointed the young

Professor Pierre d'Ailly as their advocate before the
Duke.   He did his dangerous duty like a man and
came off safe, but the plan for a Council was stifled at
its beginning.   Then d'Ailly took to the pen and wrote
a Letter from Hell.   It was signed by Leviathan, the
Prince of Darkness, ordering his vassals, the prelates,
to be careful for the maintenance of the schism.   " I
had worked in vain," he writes, " to injure the Church
while her sons loved one another, when suddenly her
prelates brought the whole heavenly Jerusalem into
confusion and began to cry, ' I am for Clement,' ' I
for Urban,' ' I for the General Council,' ' I for a union,'
' I for the resignation of both,' ' I for the Lord,' ' I
for the King,' ' I for the rich benefices I have got from
so-and-so.'   Oh, what joy for all my true subjects to
see the city thus surrendered to me!   Therefore have
I crowned my true servants, the prelates of the
Church, with glory and honor, and made them rulers
of all the work of my hands, giving them all the
kingdoms of this world and the glory thereof.   But
now, behold, a miserable remnant like mice crawling
out of their holes dare to challenge my prelates to
battle, and cry, ' General Council! let the people of
Christ come together.'   If they do not recant, kill
them, my sons.   Let no one take your crown.   No
sympathy must soften your heart, no pity cause it
to tremble; be hard as rock and let the whole earth
perish rather than give your honor to another.   Stand
by your advantage till the last breath.   I count on
you, for I know your obstinacy and stiff-neckedness.
Blessed be your wrath, that is so strong, and your
hate, that is so fixed.   Make broad your phylacteries,

and the borders of your garments great.   Love the
first places at feasts and the chief seats in synagogues.
Tithe mint and anise and cummin, but neglect the
weightier matters of the law.   Make proselytes that
are worse than yourself.   Be wise in your own con-
ceits.   Be strong and steadfast, for I am your shield
and great reward.   Run, that ye may receive the
prize.   Amen."

But these brave words were scarcely heard in the
storm of ecclesiastical politics.   The University, despairing of a Council, gave in its obedience to Clement
VII., and in 1384 d'Ailly became Rector of one of
its best colleges.   There he soon gathered round
him a band of distinguished scholars who all loved
him and became Gilles Deschamps, the " Sovereign
Doctor of Theology," Jean of Gerson, "the Most
Christian Teacher," and Nicolas of Clemanges, the
" Cicero of his Age."   D'Ailly's reputation as a wise
and forceful speaker grew, and in 1387 he was chosen
as head of a deputation to defend before the Pope the
action of the University in condemning as heretical
the theses of a Dominican applicant for a degree
who had attacked the Immaculate Conception of the
Virgin Mary.   His mission was difficult, for Thomas
Aquinas had denied the Immaculate Conception and
Urban V. had approved Thomas as the teacher of
the Church.   But, nevertheless, Clement condemned
the denial of Immaculate Conception as heretical,
and the Dominican transferred his obedience to the
other Pope.   There was wide rejoicing at this
triumph.   D'Ailly received the name of the " Eagle
of France," and at almost the same time the young

King chose him as confessor, and the University elected him Rector.

He soon had a second mission to Clement. A certain Prince Peter of Luxembourg, having been made Bishop of Metz at fourteen, and Cardinal at sixteen, died two years later, in 1387, and d'Ailly was sent to advocate his canonization. He preached twice to the Pope, once from the text, " Father, the hour is come; glorify thy Son, that thy Son also may glorify thee." The preacher proved Peter's holiness by a catalogue of 2128 miracles; e. g., dead raised, 73; blind healed, 57; cured of gout, 6, etc; his faith was illustrated by the zeal with which he flung into the fire a Dominican writing attacking the Immaculate Conception; and it was suggested as the peroration that God had given these wonderful powers to show that Clement was the rightful Pope and thus heal the schism.

In 1394 the University asked the written opinion of all its members on the schism. The result was— negotiations. And d'Ailly, being sent to the new Pope, was made to believe he would resign in due time and appointed Bishop of Cambrai.

He was succeeded in the rectorship of the University by his favorite scholar, John, born at Gerson in 1363. He had gained under his master a tendency to mysticism, a good training in theology, a love of the Scriptures, and a thorough devotion to the Church, Catholic and visible. He added to these a deep piety and an intense love of the young. The five folio volumes of his works, moral, mystic, exegetic, dogmatic, ecclesiastical, polemic and homiletic, show

how laboriously he used his powers and how faithfully he followed the bent of his genius. There is a practical turn to all his mystical and keenly critical mind thinks and feels. This Chancellor of the University used to devote much time to hearing the confessions of little boys. This learned theologian thought that all learning was only to teach the clergy to preach better. This skilful writer on ecclesiastical law was a stern preacher against the sins of the clergy, and his criticism and piety moved entirely within the self-chosen limits of the Catholic orthodox faith, which was to him a supernatural gift of God, through the Church, to every man who was obedient to God's servants. The system of faith the Church preserved, the system of government by which she preserved it, was more important to him than any opinion or any reform. Hence, like d'Ailly, in spite of the sceptical spirit he inherited with his nominalistic philosophy, he was always a *safe* theologian. And he shared not only his master's reforming zeal, but also his love for a " middle-of-the-road " policy. " It is better," he wrote, " that many truths should be unknown or concealed than that charity should be wounded by speaking of them." He anxiously warned every theological teacher to use the old forms, even if, in his judgment, he could find better. He even wished that, as the Church had one Head and one faith, so it might have only one theological faculty and be kept "safe." Naturally this was to be the faculty of Paris. He loved the Bible, but he opposed its translation into French, as full of danger of spreading heresy among unlearned folk, "as an

injury and a stumbling-block for the Catholic faith."
All these early utterances are prophecies of his tractate written over Jerome of Prague, that, when it
comes to " obstinacy in heresy against the command
of the Church, the conscience must be laid aside."

While this able successor followed him as Rector
and first orator of the University, d'Ailly was inau-
gurating reforms in his new diocese. He found
need, for in his first synodical sermon he said that,
while in our Lord's day there was one devil among
the twelve apostles, to-day among twelve baptized
there were eleven. It was from this herculean task
of cleansing, which he sketches in his convocation
sermons, that he was summoned to try and persuade
both Popes to resign. The double embassy was a
double failure, and France withdrew obedience from
both. But only for a while. Five years later
d'Ailly was summoned to preach the sermon at the
celebration of the return of France to the obedience
of Benedict—an obedience which in five years was
again withdrawn.

PERIOD I.

CHAPTER VIII.

THE COUNCIL OF PISA MAKES THE SCHISM TRIPLE—THE PROTEST OF JOHN HUSS OF BOHEMIA.

HEN, on the death of Innocent VII. in 1406, the fourteen cardinals of the Italian party met, they were evidently sincerely touched by the desperate condition of Christendom. The simple and honest way to express this feeling was to refuse to elect a Pope until it could be done by the representatives of the whole Church. For this they were not large enough. They feared lest their party should lose some advantage in the union, and after a short hesitation entered into conclave. But they bound themselves by a solemn agreement that if any of them were elected Pope he would at once begin to negotiate for union, and lay down the tiara whenever the interests of the Church demanded it. Then they chose the noble Venetian, Angelo Coraro. He was nearly eighty years old, and they thought that one so near death would not be tempted to forget duty for self—a singular want of knowledge of human nature, for all experience teaches that egotism is

79

never so all-engrossing as in the few last years left
to an ambitious or avaricious man for the exercise of
passion.   And the world soon became aware that
behind all the edifying and friendly messages sent to
his rival there was the fixed will of a crafty old man
neither to promote nor permit a union which did not
secure the gains of his party and leave him Pope.
When the pressure of France compelled both Popes
to agree to meet at Savona in September of 1408,
there began a double-sided comedy.   Each approached the place of meeting, but neither would go
there, and by letters curiously mingled of piety and
malice each tried to lay the whole blame for the
schism at the door of the other.

Then the French authorities forbade any one to
obey either Pope unless the schism were ended by a
certain day.   The enraged Benedict XIII., of the old
French faction, threatened excommunication, and the
Parliament of France and University of Paris declared
him deposed.   Gregory, triumphing over the loss of
his rival's strongest supporter, seized the opportunity
for breaking his oath to create no new cardinals, by
naming two of his nephews and two of his partisans
for the scarlet hat.   He already suspected his electors
and kept them surrounded by soldiers.   Remember-
ing the fate of the cardinals of Urban VI., most of
them fled and appealed to a Council.   Benedict
had already summoned one to his native place
of Perpignan, whither he fled for refuge.   Gregory called another to assemble near Ravenna.
Meantime some cardinals of both parties, Frenchmen
and Italians, met and called a Council, to be held at

Pisa, to arrange a basis of union and reform; and Christendom, which had so long asked for a Council, found itself overwhelmed with three.

It was a brilliant assembly that convened at Pisa in 1409: twenty-three cardinals, the prelates and ambassadors of kings, princes, and nations, the representatives of the universities, and one hundred doctors of law and theology. But in spite of its splendor and authority the council knew that its assemblage against Papal authority was an innovation, and hailed with gladness the tractates of d'Ailly and Gerson, claiming that as Christ was the corner-stone of the Church, she had power to exercise her authority without any visible Vicar if it were necessary to preserve her life. They added the characteristic and wise advice not to run the risk of adding schism to schism by electing a Pope until they were sure that Christendom would unanimously obey him.

The Council proceeded to depose and excommunicate both Gregory and Benedict as schismatics and heretics. The Cardinals then took oath that whoever was made Vicar of Christ would not dissolve the Council until the Church was reformed. And the Conclave elected Pietro Filargo. He was seventy-nine years old, came from the island of Candia, had no living relatives, and, report said, had been a beggar boy adopted by the monks to whose order he belonged. He was crowned under the name of Alexander V.; and, to use the words of a contemporary pamphleteer, the world saw " that infamous duality, now, indeed, become a trinity, not blessed, but accursed, fighting in the Church of God."

F

For the two Antipopes, each backed by his Synod, returned with interest the excommunications of the Council.   Benedict was supported by Aragon and Scotland, Gregory in Naples, Friauli, Hungary, and Bohemia.   Alexander could not conciliate them, and he had no resources to crush them.   For, as he said, " I was rich as a bishop, poor as a cardinal, but a beggar as Pope."

Baldassar Cossa, Cardinal Legate of Bologna, who succeeded him under the title of John XXIII., was popularly reported to have been a pirate in his youth and to have poisoned Alexander.   But these ought probably to be regarded as mythical details suggested by better authenticated facts of his career and character.   For these the day of judgment was approaching.   Driven by the exigencies of the triple contest to seek help from Sigismund, ruler of Germany, the Pope had no resource but to join him as emperor elect in calling a General Council at Constance in November, 1414.   And at last the middle-of-the-road policy of d'Ailly and his scholar Gerson triumphed in the call for a General Council issued by a Pope.

Meanwhile in the opposite corner of Europe another party of reform had been taking shape.   It also was national, headed by a university, and represented by two protagonists, a master and his scholar.   But nation and university were new and feeble, and both were divided on the question of reform into bitter factions.

Bohemia was a section of the empire which, by the force of the tendencies of the age, was fast acquiring an independent national feeling and existence.

It was a bilingual land, whose original German population, driven out in the eighth century by an irruption of Slavs, had since the thirteenth century been returning and mingling with them.   Germans formed the bulk of the burghers, or city dwellers, engaged in commerce, manufactures, and mining, while the peasant farmers and the nobles were Slavs.   In the middle of the century the growing national feeling had received, by the efforts of the King, two centres of expression.   The Bohemian Church was freed from the control of the Archbishopric of Mayence, whose seat was on the Rhine, and given its own Primate by the erection of a new Archbishopric in Prague; and in 1348 Bohemia became a centre of learning by the foundation of the University of Prague; the first university in Germany.

John Huss, born of a peasant family about 1369, first appears in close connection with these two organs of the national feeling.   He gained no special distinction at the University while a student, but rose steadily through the academic grades till he became a master of the liberal arts.   As a lecturer and teacher he won the respect of his fellows, and in 1402 was chosen to act as Rector or chief executive of the University for the usual term of six months.   In the same year he was ordained a priest in order to take charge of the Bethlehem Chapel, built some ten years before by a wealthy merchant of Prague, and endowed by one of the royal councillors, for the maintenance of preaching to the common people in the Slavic tongue.   He soon showed himself a not unworthy successor of the two great folks' preachers of Prague, dead about a generation before, Konrad and Miltitz. Konrad, because there was no church large enough to hold his congregation, had preached often in the great open square of the city.   He became, by the appointment of the Bishop, pastor of the largest parish in Prague, and preached repentance to the German burghers and to the clergy, denouncing sin with tremendous power.   His successor was Miltitz, a Slav, whose success was so great that he was sometimes compelled to preach five times a Sunday— thrice in Slavic and once each in German and Latin. He was so powerful in the truth that the worst street of the city, known because of its houses of prostitution as Little Venice, was abandoned by its inhabitants. The King bought and gave it to him, and he tore down the houses and built a Magdalen asylum named Little Jerusalem.   He did not hesitate in a great assembly to point out the King, his friend, and afterward still more his friend, as an antichrist who needed instant repentance.   It is not to be wondered at that one who preached in this apocalyptic strain got into trouble in those days with his ecclesiastical superiors. But he boldly went to Rome to meet his accusers. After vainly waiting for a hearing he posted on the door of St. Peter's the notice of a sermon on " The Present Antichrist."   Arrested by the inquisitor, he lay for some time in prison; but on the arrival of the Pope was released, treated with honor, and sent home in triumph.   As a preacher Huss lacked the ability, but not the courage, of these two men.

He formed his style and borrowed much of his material from the works of Wiclif.   He had already sat eagerly at the feet of the great scholastic, some of whose tractates he copied with his own hand. And now, following in the footsteps of Wiclif the preacher, he began to call men to repentance by the *law of Christ*, obedience to which was the only sign of membership in the *true church of God's chosen ones*.

Wiclif, it will be remembered, passed through three stages of thought in regard to the Church, which would be labelled by the enormous majority of his contemporaries *reform, revolution, heresy*. Huss followed him in two of these stages. And while he remained in the first stage, exhorting all ranks of the church to do their duty and rightly use their authority, he came into close connection with the second centre of national feeling, the new Archbishopric. The new incumbent, the descendant of a noble Slavic family, and skilled in everything except theology, was an honest man, for whose moral character Huss kept until the end the highest respect. He at once asked the new preacher's assistance in the reform of his province, applauded Huss's sermon before the Synod on the sins of the clergy, which did not spare even himself, and appointed him one of the commission to investigate the miracles of the blood of Christ at Wilsnach. Accepting the report upon that fraud, he forbade all pilgrimages from his province to the shrine of the alleged miracles.

But within six years, either because the Archbishop began to grow more conservative, or because Huss was becoming more radical in his criticism of the Church, a coolness arose between the two, which grew until the Archbishop removed his favorite from the

position of synodical preacher.   But the final break
with the hierarchy came when, under the lead of Huss,
the Bohemian teachers and students of the University
stood against the Bishops, and with the King, in favor
of remaining neutral in the schism of the Church and
awaiting the decision of a Council.   The three other
nations of the University voted, with the clergy, to
obey Alexander V., and the King issued a decree
giving hereafter three votes to the Bohemian nation,
and one to the Polish, Bavarian, and Saxon nations
together.   Whereupon the German students abandoned Prague and founded the new University of
Leipzig, while the triumphant Bohemians elected
Huss as rector.   Meanwhile the Archbishop had obtained two bulls from Pope Alexander V., commanding the surrender of all writings of Wiclif's and
forbidding preaching in any places which had not
acquired the right by long usage.   When these orders
were published, Huss, before a large assembly in the
Bethlehem Chapel, entered his protest against both
points, and appealed to the Pope.   A month later the
Archbishop excommunicated Huss, and two months
later two hundred volumes of Wiclif's writings were
publicly burned.   The students resented the first by
singing mocking songs about an " A B C archbishop
who burned books and didn't know what was in
them."   And the people resented the condemnation
of their favorite preacher in sterner fashion.   A
tumult in the cathedral broke up the high mass and
compelled the Archbishop to withdraw.   And in St.
Stephen's Church six men with drawn swords fell
upon the priest as he read the excommunication of

Huss and drove him from the pulpit.   Then the Archbishop used his last weapon, the dreaded interdict that forbade baptism, burial, marriage, and the Lord's Supper in the rebellious city of Prague.   But Huss stood by his post, and the sudden death of the Archbishop, and the appointment of the King's physician and trusted friend as his successor, brought peace.

A new cause for war soon followed.   John XXIII. proclaimed a crusade against Gregory XII., and an agent of the Curia appeared in Prague to cause the proclamation from every pulpit of a sale of indulgences to raise funds, and an enlistment of soldiers for a holy war in the name of the Vicar of Christ.   Huss, like Wiclif before him, sprang to his spiritual arms.   His pulpit rang with denunciations, and in university disputation he and his friends, notably the eloquent Jerome of Prague, attacked the crusade and the sale of indulgences against the majority of the theological faculty.   The excitement spread.   A mock procession, organized by a well-known nobleman, drew through the streets a wagon on which sat a woman of the town with the Pope's bull around her neck. Halting for a while before the palace of the Archbishop, the huge rude train went to the market-place, where the bull was laid on a scaffold and publicly burned.   The King did not punish the act, but forbade all disorder in future, under pain of death. Three young men of the common people, in spite of this edict, interrupted the services of several churches by denouncing the indulgence as a cheat and lie. They were arrested by the magistrates and beheaded. The people gathered the bodies, and in a procession, headed by a band of students chanting the song of the breviary for the commemoration of the martyrs, "Isti sunt sancti," bore them to the Bethlehem Chapel for a solemn funeral service. The German City Council endeavored to suppress Huss's preaching by force, and his congregation appeared in arms for his defence. Then, to relieve the city from the interdict and avoid the chances of riot in the streets, Huss, at the request of his King, withdrew to voluntary exile, leaving behind an open letter in which he appealed from the Curia to Christ.

Soon after he was visited by two messengers from Sigismund, who invited him, under promise of a safe-conduct, to appear before the General Council at Constance, where he might have an opportunity to clear himself of the charge of heresy and save the ecclesiastical honor of Bohemia. Nothing could have pleased Huss more. He had himself appealed from the Pope to a Council, and his one desire had always been to persuade the Church to accept his ideas, or at least permit them. Nevertheless, forebodings of evil haunted his prophetic soul. His letter to the Emperor spoke of his desire to confess Christ, and if need be suffer death for his true law. He wrote his will and gave it to a favorite scholar, with directions not to break the seal until he heard of his death. And he left a farewell letter to his friends in Bohemia, in which he asked for their prayers that he might stand firm, and if need be suffer death without fear. They shared his anxiety. A shoemaker of the city bade him, "God-speed; I think you will not come back, dear, true, and steadfast knight. May the heavenly King, not the Hungarian, give you the eternal reward for the faithful care you have given to my soul."

Sigismund appointed three Bohemian nobles as imperial deputies to enforce the safe-conduct which protected him against illegal violence, and Huss set out for Constance.

PERIOD I.

CHAPTER IX.

THE COUNCIL OF CONSTANCE AND TRIUMPH OF
THE PARTY OF CONCILIAR AUTHORITY: (1)
THEY DEPOSE THE POPES AND FORCE UNION;
(2) THEY REPUDIATE THE BOHEMIAN PRO-
TEST AND BURN HUSS; (3) THEY FAIL TO DE-
TERMINE THE REFORM OF THE CHURCH IN
HEAD AND MEMBERS.

LMOST the first to arrive at the fair little
city by the lake was the Pope, who had
ridden up from Italy with a splendid train
of nine cardinals and many prelates. He
entered the gates in state, with two great
nobles walking at the bridle-reins of his palfrey, while
the burgomaster and rulers of the city carried the
glittering baldachin over his head. And for three
months the boys of Constance must have revelled in
the almost daily spectacle of some stately entry. The
legates of Gregory and Benedict, who had been
courteously invited to come to the Council, princes,
ambassadors, great nobles, archbishops and splendid
prelates, little companies of University doctors, all
with as many horses and servants in their train as

they could muster, straggled through the streets in spasmodic parade. The Emperor came by torchlight on Christmas eve. He was accompanied by the Empress and several Princes of the Empire, and followed by a thousand horses laden with articles of luxury, from his service of table silver down to many pack-loads of embroidered pillows, silk bolsters, and carpets. Before midnight, clothed in the dalmatic and with his crown on his head, he read the Gospel for the day as deacon, while the Pope conducted mass in the cathedral.

One meeting had already been held, but nothing done, except formally open the Council, arrange for proper secretaries, and discuss the order of business. The first important question was the manner of voting, and its discussion plunged the Council into the troubled sea of curial politics. The Italian prelates numbered almost half the voters, for Italy was cut up into many petty bishoprics. If the Council voted in a mass, the Pope held the balance of power. The friends of union and reform therefore rejected this usual custom, and it was decided that all present should be divided into four nations, German, English, French, and Italian. (The Spanish was added afterward.) Each nation was represented by a fixed number of deputies, with a president, changed every month. All questions were first discussed in national assemblies. The results were communicated and discussed in common meetings of the deputies. Any point on which all agreed was then discussed in a general congregation and, if adopted, solemnly affirmed in the next General Session of the Council.

Armed with this conclusion, the friends of union proceeded to deal with John.

They had no easy task to force him to face the situation. It was hard for such a man, an adventurer fighting for his own hand, to whom the idea of duty was unknown, to get any glimpse of what it meant to be head and servant of a great institution. He knew no better than to keep on as Pope doing what he had done all his life—use every circumstance and event as something to be squeezed for his own gain. Nor was he without support. The cardinals probably had no illusions in regard to him as a man, but it was natural they should stand by him as Pope. For when men have risen by work or fortune to the top of any institution, it takes unusual greatness of mind or character to be very much dissatisfied with it; and they are always apt to be disinclined to any changes not absolutely necessary to its life. D'Ailly, therefore, stood almost alone among the Princes of the Church in desiring thoroughgoing reform—reform checked and guarded at every point, but reform based, if need be, on amendment of the constitution. He stood by his order, of course, but Gerson working without and he within, soon forced upon John, in spite of every subterfuge and attempt to dissolve the party by personal diplomacy, the solemn declaration " to give peace to the Church by the method of simple cession of the Papacy whenever Benedict and Gregory, either in person or by proper procurators, shall do the same." But already the report was in the air that John would break up the Council by flight. Several princes warned the Archduke of Austria, whose dynastic ambition would be flattered by having a Pope to protect and control, to keep out of any such plot, and Sigismund visited John and bluntly told him of the current suspicions. It is even said that the Bishop of Salisbury, who was in the Emperor's train, forbade the Pope to his face to dare any such rebellion against the authority of the Council. John promised " not to leave before the dissolution of the Council "; which his party afterward excused by the statement that the absence of the Pope *ipso facto* dissolved the Council.

Two days later the evasion was skilfully carried out. By this time a crowd of one hundred thousand strangers, with thirty thousand horses, was assembled at Constance. It was a mixed assembly of members of the Council and idle sight-seers, and was anxious to be amused. Musicians and jugglers, estimated at seventeen hundred, ministered to the pleasure of the visitors, and a great crowd of the victims and tempters of the vices of society served its sins in a commerce of evil which, to the great scandal of all honest men, even involved some of the worldly prelates of the Church. The princes, in the spirit of perpetual circus day which was common to the time, vied with one another in display at feasts and processions; and when the Duke of Austria gave his great tournament on the 20th of March all Constance went to see. At nightfall the Pope, dressed like a groom, mounted on a mean horse with an arquebuse at the saddle-bow, and, covered with a coarse gray cloak, coolly rode out of the gates with only one boy in his train. Two hours later a hungry traveller asked food of the village pastor of Ermatingen, and getting into a little boat, was carried across the sea to Schaffhausen, where he was joined the next day by the Duke, its Sovereign. The news of this evasion, brought by a letter from John to the Emperor, threw all Constance into panic. The timid members of the Council prepared for instant flight. The mob began to plunder, and rumor reported an army at the gates. It seemed as if the Council would break up at once. Sigismund first rallied the terror-stricken city. Riding through the swarming streets, he put down disorder with a strong hand, scoffed at the idea of an assault, and bade every one be of good cheer. He called two assemblies, one of the German princes, and another of the four nations. In the first he announced his purpose to hold the Council together if it cost his life, and by deputation obtained from the cardinals the promise to join in conducting business, if necessary, without the Pope. They even agreed to abandon him altogether in case his continued absence prevented union and reform. Meanwhile they asked that all action against him be suspended until an embassy could confer and report.

The Council itself was steadied by a sermon from Gerson on John xii. 35, which maintained that the Church might take counsel without the presence of the Pope and, if need be, force him to close the schism. The cardinals refused to be present at the sermon, and the Council, after waiting in vain for their co-operation, proceeded to a General Session without them. Only two of them seemed to have been aware of the danger. The Council at Pisa had met without a Pope, but here was the more fatal innovation of a Council without cardinals. D'Ailly, the most progressive, and Zabarella, one of the more conservative of the body, were alike too old and trained ecclesiastics to be so caught. It was bad to be outvoted; it was worse to be ignored. While their brother princes sulked in their tents, they rushed at once to the Hall, where one acted as President, and the other read the conclusions of the Nations.

In the next two sessions, under presidence of the cardinals, and after heavy debating carried on amid a double fire of pamphlets, it was decided that the Council of Constance, as a true Ecumenical Council, held its power direct from God; that every Christian, even the Pope himself, was bound to obey it in all that concerned faith, the destruction of the schism, and reform in head and members; and therefore "it was not dissolved by the blameworthy and scandalous flight of the Pope, but remained in all its integrity and authority, even though the Pope should declare the contrary." Thus the party of union and reform threw down the glove before the defenders of an autocratic Papacy. Their victory was certain.* As long negotiations made plainer and plainer the unwillingness of John to forget himself in his duty, even the cardinals, who wanted to stand by him as long as possible, yielded to the pressure of circumstances or the logic of events, and in the eleventh sitting, on the 29th of May, the President of the College of Cardinals added their placet to the decree by which John XXIII. was solemnly deposed from the Papacy as a notorious simoniac, a squanderer of the goods of the

Church, an evil steward, and a man whose horrible life and indecent manners both before and after his election had given scandal to the Church of God and all Christian people. The first stumbling-block on the way to union and reform was removed.

Then the Council proceeded to remove the second : the heresy so wide-spread in Bohemia. For though Huss hoped to appear at the Council as a man slandered by a charge of heresy, but really representing a great body of true Catholics desiring to persuade the Church to necessary reforms, his Bohemian enemies and the leaders of the other parties were too clever to let him appear in any such light. They did not propose to have a discussion, but a trial, and they made up their minds that, in spite of the imperial safe-conduct, Huss's first public appearance must be as a prisoner.

The 21st of November, three weeks after his arrival, two bishops appeared in Huss's lodgings to lead him to an audience with the cardinals. Baron von Chlum, as the representative of the royal honor, at once interfered and declined to allow anything to be done in Huss's case until Sigismund had arrived. The Bishop of Trent replied that no harm was intended to Huss; the invitation was simply a friendly one. Whereupon Huss at once agreed to go. They took him to the palace of the Pope, where he had an audience with the cardinals, and in the afternoon the Baron von Chlum was informed that he might withdraw whenever he desired, but Magister Huss must remain. The knight at once demanded to see the Pope, and using the respectful forms of address due to his office, accused him of treachery and falsehood.   For he did not fail in duty or friendship. Influential noblemen, prelates, and burghers of Constance were shown the safe-conduct, and begged to defend the royal honor.   Then, unable to do more, he nailed his public protest, in Latin and German, on the door of the cathedral.   Meanwhile Huss was put into a cell of the Dominican cloister so unwholesome that in a short time he fell ill, poisoned by sewer-gas.   When Sigismund, met on the road to Constance by John von Chlum, heard of Huss's arrest without any legal process, he flamed into wrath and sent an order for his instant release, with a threat to break the doors of his prison and fetch him.   But before the resistance of the Curia his purpose melted, and even when the flight of John put the keys of Huss's prison into his hands, he simply sent them to the Bishop of Constance, and the prisoner, worn by illness, was thrust into the tower of the episcopal castle at Gottlieben, near Constance, badly fed, compelled to carry chains by day, and to sleep with his hands fastened to the wall beside his bed.   Meantime the Council had condemned forty-five propositions drawn from the works of Wiclif, and declared him a hardened heretic whose body ought not to rest in consecrated ground ; a sentence carried out twelve years later by the Bishop of Lincoln, who dug up his bones.   Then, as soon as the Pope was deposed, Huss was summoned before the Council for his first public hearing.

Public rumor and the efforts of the emissaries of the Bohemian clergy, the majority of whom were

G

contributors to a fund to pay the costs of Huss's prosecution, had surrounded him with such an air of heresy and violent revolution that in the minds of the Council he was condemned before he appeared, and they listened with scant patience at his first informal hearing. He was interrupted by exclamations. When he claimed that he had been misquoted they cried, "Stop your sophistry; answer yes or no." When he kept silence they said, " Silence gives consent." And such an uproar finally arose that it was thought best to dismiss the assembly. In future hearings there was fair play, for the presence of Sigismund kept order. But his words told strongly against Huss; for he declared that any single one of the propositions from his books on which he was arraigned was enough to prove him a heretic, and demanded that if he did not recant he should be burned. He warned them not even to trust his recantation, for if he was not forbidden to preach or see his friends he would resume his heresy on his return to Bohemia. If there was any lingering doubt about his fate this speech sealed it.

John von Chlum stood by him like a man, and as he left the assembly seized him boldly by the hand and bade him be of good cheer. There were others who would have saved him if they could. He was visited again and again in his prison, and the utmost was done to frame a formula of adjuration he would accept. The final result was skilful and fair, for it limited his recantation to literal transcriptions of propositions from his books, and, embodying his denial of utterances put into his mouth by witnesses, simply rejected them hypothetically. To lead him to accept this formula the leaders of the Council sought the intercession of John von Chlum and his companion, von Duba. John visited Huss in company with many prelates, and said: "See, Magister John, we are laymen and cannot advise you. But if you are guilty you must not be ashamed to be taught and recant. If, however, you do not feel yourself guilty, you must on no account disobey your conscience and lie before God, but rather stand steadfast in the truth till death." These words of honest friendship were good to the prisoner who had written to the University of Prague that he was determined to retract nothing unless it were proved to be false by the Word of God, and failing acquittal, he would appeal from the Council to the judgment-seat of Christ. Such an attitude, denying the authority of the Church to determine belief and rule conduct, was in itself heresy and, according to the law, a sufficient ground of condemnation.

Huss was brought before the Council for sentence the 6th of July, 1415. He was clad in the garments of a priest about to say mass, and the pieces were taken from him by the bishops, according to the usual formula. When they took from his hand the cup they said, "Judas, who hast left the councils of peace and joined thyself to the council of the Jews, we take from thee the cup of salvation." To which Huss answered with firm voice, "I trust in the Lord, the Almighty God, for whose name's sake I patiently bear these blasphemies. He will not take from me the cup of salvation, and I hope to drink it with him even to-day in his Kingdom."

Arrived at the place of execution, he fell on his knees at sight of the stake, crying, " Lord Jesus Christ, I will bear this horrible and shameful death humbly and patiently for the sake of thy gospel and for the preaching of thy Word." He was bound to the stake, and wood and straw piled around him as high as his chin. Pappenheim, the Marshal of the Empire, begged him to recant and save his life. Huss refused, and the fire was lighted. The smoke rolled up, and before his Latin prayer, " Jesus Christ, Son of the living God, have mercy upon me," could be three times intoned he died. They gathered the ashes from around the stake and cast them into the Rhine.

Eleven months afterward Jerome of Prague, having once recanted and anathematized the works of Wiclif and Huss, was called to a second trial on new charges. He closed his defence by declaring that " the writings of his master were holy and right, like his life," and, refusing to recant, was burned as " a sharer in the errors of Huss and Wiclif."

Huss and Jerome died when they were condemned, because heresy was as much a crime by the law as stealing or murder. Their condemnation was inevitable, because, when they met d'Ailly and Gerson, two types of men stood face to face. Huss and Jerome were not, indeed, wanting in reverence for inheritance of the past and the institutions of society. Their defence was full of quotations from the men of old, and they came to Constance of their own free will, because they loved the Church. But to them the truth was greater than the symbol and religion more

vital than any of its institutions. They felt that
Christ had left in the world a teaching, not a visible
authority, and it was the duty of every man to do
and believe what his mind and conscience told him
was in accord with that teaching. D'Ailly, Gerson,
and their followers were, on the other hand, not in-
different to truth. Gerson's mystic piety was deep,
and we may well believe that he would have died for
the truth as freely as the two Bohemians. But he did
not believe that the truth could continue to exist apart
from the visible authority of the institution he served.
Neither Huss nor d'Ailly were without personal ambition. The acute Frenchman tried to catch the
debate-loving Hungarian in a scholastic dilemma over
universals and prove him a heretic on the doctrine of
the Trinity. And Huss writes with unmistakable glee
to his friends how he escaped the subtle snare and
silenced "the chief Cardinal of them all." D'Ailly
was so well contented to be the chief Cardinal that he
was willing to give a despised heretic the last word.
But after all, both judge and prisoner, in spite of the
weakness of the flesh and the *gaudium certaminis*,
stood resolutely and honestly for their convictions.
Both believed in reason and conscience; but the one
submitted his reason and conscience to the invisible
Christ, the other to the visible Christ, the Holy
Church.

What was expected of Huss had he been an orthodox Roman Catholic has been plainly exemplified in
this generation by those prelates who, after combat-
ing the dogma of Infallibility at the Vatican Council,
afterward felt it their duty to accept it for the sake

of charity and on the authority of the Church.   The
Bohemians died for refusing this authority.   They
indignantly asserted their fidelity to the entire received doctrine of the mass.   Jerome began his defence by invoking the Virgin Mary and all the saints,
and when bound to the stake sang the creed as a
proof that he died in the true faith.

Huss was not a great thinker.   The parallel column
has shown unmistakably that the chief of his new opinions, and even the forms of their expression, were borrowed from Wiclif.   It has been mistakenly claimed
that he shared in the theological scheme afterward asserted by Luther, the *solafidean.*   But his writings refute
the claim, and his dying assertion of faith in Jesus Christ,
a quotation from the prayer-book, is no more a proof
that theologically he was an " evangelical " than the
similar dying confession of St. Catherine of Siena,
or a score of other orthodox Roman Catholic worthies
of all ages.   He did not possess the force or originality of intellect needed to express religious experience in new theological formulas.   And this makes
clear his courage and illuminates the significance of
his death.   He sealed his fate when he cried, " I appeal from the Council to Christ."   More plainly, perhaps, than any man in the history of the Church, he
and his friend died for the dignity of the individual
soul and the idea that, in the last analysis, religion is
a personal matter between the Teacher sent from
God and every disciple.

The result of the death of Huss and Jerome was the
revolt of Bohemia against the commands of the Church

and the Empire. When their King died the peasants and nobles refused to receive his brother Sigismund as King because he had broken his word and betrayed Huss to death. He has never lacked for apologetes, and they have a case, because the formal safe-conduct was not intended to protect against the law, but only against violence. But the instant they step outside of those formalities by which gentlemen of every age and people have always declined to limit their honor, Sigismund's defenders are in great embarrassment. Huss came to Constance on reliance on his word. The least Sigismund could have done was to secure fair play, to defend him against being cast into a noisome dungeon without due process of law, to have stood by him to the end, and not to have sealed his fate even before he was condemned. Charles V., when he was urged to permit the arrest of Luther, who came to Worms under his protection, refused because he did not care to blush like Sigismund. For it is said that Huss, before he left the cathedral on his way to the stake, turned and looked at Sigismund, who looked down and colored. History finds no basis for the anecdote, but the judgment of most honest men is that if Sigismund did not blush he ought to have blushed.

The war in Bohemia, animated by the two forces of race hatred and religious zeal, soon took on a character of singular ferocity. When the crusade was proclaimed against the heretics, adventurers of all nations, led by the offer of indulgences and the promise of plunder, joined the German army. The Bohemians met the cross, now become the sign of oppression and cruelty, with the symbol of the cup.   It signified their habit of communing in both kinds.   In the orthodox Roman Catholic communion only the bread is given to the people, and the wine is drunk by the priest.   This custom, originally caused by the fear lest the blood of Christ should be spilled, had come to be associated with the special privileges of the clergy as priests needed to mediate between the people and God. The habit of giving the cup to the laity started in Bohemia during Huss's captivity.   After some hesitation it was approved by him as agreeable to the example of our Lord and his apostles.   It soon became to the people the visible expression of that appeal from the authority of tradition to the word of Christ found in the Scriptures and interpreted by reason and conscience, for which he had died. Under this rallying signal they hurled back five crusades in slaughterous defeat; and crossing the borders, ravaged Germany almost to the Rhine with fire and sword, so that the name Bohemian or Hussite remained for generations in German villages a word to frighten children.   It was eighteen years before the Bohemians came back again to the fellowship of the Church.

The Council, having thus decided that the centre of ecclesiastical authority was in itself, having deposed one Pope and received the resignation of another, having cut off the heresy which denied the supreme authority of the Church, was free to proceed to that task for which all these things were only the preparation —the reform of the Church in head and members.

The general good will for this work is suggested in three sermons, preached in the end of August and beginning of September, 1416. The first one asserted that the Roman Curia is diabolic and almost all the clergy of the Church subject to the devil. The second, by Professor Theobald, going into particulars, accuses the clergy of open vices, and sums up the situation in the phrase, " Prælati nutriunt tot meretrices quot familiares." The third, delivered by the representative of the University of Vienna, on the word of Christ to the leper, " Go show thyself to the priests," cited the entire clergy, patriarch, archbishops, bishops, etc., as being afflicted with the leprosy of worldliness, dissoluteness, avarice, and simony, and called on the Council to heal this foul disease.

They began with the deposition of Benedict XIII. An embassy was sent to his mountain fortress of Paniscola to announce it. The old Spaniard's will was unbroken by isolation and the weight of over ninety years. He received the embassy of assembled Christendom in full regalia, and they began to read the sentence of the Council. The words " heretic " and " schismatic " brought an outburst of wrath. " It is not true; you lie. Here," he cried, beating the arm of his chair with his hand, " here is the ark of Noah. I am the true follower of the unity of the Church. Those at Constance are heretics and schismatics, not I." For eight years longer the unconquerable graybeard held his empty state, and bound his two remaining cardinals, under penalty of his dying curse, to elect a successor. They solemnly shut themseves into conclave and elected the

Canon Mugnos, who maintained the pomp and circumstance of the little mountain Papacy for four years more and then resigned, A.D. 1429.

The evils which demanded reform at the hands of the Council were of two kinds: the unworthy character and irregular lives of the clergy, and the exactions and corruption of the administration of the Church by the Roman Curia. To meet these evils the party of which Gerson was the ablest spokesman demanded the reform of the Church in head and members. The cause of this corruption, so far as it exceeded that measure of weakness and personal ambition which may be expected in all institutions managed by men, was the same as that which lies at the root of the worst corruptions of our politics, the temptations of an enormous patronage. The Church was a very wealthy institution. Its property was not dispersed by inheritances, and grew constantly by gift and bequest. The ecclesiastical lands in England, for instance, were reckoned at a third of the entire real estate of the kingdom. Much of this wealth was honestly spent in the care of the poor and the building of those mediæval churches which are among the most beautiful things ever made by human hands. Much of it was spent in luxury and display, by which numbers of unworthy men were tempted to enter the priesthood and the manners and morals of the clergy corrupted. By steady usurpation of privileges the Roman Curia had succeeded in imposing a heavy burden of complicated taxes on the ecclesiastical salaries and incomes of the world. The foundation of direct taxes was the so-called right of reservation, by which the Popes had acquired the right to fill vacancies in a large number of bishoprics and abbacies by direct appointment. All such appointees were compelled to pay heavy taxes—the first year's income of the benefice, and various other sums—to the Papal treasury. A second kind of tax, direct and indirect, was indulgences; by which the Pope, usurping the rights of local discipline, sold by his agents all over the world dispensations from the Church penance imposed upon various sins. The right of appeal to Rome in all ecclesiastical causes was another great source of revenue. For dispensations were sold through the dioceses of the world, by which a clergyman of lower rank was freed from some given claim or right of his superior, and made secure of acquittal in the event of an appeal to Rome. Then exemptions against these exemptions were sold to the ecclesiastical overlord, until the rights of some of the bishops were so tied up with a tangle of Papal bulls that it would have puzzled the shrewdest canonical lawyer to define just what power remained to them in many cases. To these abuses of the power of provisors and indulgence were attached two scandals which everybody had denounced and no one dared to defend for generations, and yet which had steadily increased—plurality of benefices, resulting in absenteeism and simony or the sale of the offices of the Church. It was common for one man to hold several offices and perform the duties of none. There were bishops who knew nothing of the state of religion in their dioceses, and cared less, canons who had never seen the cathedral to which they belonged, and priests who had never entered the bounds of their parishes. And the sale of the salaried positions of the Church, from the Papacy and the red hat of a cardinal down to door-keepers of the churches, was notorious.

To drive out these tables of the money-changers from the house of God the Council needed something more than invective. The times demanded the repression of the usurpations by which the Curia had encroached upon episcopal rights, and the restoration of local government throughout the dioceses; an absolute prohibition of pluralities, and rules strictly regulating absenteeism; the devising of some means to convict simoniacs and enforce upon them the stern penalties of the canon law, so long mere dead letters. But ecclesiastical assemblies, always apt to be cautious, are often cowardly. And against the advocates of a thorough and sure reform, those whose principles or whose interests led them to defend the privileges of the Curia could appeal to the fears of the conservatives that reform would become revolution. They had two arguments to use. The Papal States were in rebellion and but little income came from them. If the Papal taxes were reduced, how could the Church have any Pope and cardinals at all? Secondly, though the Council had rightly deposed the Pope for the preservation of the Church, the Church was only rightly constituted when she had a head, and reform ought to be preceded by the election of a Pope.

After long discussion the twenty-three cardinals, accompanied by six deputies from each of the five nations, Spain, Italy, France, England, and Germany, went into conclave on the 4th of November, 1417. The great hall of the merchants' house had been divided into fifty-three little rooms by canvas walls. All access to doors or windows was shut off by guarded barriers, and no ship might approach within bowshot of the walls. Two bishops sat before the door to inspect all food carried in, lest notes might be concealed in it; but the ancient rule that after three days they were to receive only two meals a day, and after eight more only one, was suspended—perhaps out of consideration for the carnal weakness of the deputies associated with the cardinals in the conclave. On the third day the anxious city learned that after a long strife between the five nations, each of which wanted a Pope of its own tongue, the unanimous choice had fallen upon the Cardinal Deacon Otto, of the ancient Roman house of Colonna, a man of ability and honorable record, with a fine personal appearance and dignified manners. The Emperor rushed into the conclave and kissed his feet, hailing him as the morning star that at last had risen out of darkness, and all Christendom rejoiced that the schism was safely closed. Five months later the Cardinal Deacon Raynald called out, " Domini ite in pace," all answered, " Amen," and the great Council was over. But the reform of the Church in head and members was scarcely begun. For the curial party, under the lead of Martin V., had but little difficulty in foiling every attempt to unite the nations in any plan of general reform. Amid distrust and despair, each began to scramble for national privileges, secured to them in a series of concordats signed by the Pope. And these compromise reforms recognized the rights of the Pope in the matter of the very usurpations and abuses they abated.

The Council of Constance has involved the orthodox Roman Catholic theologian and canonist of this century in considerable embarrassment. The Papal succession depends upon its ecumenical authority, for it deposed two Papal claimants as schismatics, compelled a third to resign, and elected a new Pope by an untraditional method. But the decree necessary to its work, that the authority of a General Council was greater than the authority of a Pope, is of course a denial of that dogma by which the Vatican Council of 1870 completed the Catholic system and defended it against all change—the Infallibility of the Pope. The judgment of the learned Bishop Hefele, in his great "Conciliengeschichte," is characteristic: "There can, therefore, be no doubt that, according to the ecclesiastical law of to-day, which considers the approbation of the Pope upon General Councils necessary to constitute them such, all conclusions of Constance which do not prejudice the Papacy are to be considered ecumenical, but all, on the other hand, which infringe upon the privilege, the dignity, the preëminence of the apostolic chair are to be held for reprobated."

PERIOD I.

CHAPTER X.

THE PAPAL REACTION—THE STRUGGLE FOR THE PATRIMONIUM—MARTIN V. AND EUGENIUS IV. REËSTABLISH THE PAPAL SUPREMACY WITHOUT GRANTING REFORM—THE PROTEST AND ABORTIVE SCHISM OF THE COUNCIL OF BASLE.

HE new Pope was face to face with a situation that might well have daunted a bolder man. He entered Rome by streets almost impassable, past ruined churches and empty or fallen houses, through a crowd as wild and miserable-looking as their city. The States of the Church were all but dissolved into strange or hostile municipalities and communes, while petty tyrants and soldiers of fortune were striving to make principalities for themselves out of the patrimony of St. Peter. And behind this was the task of the reform of the Church in head and members, to which he was solemnly pledged.

To meet his political difficulties he was fitted by many characteristics. He was firm, clever, had an engaging personality that inspired confidence, and lived simply; for he desired the reality and not the shows of power. Rome began to become prosperous; the citizens rebuilt their houses, streets and bridges were repaired, and, led by his example, some of the cardinals rebuilt their titular churches. Order was restored around the walls of the city by the destruction of robbers, and an annalist exclaims with wonder that one could go through the country with gold in the open hand. Teachers of religion began to appeal with success to the people. Bernardino of Siena, for instance, came to Rome three years after Martin's return, preaching repentance. He was the son of a noble family, who, feeling in his heart the call to preach Christ, entered the order of St. Francis while still a youth. He had acquired great influence throughout various cities of Italy, and his success at Rome was striking. Many blood-feuds were reconciled by him. He was accustomed to denounce the luxury of the times as a chief cause of sin, and on the 25th of June, 1421, he publicly set fire to a great scaffold on which was piled false hair, cosmetics, instruments of music, worldly books, and many other articles of luxury. Three days later another pyre was lighted in the presence of all Rome, which was crowned by a living woman, burned for witchcraft.

In the attempt to recover the Papal State lost to tyrants and rebellious vassals, Martin's chief opponent was Braccio Fortebraccio, a condottiere, or soldier of fortune. For the Breton or German leaders of the Free Companies of the fourteenth century were now quite largely replaced by Italians trained in their troops and rising from the ranks. The two most celebrated of these were Jacopo Sforza and Braccio Fortebraccio. Sforza, the son of a peasant, had run away from home and enlisted at the age of thirteen. Rising to fame, he had used his twenty brothers and sisters to extend and hold his power. His frank manners, strict honesty in all money engagements, the care with which he protected the peasants from pillage, and his reluctance to destroy conquered cities made him respected even while feared, and he was called "the common father of the men-at-arms." His rival, Braccio, seems to have been a rougher sort—a breaker of his word, a layer of plots, and a burner of harvest-fields, who put the country-side in terror. But he was firmly fixed in his usurpations, and the Pope could only get into Rome by receiving him at Florence and naming him Vicar for the rule of some of his best cities.

Two traits prevented Martin from having a good will for the reform of the Church—pride and the greed of gold. The latter was so notorious that a celebrated writer among the curial secretaries hesitated to publish an essay "On Avarice," lest it should be thought an attack on the Pope. No avaricious Pope could honestly desire reform. Nor would the head of the Colonna consent to lessen the wealth and power of the city which was the background of the dignity of his race. His nepotism was as marked as that of poorer Popes, who thought it necessary to create great relatives for their own support. And during his life the family of Colonna were everywhere advanced and enriched. The sale of benefices and the whole system of fees and perquisites, which crushed all poor appellants to the justice of the Papal court, increased, and the Papal usurpations

H

of episcopal rights on which these abuses were founded were silently maintained, in spite of the protests and agreements of Constance. It was not to be supposed that this was done without opposition. It had been agreed at Constance that a new Synod was to be assembled at Pavia within five years, but its temper was so dangerous when it met that the Pope adjourned it to Siena, and then closed it to await the General Council which had been appointed for the tenth year after Constance. Meantime he pleased Christendom by appointing to the College of Cardinals half a dozen men whose wisdom or piety fitted them in the eyes of all for the dignity of Princes of the Church. Then, just on the eve of the assembly of an Ecumenical Council at Basle, he died (1431).

Martin had in every way repressed the powers of the cardinals, and before they proceeded to a new election, the College, the most weighty and dignified for many years, passed the first of the capitulations which hereafter every Pope was compelled to accept. It was an attempt to preserve the Papacy in the form of an aristocratic oligarchy where the Pope was the first of the cardinals, and to defend their rights as a senate governing the Church with him. In practice, however, it always failed of its purpose and never seriously checked the growing absolutism of the Papacy.

The so-called rhythm of the Papacy, by which the opposition party generally elects the new Pope, gave the votes to the candidate of the Orsini, the Roman family which rivalled the Colonna. Eugenius IV. was forty-eight years old and had been made Cardinal by his uncle, Gregory XII., in 1408. His appearance, writes a chronicler, was so majestic that once, when he appeared upon a platform to intone the prayer in a service at Florence, the people who crowded the great square were moved to tears before the figure " of the Vicar of Christ, who seemed to be he whom he represented." His pious habit never varied. Amid all his business, four monks, two of his own order, were always with him to conduct the proper offices of day and night, in which he never failed to join. He was free from nepotism and avarice. His relatives, who flocked to him, received nothing from the goods of the Church. He answered that he could not give away what was not his. But many stories are told of his generosity. Once he offered to a poor Florentine who begged for help a purse of gold pieces and told him to help himself. The abashed man took only two or three. " Oh," laughed Eugenius, " put your hand in. You are welcome to the gold."

The nepotic and avaricious Martin had ruled Rome in peace, but the generous and unworldly Eugenius lived in the midst of civil war. For the sins of his predecessor were visited on his head. The castles and cities of the patrimonium were garrisoned by the soldiers of the Colonnas; the Papal jewels and a large part of the treasure of St. Peter were in their hands. When summoned they declined to surrender them to a Pope who had been the candidate of the rival family of Orsini. When Eugenius became peremptory they assaulted the city, seized and held one of the gates, and the slaughter and burning of civil war filled the streets of a part of Rome for a month.

Scarcely was this bloody trouble ended by the entire submission of the Colonna and the surrender of everything claimed by the Pope than the Council met at Basle, and the Papacy had to face again that great episcopal system whose rights it had so continuously usurped. The prelates reaffirmed the decision of Constance that the Council was independent, indissoluble, except by its own consent, and superior to the Pope, and summoned Eugenius to appear within three months for trial. These things strengthened the local enemies of the Pope. Different bands of condottieri, the chief of whom called himself General of the Holy Council, besieged him in Rome. Thus driven to a corner, Eugenius recalled the bulls dissolving the Council, acknowledged it as the highest authority, and put himself under its protection. By this time many prelates, including seven cardinals, were assembled; the Council was supported by all the powers, and it seemed that the principle of Conciliar Authority had obtained a second and lasting victory over Papal absolutism.

But Eugenius could not make his peace with the Romans. Wearied by the endless war which wasted their lands, they rose with the old cry of "The folk, the folk and freedom!" established the Republic, and forced the captive Pope to renounce the worldly power. Then Eugenius fled. A reformed pirate, Vitellius of Ischia, had recently been taken into the Papal service, and his galley lay at Ostia. Disguised as a Dominican monk, the Pope slipped out of the back door, while some bishops appeared to wait his immediate coming to the audience-chamber. A mule brought him to the river-bank, and a servant of the ex-pirate carried the Pope on his back through the shallow water to a boat. But suspicion was aroused, for it was full daylight, and a great crowd pursued. They put the Pope in the bottom and covered him with a shield, and the seamen of Vitellius rowed down the river amid a storm of stones and arrows until they distanced the cursing Romans and landed their passenger on the galley. The Romans had often driven the Popes from Rome and called them back again, for they were a folk impatient of authority and incapable of self-rule; but it might have comforted Eugenius, as he lay under the shield, could he have known that none of his successors for four hundred years would again be compelled to flee before an insurrection of their own people.

In June, 1434, the Pope sought the protection of the Republic of Florence and took up his residence in that city. Every petty tyrant in the Papal States, suppressed or appeased by the policy or strength of the family of Martin, now seized the opportunity given by the rebellious Colonna. And once more it was evident that if the Vicar of Christ was to be ruler of a kingdom of this world, the Church had need of a prince who could hide the silk glove of a cardinal in the gauntlet of a man-at-arms. He was at hand in the person of Giovanni Vitelleschi, who began life as the clerk of a condottiere, afterward went into ecclesiastics, and had become Bishop of Recanati. He had already been Papal legate in the march of Ancona, where he had displayed skill in war and a ruthless temperament. Eugenius gave him the task of destroying petty tyrants, rooting out the condottieri and subduing Rome. The terrible priest, who had already shown himself not slow to shed blood, fought fire with fire. One by one the fierce barons were bribed or forced to peace. The Prefect of Vico, descendant of a family which had been a thorn in the side of the Popes for three hundred years, was besieged, forced to surrender, and beheaded. Rebellious Rome, half frightened, longing for the money spent by the Curia, and envious of the glory given to Florence by the presence of the Pope, invited him to return. And Vitelleschi, reporting his successes to Eugenius, was made Archbishop of Florence and Patriarch of Alexandria. Then he was sent back to finish his work. He hung, beheaded, and strangled the tyrants wherever he could lay hands on them, and with patient destructiveness levelled the walls, churches, and houses of some of the feudal strong places whence the fierce nobility had for generations threatened the supremacy of law and made stable government all but impossible. The head of a second conspiracy in Rome was drawn through the streets on a hurdle, torn with red-hot pincers, and then quartered. Thus a stern will made stillness rest upon a land of wasted fields and the ruins of thirty destroyed cities. The thoroughly cowed Roman burghers voted him an equestrian statue on the Capitol, inscribed to "Giovanni Vitelleschi, Patriarch of Alexandria, the third father of the State after Romulus." The Colonna were humbled to the very dust, and of their family city fortress not one stone was left upon another. Then the riches and power of the man who had done this work excited suspicion. . Vitelleschi, now become a Cardinal, was on his way to Tuscany, and crossed the bridge of San Angelo in the rear of his army. The portcullis was suddenly dropped on one end and a chain drawn across the other. The men-at-arms from the castle of San Angelo fell upon him, and, in spite of a desperate defence, carried him a wounded prisoner into the castle. When his army turned back in rage at the news, they were met by the closed gates and cannon of the castle, while the governor waved over the battlements the parchment order for their general's arrest, stamped with the Papal seal. A month later Vitelleschi was dead. He was a striking representative of the class created by the Dominium Temporale, the fighting priest whose prototype was the fighting Pope Julius II., who at the beginning of the next century was to set up over the church door of a conquered city a statue of himself cast from captured cannon.

Meanwhile, strengthened by the iron hand of his servant, Eugenius had resumed resistance to the Council of Basle with great success. At first the party of reform had things all their own way. But for reasons which seem not at all clear, their sweeping decrees for reform produced a powerful reaction. And the Papacy found able and worthy defenders in Juan Torquemada, who asserted its infallibility, Ambrogio, Travasari, and the noble Cardinal Cesarini. Eugenius had been in negotiation for union with the Eastern Church, and had succeeded in procuring submission to the Chair of St. Peter as a condition of the military aid of Western Christendom in resisting the Turk.

The necessity of having a meeting-place more convenient for the embassy of Constantinople enabled him to carry off the most influential, though the smaller, part of the Council to Ferrara and then to Florence. There, in July, 1439, the Patriarch of Constantinople kissed his hand, and the Emperor formally acknowledged that the Patriarch of Rome was the Vicar of Christ and the supreme head of the entire Church. This reconciliation was merely a political necessity, shortly after renounced by the entire Greek Church, but for the time it strengthened the cause of Eugenius. And when the Council of Basle, having deposed him, elected a new Pope, Felix V., in November, 1439, the powers of Europe, shrinking in horror from a new schism, refused to recognize him. France, indeed, had the courage to adopt all the decrees of Basle in the Pragmatic Sanction passed by a national Synod at Bourges, and to compel from Eugenius as the price of her support the recognition of the episcopal rights of the national Church. Germany tried to do the same thing. She declared her neutrality in the schism, and demanded needed reforms before she would declare obedience to Eugenius. The embassy from the princes and prince bishops obtained an acknowledgment of the preëminence of the Council and the promise of reforms; but the Pope, before he handed the bulls to the ambassadors from his death-bed, had signed a previous bull providing that his concessions, which were made at a time when his judgment was weakened by illness, should be null if they in any way injured the teaching of the fathers and the rights of

the Holy Chair of St. Peter.   But his successor did
not need to appeal to it.   The jealous strife between
the petty German princes gave too broad an opening
for the diplomacy of clever legates.   The Roman King
(title of the Emperor elect) had already sold his support for a paltry bribe in money and patronage; the
princes and bishops were only too ready to be bribed,
and in the concordats of Aschaffenburg and Vienna
(1447–1448) they signed away the national rights
which the French episcopate had successfully defended.

CHAPTER XI.

THE SPREAD OF HUMANISM.

WHILE the Papacy, using an ecclesiastical reaction and the skilful diplomacy which surrendered individual aggressions to reserve the principle of Papal autocracy, had resisted reform and weakened the power both of the College of Cardinals and the advocates of Conciliar Authority, the movement of the New Learning was finding broader and stronger expression. The light centred in Florence by the three first followers of Petrarch—Boccaccio, Marsigli, Salutato—and their friends had been spread over all North Italy by the efforts of a race of wandering teachers. These pioneers of learning may be represented in short sketches of two, the most characteristic of their generation.

Giovanni di Conversino was a poor boy who won distinction in the school of Donato at Venice, and was sent to Petrarch to act as copyist. He left that barren employment because he wanted to learn Greek and see the world, and led henceforth a restless life, whose hopes and pride were always larger than its fortunes. The poor fellow never fulfilled his early ambition to learn Greek, but went to Florence, to Rome, to Belluno, Padua, Ragusa, Udine, to Padua again, and back to Florence. Now he was private secretary, now notary, now lecturer on Cicero, now master of a Latin school. He must have had some of the elements of a great teacher, for we are told by one of his scholars that he "led the way to virtue not only by showing the examples of the ancients, but by his own walk and conversation." Two of the greatest teachers Italy ever had, Guarino and Vittorino, sat at his feet, and it is a pity to think of the· impossible man passing through so many good positions to earn the scanty bread of his old age as a giver of lessons in Venice to any scattered pupils he could pick up.

A still more striking figure is Chrysoloras, the first of the line of learned men who were to flee from Constantinople, then tottering to its fall before the assaults of the Turk. The Greek scholarship of Constantinople does not seem to have had within itself the seed of growth; but it possessed by inheritance the manuscripts in which were recorded the origins of our poetry, our philosophy, and our religion, and the knowledge of the language in which they were written. Italy had long desired to know Greek, and when news came that Chrysoloras, a distinguished teacher of rhetoric and philosophy, had landed in Venice to seek aid for the Empire against the Turk, two noble Florentines went at once to see him. One of them returned with him to Constantinople. The other brought to Florence so glowing a report of his learning and personality that Salutato induced the city to call him for ten years as a teacher of Greek, with a salary of one hundred florins and fees. In 1396 he came. A great crowd went to hear his instruction, but it is melancholy to find that none of the older men, like Salutato, who had longed so earnestly for this treasure, were able to master the difficulties of the tongue. Chrysoloras formed in Florence some able young scholars, and wandered to Pavia, then back again to Byzantium, and returned once more to Venice and Florence on his way to Rome. From thence he visited France, Spain, and England, came back to Rome, and was sent by the Pope on a mission to Byzantium. Returned, he was despatched to Germany, and finally died at the Council of Constance. Thus the long beard and flowing garments of the Greek reminded the students of the world that the tongue of Homer, Plato, and John might be learned and its lost treasures recovered.

A little army of such scouts of learning, most of whose names are long forgotten, wandered from city to city, seeking or giving knowledge. And through their labors there were soon scattered over Italy knots of men who loved to live laborious days in the pursuit of truth and beauty.

The leaders in this love of learning were of the country of Dante, Petrarch, and Boccaccio, and the capital of their little state was not only the defender of liberty, but the Athens of Italy.

Florence, like London to-day, was the centre of trade and the financial exchange of the world. The most remarkable of her merchant princes and rich bankers was Cosimo de' Medici. His father, Giovanni

de' Medici (died 1428), left to his two sons, Cosimo
and Lorenzo, a fortune acknowledged as 179,221
gold florins. This wealth was enormously increased
by Cosimo's skill as a merchant and banker. The
figures will indicate what this means. Lorenzo, who
died in 1440, left 253,000 florins. Piero, Cosimo's
son, who died in 1469, left 238,000; and, besides the
expenses of living, the family had spent between 1434
and 1471 in taxes, benefactions, and public buildings
664,000 florins, of which Cosimo, who died in 1464,
paid 400,000. So that, besides the expenses of living,
the 180,000 florins of the grandfather had in less than
fifty years gained for his descendants 1,000,000
florins, or one half the total coined money circulating
in the Republic in 1422.[1] It was the rule, so well
illustrated in the history of some American families,
that money skilfully handled breeds money; but
more than two thirds of the increase of two generations of the Medici accrued to the public
benefit in taxes, charities, and gifts to learning or
the arts.

The relation of Cosimo to his city can be easily
appreciated by the Americans of to-day. He was
the boss of the little Republic of Florence, then a
city of about ninety thousand inhabitants. His
family were among the hereditary leaders of the
democracy against the party of millionaire manufacturers and middle-class merchants who desired to
retain power in order to control the tariff. And
they had been very influential in the uprising of

---

[1] These figures do not mean much to the modern reader. The
florin was worth about $2.50, but the cost and scale of living are dif-
ficult to estimate. In 1460 the Patriarch of Aquileja was called the
richest man in Italy. He left 200,000 florins.

1378, which resulted in the extension of suffrage to the working-man.   Cosimo was simple in his habits, given to hospitality, liberal in sharing the enjoyment of the treasures of art and learning with which his palace was filled, generous where it would do the most good, reserved, but affable of speech. Hiding his secrets behind an impenetrable veil of invariable courtesy, he gathered into his hands all the wires that moved Florentine politics, and, seeking no public honors for himself, was nearly always able to control the City Council and quietly shape the policy of the Republic.   His hands were free from taking bribes, though he did not scruple to handle for its full value the patronage he controlled.   And doubtless one great cause of his success as a money-lender and merchant was his early and intimate knowledge of political movements.   His commercial correspondents were scattered over all Europe, the Levant, and even in Egypt.   He had loaned money on the security of the public income to the State of Florence and to every burgher who wished to borrow of him. And yet he used his power so gently that he conquered envy and received by public decree the title of " Father of the Fatherland."

The Florentine merchant nobility had long been in the habit of protecting and enjoying art and literature. It was natural, therefore, that Cosimo should employ his striking critical taste, trained by reading and discussion, his enormous wealth, his knowledge of men, finished by travel and the conduct of affairs, his correspondence, spread over all countries of the world, in forming collections of books and manuscripts, in employing men of genius, and becoming the leading patron of art and letters in Italy. The most efficient of his friends and protégés in this work was Niccolo de' Niccoli. He was the son of a small merchant of the city, who, inheriting a very modest fortune, abandoned business and gave himself up to the profession of a connoisseur and collector of manuscripts and objects of art. The stout little man who always dressed with scrupulous care was very fond of society, and the soul of every company; but somewhat feared withal, because of a touch of sarcasm in his irresistibly funny speeches. He was a good deal of a beau in his younger days, and we learn from letters that he and his friend Bruni used to wait round the doors of the churches to see the pretty girls come out. But he never married, because he knew that if he had a wife he must give up collecting books. He was more than consoled by forming out of his moderate income the best library in Florence—eight hundred manuscripts, all rare, some of them unique. When an over-enthusiastic purchase, as, for instance, the library of Salutato, had reduced him for the time to poverty, he hung on to the books and economized until he could pay for them. He had, besides, a small but good collection of gems, statues, coins, and pictures. But he lived no comfortless life of the traditional old bachelor. He loved to see a piece of fine linen, a crystal goblet, an antique vase, some bits of choice pottery on his table.

He was the centre of correspondence for the Humanists of his day, and not to know Niccoli was to be unknown in the realm of letters. He was the greatest living authority on manuscripts, with an infallible eye for an old codex, and an extended practical knowledge of the then unknown science of diplomatics. He was the first collector who let his uniques be copied, and showed a liberality in regard to his treasures absolutely unequalled. At his death it was found that two hundred of his volumes were loaned. His house was always open and was the meeting-place of the literati and artists of Florence. It was also a sort of free school, for sometimes there were ten or twelve young men reading quietly in the library, while Niccoli walked about the room, giving instructions or asking now one and then another his impressions of what he read. And yet he was no easy man to get on with. His spirit was intensely critical, and a friend writes that even of the dead he never praised any but Plato, Virgil, Horace, and Jerome. He was neglectful of formalities toward others and exceedingly touchy in regard to himself, and the later years of the peppery old man were filled with quarrels. Cosimo did everything for him. His word was law in regard to appointments and dismissals at the High School of Florence. And it was understood that whenever he was unable to pay for a book he had only to send a note to Cosimo's cashier, who had standing orders to discount it at once—a graceful way of making a gift, for Niccoli died five hundred florins in his patron's debt. He had always been wont to rebuke the jests against religion of the free-thinkers among his literary friends, and he made an edifying end. His last words gave directions as to what was to be done with his books.

Men like these—for Cosimo and Niccoli were only the most skilful of many connoisseurs of art and letters in Florence—searched the world for the remains of classical antiquity. And there was no lack of patient explorers who gladly gave their years to this service. We have a suggestion of such toils and pleasures in letters describing the book-hunts of three young secretaries at the Council of Constance. One day, for instance, they took boat to the Benedictine abbey on the island of Reichenau. On another they crossed to the north shore of the lake and rode eighteen or twenty miles inland to the old abbey of Weingarten. Sometimes they got much, sometimes little; but, like fishermen, they never let success suffer in the telling of it.

Their best trip was to the abbey of St. Gall. This abbey, founded in the seventh century, had been for generations, through its convent school, a centre of light, but the degenerate monks were so forgetful of the ancient glories of their house that the library was thrust into a dusty tower and left to worms and decay. Doubtless much was already gone, but the indignant friends found something to fill Florence with joy—a perfect Institutes of Quintilian, only known to Italy in fragments. Poggio got permission to carry it to Constance, and spent fifty-three days copying it. Their net took other smaller fish. Some books of Valerius, Flaccus, a commentary on five speeches of Cicero, Statius's Woods, a book of Manilius, and a short work of Priscian. And they

I

copied these too.   But it was the news of the
Quintilian that drew from Bruni, soon to be chosen
as the worthiest successor of Salutato in the Chan-
cellorship of Florence, the answer, " O vast gain! O
unhoped-for joy!"

Another very useful man in this book-collecting
was Giovanni Aurispa, not much of a scholar, but a
skilful buyer, particularly of Greek manuscripts. There
was great excitement in Florence when he landed in
Venice with two hundred and thirty-eight books in
his chests.   To pay for them he had sold all he had
except the clothes he wore, and still owed fifty florins
for freight and other debts.   Cosimo's brother immediately advanced the money.   But the shrewd
Aurispa would not visit Florence till, by sending an
occasional volume and an imperfect list of his treasures, he had roused the appetite of the literati to
fever-heat.   Then he doubtless came well out of his .
speculation.

What these men and their patrons were doing for
the writings of antiquity Ciriaco of Ancona did for
its art.   Having picked up Latin while clerk of harbor repairs in his native city, he was seized, while on
a visit to Rome, by the passion of the antiquary, and
gave his life to gratify it.   Sailing in the Levant as
supercargo, he bought in a convent a manuscript of
the Iliad and learned Greek out of it.   When he
came to Rome to visit Pope Eugenius his chests
were laden with interesting things: splendid bronze
vases with silver inlay, a complete Greek manuscript
of the New Testament, marble heads, cut gems, gold
coins of Philip and Alexander, Indian water-cans of

porcelain decorated in gold, and a long list of copies of ancient inscriptions. He saw and was seen by the literati of Rome, and went to Florence, where he settled down in the library of Niccoli as the choicest spot in the world. But he never stayed long in any place. He visited every important ruin in Italy merely in the intervals of journeys that carried him to the limits of travel. He went to the pyramids, where he copied an inscription in an unknown tongue to send to his friend Niccoli. Then he turned back, lingering, and longing to go farther up the mysterious river. For his dearest plans always failed. At Damascus he was very anxious to accompany the son of a rich merchant to Ethiopia and India, but could not. He was also obliged to give up a trip to Persia with a Genoese merchant he met in Adrianople. And he tried in vain to get money from the Pope and Cosimo for a visit to the Atlas Mountains and the Island of Thule at the end of the world. But Cosimo did give him an open credit at the Medici bank to invest in antiques. And Ciriaco must have spent on his heavy chests more than he earned, for he was no mere trader, but loved to give a gold coin of Trojan to the Emperor, a bit of amber with a fly in it to the King of Naples, drawings of temples and copies of mosaics to his friends. He was full of pomposity and conceit, published an extraordinary prayer made to Mercury on the way from Delos to Mycenæ, liked to tell everywhere how he once mystified a stupid priest by the saying, "My art is to sometimes waken the dead from the grave," and altogether took himself too seriously. So they laughed at him a good deal, called him "Resurrectionist" and "Mercury of Ancona"; but the ablest of the brilliant circle of which he loved to rank himself a member knew his real services to learning, and his lost collections of carefully copied inscriptions would doubtless fill many a gap in antiquarian knowledge.

These collectors and the patrons whose homes sheltered the inheritance of the past were surrounded by a swarm of teachers and writers, and the wandering masters found more dignified successors in the incumbents of new schools founded in many parts of Italy. The greatest of this generation of teachers are Vittorino da Feltre (1377–1446) and Guarino da Verona (1370–1460). In his youth Guarino had gone to Constantinople to learn Greek of Chrysoloras, and when he was called to Ferrara as tutor to the princes of the royal house he had taught in many cities and was sixty years old. But, old as he was, the real labor of his life, that was to make his name gratefully honored throughout Italy, was just begun. He was lecturer on poetry to the University, and the hearers who soon filled the room included men as well as youth, and not infrequently women. But his genius as a teacher was best displayed in his private school. And his house gathered scholars from all parts of Italy, Dalmatia, Germany, Hungary, Bohemia, Poland, France, England, and the islands of the Levant. It was a gentle discipline, that of the learned and kindly man, who loved a joke as well as the wildest lad among them. The pupils were brought up with his own sons, who all grew up to be scholars, and became the ancestors of a numerous race distinguished for ten generations in poetry and the Humanities. He was very much opposed to the use of the rod, saying that it enslaved boys and made them hate learning. Nor was he a believer in " the drilled dull lesson, forced down word for word." He taught his pupils the elements of grammar, and then threw them on their own resources, to read steadily and continuously, with the help of a translation. This method, for lack of which generations of American college students have wasted the best years of their lives over Greek and Latin without learning to read either with pleasure, had astonishing success. There are recorded instances of men, young and old, who, beginning Greek, could, after less than a year in Guarino's house, read it freely and with pleasure. At the age of ninety he called his sons around him, blessed them, and crowned a life of gentle labor with a peaceful death.

Even more beautiful is the personality and life of Vittorino da Feltre. His parents were poor, and he had to help himself to an education by tutoring and studying at the same time. But in spite of his hard work he was more than a mere dig, for he did well in the sports of his fellows and sang the praises of his sweetheart in Latin and Italian. He had a little school at Venice for a while, and then lectured at Padua, his alma mater, in rhetoric and philosophy. His success brought him a call to Mantua in 1423. The Duke, a great soldier, but a friend to learning, had built for an academy a stately house in the midst of a green meadow on the bank of a little lake not far from the city. It was generously planned, for the halls were decorated with frescoes and the courts with fountains.   Here, and in the neighboring house which Vittorino built from his profits, assembled a strange medley of pupils, sons of princes and noblemen side by side with poor scholars Vittorino had picked up, who could bring nothing but their love of learning.   He had a large number of masters, including teachers of painting and music, riding, fencing, and ball-playing.   He was always in debt, for he never could resist taking promising lads who were poor, or practise economy when it was possible to improve his school.   His own large salary he gave away, and left so embarrassed an estate that his heirs refused to accept it.   But he had a ready resource, for his noble master never could resist the smile with which Vittorino was wont to confess that he had spent several hundred gold pieces extra for the needs of the school and hoped it would be supplied.   He himself never thought of money.   He had no pleasures except those he shared with his boys, and the only thing in the world he kept to himself was a tiny house and garden on the hill where Virgil was said to have been born.   When his friends advised him to marry and told of the joys of the family, he pointed to his scholars and said he had children enough already.   The boys were brought up with freedom, but under a stern law, and they feared his rebuke.   His special dislikes were lying, profanity, laziness, and dandyism.   The son of the Duke, almost a young man, blasphemed on the ball-field, and Vittorino instantly called him and boxed his ears.   His piety was very deep, and he taught his scholars the strict observance of the customs of worship. At the school table prayer was made before and after meat. The older scholars heard mass every morning, went to confession every month, and kept honestly all the prescribed fasts of the Church. But the asceticism of his system was based on classic rather than on monkish ideas, and endeavored to subdue the body by training it. The boys had to play and exercise every day in the open air in running, wrestling, swimming, riding, ball-playing, or shooting with the bow. Sometimes they were divided into two armies which fought battles. Sometimes they were sent hunting or fishing, or, in summer, taken on long tramps to the Alps.

He never wrote anything, saying " the ancients had written enough ; it was better to read them "— probably only his excuse to himself for giving his whole learning to his boys, for he always praised and admired the writings of others. He had his reward in the tears of joy that were seen in his eyes when one did well in the crowning exercise of the school, an elegant rendering of Greek into Latin, before visitors, and in the universal love and respect which came to him from all men in an envious and quarrelsome age. The best medallist of the day gave to the medal in his honor this legend : " Father of Classic Learning."

Then also the three great Florentines around whom we grouped the first generation of the followers of Petrarch in the ways of the New Learning found worthy successors each in his kind.

Marsigli, the Augustinian monk, friend of Boccaccio and Salutato, is represented by Traversari the Camaldulensian. Abroad he was the churchman, General of his Order, ambassador of the Pope, and powerful advocate of the Papal authority at Basle. But in Florence he was one of the little band who sat at Cosimo's table for a feast of reason. He was a sworn friend of Niccoli, who was forever urging him to read less theology and more classics. When Niccoli went on his travels he always left to Traversari the keys of his iron-bound manuscript chests, and his clothes, which, to please the dandy antiquary, had to be shaken and brushed at regular intervals by a brother of the order. He had a hard time between the rules of his convent and his taste for heathen poets and literary distinction. When he had translated for Cosimo so apparently unsatanic a book as Diogenes Laertius's Sketches of Distinguished Philosophers, he could only quiet his conscience for not having spent the time on Church fathers with the reflection that even this work might help religion by its moral examples.

Leonardo Bruni, a poor orphan boy brought up under the protection of Salutato, became, after serving as curial secretary, a worthy successor of his patron as Chancellor of Florence. He was accounted the best Grecian of his day, and left seventy-four works in Greek and Latin. He seemed, as he strode majestically through the streets in his long red robe, one of those ancient Roman worthies whose tongue he wrote so clearly and beautifully in letters, or rolled out in the strong and stately phrases of his festal orations. He was third of an illustrious roll of chancellors, which numbers between Salutato and Machiavelli some of the chief names in the literature of successive generations.

But it is in Poggio and Filelfo that we see the typical figure of the Humanist, the successor of Petrarch, a scholar and writer living by his knowledge and his pen, not directly through teaching or the sale of his books, but by the presents and sinecures offered by admiring patrons.

Poggio Bracciolini (1380–1459) walked into Florence, like Franklin into Philadelphia, with only a few pieces of silver in his pocket. But he soon found a friend in Salutato, who put him in the way of earning a living as a copyist of classical manuscripts; and his beautiful handwriting brought him plenty of work. Niccoli lent him books and money, and, guided by the advice of both, he hammered out for himself without teachers a mastery of Latin and a passable knowledge of Greek. While still a youth he got a position as secretary of the Papal Curia, which he held for fifty years. But his heart was always in Florence, where his treasure of books was, either stored in his little villa, or under the care of his friend Traversari. There he married, when over fifty, a young girl of eighteen, a match which, to the amazement of all his friends, was the happiness of both. He was forty before the discovery of the Quintilian at St. Gall brought him anything like fame, and it was afterward that he was ranked among the first scholars and stylists of his day. Poggio did not serve Minerva for nothing. He wrote, it is true, essays on "Avarice" and "The Greed of Gold," but

both as curial secretary and litterateur he understood
perfectly the art of feathering his nest.   His pride
was of the vulgar stripe which keeps constantly
asking for something, not the noble self-respect of a
Salutato, which is always content with its wages and
stands aside to watch, half in scorn and half in
amusement, the universal struggle for the almighty
dollar.   Until the time when he gave it up and married he was, like Petrarch, a patient hunter of benefices, and no rich patron in Italy need despair of the
services of his pen, most skilled in eulogy.   Nor did
he scruple to skilfully solicit this kind of business.
When he had translated the " Cyropædia " of Xenophon he hinted with increasing plainness to those in
the court of Alfonso of Naples his desire to dedicate
it to that generous Mæcenas.   When the bait was
not even nibbled at, he wrote a dedication in his
warmest tone and sent a splendidly bound copy of
the work.   But Alfonso made no return and the indignant scholar began to hedge violently in his opinion of the King whom he had just lauded to the skies,
questioned his taste and the honesty of his devotion
to literature, and struck his name out of the copies
of his book so that the dedication might serve for
any prince.   Then Alfonso sent him six hundred
florins, and begged him if he wanted anything else
not to be afraid to ask.   Immediately the tide of
Poggio's admiration swelled to high-water mark, and
at the first opportunity he sent an open letter begging Alfonso to raise all Italy against the Turk, and
calling him a model of every royal virtue in peace
and war.

He was even more skilled in invective than in eulogy. And woe betide the man who in the smallest way crossed Poggio's path. He was pilloried in Latin letters whose style spread them all over Europe. To this rule Guarino was the sole exception. His character awed even the pen of Poggio, and their dispute as to whether Cæsar or Scipio was the greatest man was carried on, if not with all the courtesy of an old-fashioned village debating society, yet with what for Poggio was decency. On the other hand, in defending his patron Cosimo against Filelfo he stopped at no personality. No member of his adversary's family was left untouched by dirty accusations. And there was scarcely a crime so mean and unmentionable that he did not accuse his opponent of it. Some allowance must be made, of course, for the contemporary customs of dispute. But even a tough-skinned generation shrank before the poisoned bitterness of Poggio's darts.

Francesco Filelfo (1398–1481), when he landed in Venice in 1427, had served for five years as secretary to the Emperor John in Constantinople, whither he had originally been sent by the Venetian State as secretary of the trade-house—a sort of consul. Two years later he brought his chest of Greek manuscripts and his beautiful young Greek wife, the grand niece of Manuel Chrysoloras, to Florence, to lecture in the employ of the city on Cicero, Livy, Terence, Homer, Thucydides, and Xenophon. He did not stay long. For it is not to be supposed that continual peace brooded over the Florentine garden of the Muses. Scholars and men of letters are notoriously difficult, and petty jealousies and quarrels were as common in Florence as in a modern college faculty. Then the immeasurable vanity of Filelfo, who thought the street curiosity that stared at his Eastern beard and robe a tribute to his learning, struck like flint on steel against the sarcastic humor of Niccoli. But the man who bore the triple reputation of one of the first Latinists, the ablest Greek scholar, and the most skilful poet of Italy had no trouble in finding a new home. He went to the High School of Siena, and the war of words passed to knives; for after Filelfo's life had twice been attempted by assassins, hired, as he charged, by Cosimo and his friends, the great Grecian joined with other exiles of the "noble" party of Florentine politics to hire a band of murderers to kill Cosimo and Marsuppini. Filelfo added a special promise of twenty-five florins for the death of Marsuppini. But the assassin was caught, had both of his hands cut off, and was driven from Florentine territory; and it was decreed that if Filelfo were taken he should have his tongue cut out. Filelfo's answer was to pillory the Medici in an invective, and Cosimo, touched by the only spot on his good fame, sought to make peace through Traversari; an overture to which Filelfo replied: "Cosimo has poison and dagger against me. I have brains and pen against him. I do not want his friendship and I despise his hostility." But it was not many years before he again sought Cosimo's patronage, promising to destroy all his invectives. And at the end of his life, when he hoped to gain from Lorenzo, Cosimo's grandson, a position at the new university at

Pisa, he planned a great eulogy of the Medici in ten books, of which he sent a flattering preface as a sample. And at eighty-three years he was actually recalled to Florence, to die almost on reaching it. Meanwhile he had not suffered. He was always complaining of poverty, even when he had six servants or kept six horses and dressed in silk and fine furs. And his measureless importunity supported this state. For it was actually the belief of the age that the key of the heaven of fame was the pen of the Humanist, and the sale of their eulogies has been well compared to the sale of indulgences by the Church. We have seen how even Cosimo feared to have his name mentioned with disrespect in Filelfo's immortal letters, and to obtain honorable mention in them many a prince was willing to fill his hands with gold.

For the rest Filelfo and Poggio were pretty thorough heathen. They did not quarrel with the Church, for it was dangerous. The very fury with which Petrarch, Boccaccio, and Salutato had attacked ecclesiastical abuses showed their love of the Church. But Filelfo and Poggio did little else but sneer at her wrongs and weaknesses. A Bruni, a Niccoli, a Guarino, a Vittorino showed by their attitude toward her worship their faith in the great institution which handed down the teaching of Christ. . But these two most typical Humanists, who sought the glory of men through the glory of letters, and lived by patronage, looked upon the priests as Cicero on the augurs. They dropped altogether the sense of sin which Jesus of Nazareth brought into the world, and when they thus turned to the Greek ideal they did not replace the penitence issuing in the love of God and man of his doctrine by the stoic self-respect which had produced an Epictetus and taught Marcus Aurelius to write that " even in a palace life might be well lived." A few of their successors in the New Learning put on the simple garb of that philosophy. But the typical Humanists of this generation, with most of their successors, set up nothing in place of what they abandoned, and, borrowing one of the worst traits of classic life, stamped with the authority of culture and good taste those vices which constantly threaten to rot society to the point of dissolution. Filelfo's " De Jocis et Seriis " has never been printed. His biographer (Rosmini, 1808) was ashamed to quote it because of its " horrible obscenity." Poggio tells how a knot of choice spirits among the Papal secretaries, all of whom belonged to the clergy, used to meet after work in a remote room of the palace. They called their informal society " Bugiale," or " The Forge of Lies," and he collected and published the tales he heard there under the title of " Facetiæ." It went through twenty-six editions in sixty years. Any one attempting to circulate an English translation through the United States mail could be sent to the penitentiary. Nor was this all. The worship of lubricity became deliberate. In Valla's dialogue, " De Voluptate," while the formal victory remains with virtue, the freshness and strength of argument are all on the side of the Greek view; and the conclusion, " Whatever pleases is permitted," lies near to every reader.

But in Beccadelli's "Hermaphroditus," by which the author won instant fame at the age of thirty-one, the astonished modern reader finds a veritable Priapean orgy. The polished Latin verses, decorated with all the skill of a poet and rhetorician, have for their subject those things which St. Paul says it is a shame even to speak of. It was received with a perfect storm of applause, and gained for Beccadelli the laurel crown of a poet from the hand of the Emperor Sigismund. Not, of course, without protest. For the leading folks' preachers, Bernardino of Siena and his associates the Franciscans, thundered against it and publicly burned it with the picture of the author in the market squares of Bologna, Ferrara, and Milan, while the Pope excommunicated any who should dare to read it. But the more it was attacked the more it was read. And though in later life the author mildly expressed his regret, it was the chief support of his fame. The claim of apologetes that Christianity has obliterated that shame of the classic world has never been justified by facts in this or any other age. But it is certainly a sign of additional corruption to find a crime, now stamped as infamous by every statute-book of Europe, and then punished by death in France, openly praised with more than Turkish cynicism amid the applause of men who assumed to lead taste and learning.

The Laurentius Valla alluded to was born twenty-seven years later than Poggio, and together with Beccadelli formed the chief ornament of the cultured court of Alfonso of Naples. He became one of the ablest critics the world has ever seen. It was difficult for any mythical humbug or traditional fraud to escape his sharp eye and tongue.   When Beccadelli showed King Alfonso the skull of a dragon, Valla proved that it was nothing but a crocodile.   No adherent of the New Learning had yet struck such resistless blows at the traditional methods of scholasticism, which enslaved so much of the teaching at the universities and schools.   Though it was two generations since the death of Petrarch he made the beginnings of a scientific Latin grammar and syntax.   He denied the right of the monks and nuns to their exclusive title "religious," and the claim on which it was based, that an honest monk could expect a higher reward from God, simply because of his monkish vow, than an honest layman.   He exposed as a forgery the letter of Abgar, King of Edessa, to Christ, mistakenly quoted by Eusebius as an original. He attacked the catechism of the Franciscans as false because it said that the Apostles had in person composed the different articles of the so-called Apostles' Creed.   He demanded that the Vulgate, or Jerome's Latin translation of the New Testament, should be compared with the original Greek and corrected.[1] These assertions are commonplaces now.   They required the originality of genius then.   But in the moral courage to sustain his originality Valla was absolutely deficient.   When he was summoned before an ecclesiastical court and confronted with a charge of heresy he escaped by saying that " Mother Church

---

[1] The manuscript containing this demand was never published until Erasmus found it in Belgium and had it printed in 1505.

did not know anything about it, but nevertheless he thought in these matters entirely as Mother Church." And when he wanted a sinecure on the staff of Papal secretaries his letter to the Pope humbly retracted every conclusion of his scholarship and promised hereafter to write entirely in his interests.

It has seemed necessary to interrupt the account of the attempted reform of the Church in head and members by the three parties of the radicals (Wicliff and Huss), the middle party of conciliar reform (Gerson, d'Ailly, and the fathers of Basle), and the orthodox, ascetic folks' preachers (Catherine of Siena, Bernardino of Siena, etc.) by this long account of the second generation of the men of the New Learning, because the success of their movement finally brought about the end of the drama in the triumph of reform. Neither the protesting Reformation of Luther nor the Catholic Counter-reformation of Trent would have been possible but for the victory of the New Learning over the traditions of scholasticism. And curiously enough this relation, which it might be tedious to demonstrate abstractly, has been clearly suggested in a letter from one of the Humanists we have described.

Petrarch, the founder of the New Learning, did three things: he tested tradition by reason; he awoke self-consciousness—made man cease to be a member of a class and an institution to become an independent personality; and he evoked the historical sense and turned it to study the records of the past. We have seen that John Huss, appealing from the Council to Christ, died for the dignity and indepen-

J

dence of the individual soul, in defence of the truth that Christianity is in the last analysis a personal matter between each disciple and his Master.   And Jerome died because he stood by Huss.   Poggio, that careless Gallio who cared for none of these things, wrote, among the letters from Constance about his book-hunts, one to Bruni, describing the trial and death of Jerome.   And the unheroic Humanist, not himself the stuff that makes martyrs, cannot conceal his intellectual sympathy for the man who stood in the name of reason and conscience against Council and Emperor, the combined traditional authority of Church and State.   The letter is so characteristic of one type of Humanist, and so illustrative of the secret and unseen interaction of the forces of history, that it seems wise to give the reader a free and condensed but true translation, one third the length of the original.

"Poggio sends his best greetings to Leonardo. When I had been several days at the baths I wrote to our friend Nicolas a letter which I hoped you would read.   Then when I had returned to Constance the case of Jerome was under discussion.   I confess I have never seen any one who approached more nearly to the much-admired eloquence of the ancients. The diction, the skill, the arguments, the expressive countenance, the confidence with which he answered his adversaries were wonderful.   And it is a pity that so noble an intellect should have turned to heresy, if, indeed, those things are true of which he is charged.   Nor, indeed, is it my business to decide so great a question.   I yield to the judgment of those who are accounted wiser. It would take too long to give you an account of the whole affair, but I will touch on some of its more remarkable features.

" The charges were read from the pulpit, head after head, and he was given an opportunity to defend himself. It is impossible to tell you how calmly he answered and how skilfully he defended himself. Nothing came from his lips unworthy of a good man. His answer to some was a witty saying, to others a sarcasm; he compelled many in the midst of this sorrowful affair to laughter, returning their fierce interruptions with a joke. To a Dominican crying out bitterly against him he replied, ' Be silent, hypocrite.' To another swearing by his conscience, ' That,' he said, ' is the surest way to deceive.' A certain chief among his adversaries he never addressed save as ass or dog. When at last, on the third day, he was given permission to speak at length, he began with praying God to grant him such a mind and skill in speaking as should be for the gain and salvation of his soul. Then he pointed out that many excellent men, overwhelmed by false witnesses, have been condemn d by unjust judgment; referring to Socrates, unjustly killed, the captivity of Plato, the flight of Anaxagoras, the torture of Zeno, the exile of Rutilius, the death of Boethius, and others. Then he passed over to the history of the Hebrews; spoke of Moses, Joseph, Isaiah, Daniel, and almost all the prophets, oppressed by unjust judgment as despisers of the gods and seducers of the people. Coming down to John the Baptist, our Lord, and all the Apostles, he showed that they died by false

accusation as evil-doers.   His voice was sweet, full,
and resonant.   There was great dignity in his ges-
tures either to express indignation or to excite pity,
although he did not ask pity.   He stood intrepid
and unflinching, not only despising death, but even
seeking it.   You might have called him a second
Cato—a man worthy of eternal memory among men
(I do not praise anything in him contrary to the institutions of the Church).   Obstinate in his errors, he
was condemned as a heretic and burned.   He approached death with a pleasant and smiling countenance.   But this was a particular sign of a steadfast
mind.   When the executioner would have started
the fire behind, that he might not see it, ' Come here,
he said, ' and light the fire in front.   If I were afraid
of it I would never have come to this place, which I
could have escaped.'   I saw this ending and watched
each act of this drama.   And having leisure I wished
to tell you this affair a little like the stories of the
worthies of antiquity.   For not Mutius himself suffered his hand to be burned with so steadfast a spirit
as he the whole body.   Nor did Socrates drink the
poison so willingly as he endured the fire.   Farewell,
my dearest Leonardo."

PERIOD II.

FROM THE ACCESSION OF THE FIRST HUMANIST POPE TO THE FRENCH INVASION OF ITALY (1447–94).

PERIOD II.

CHAPTER XII.

NICHOLAS V., THE FIRST HUMANIST POPE, MAKES ROME THE HOME OF THE MUSES—THE WAR OF THE MONKS AND THE HUMANISTS.

HE death of Eugenius in 1447 left the Church in the care of a strong and representative body of cardinals—eleven Italians, four Spaniards, two Greeks, a German, an Englishman, a Pole, a Hungarian, a Portuguese, and two Frenchmen. After a short conclave they elected, to his own great astonishment, the youngest, but one of the ablest of their number, Tommaso Parentucelli, of Sarzana, Cardinal of Bologna, who took the title of Nicholas V. There was no churchman who represented more unmistakably the training and ideals of the New Learning. After attaining a master's degree at Bologna in philosophy and the liberal arts, he lived for several years in Florence as tutor in the houses of the Albizzi and Strozzi, and breathed deep the air of the New Learning that filled the homes of their friends. A further course of study gained a degree in theology, and he became for twenty years the friend and helper of the Bishop of Bologna, one of the most faithful

prelates of his day, whose character earned the red
hat and nominated him to important legations.   On
these missions Tommaso added the culture of travel,
distinguished conversation, and the conduct of great
affairs to the culture of books, and acquired such
readiness that he talked on any subject as if he had
given his whole life to its study.   After he was made
a cardinal for closing the negotiations which brought
rebellious Germany to the bedside of the dying
Eugenius, he had been called the " Second Pope,"
and his election was hailed with joy.

He was a little man of choleric temper, with considerable power of self-control in emergencies, but
quick and impatient at small carelessness or stupidity.
He disliked ceremony intensely so far as personal intercourse was concerned, and his manners were pleasant and friendly.   His conversation was always frank
and often merry.   He never forgot old friends.   And
his old friends at Florence sent a great embassy with
a hundred and twenty horses to congratulate the new
Pope.   Among them was the bookseller Vespasiano
da Bisticci, and to him Nicholas confided his ideal:
" So long as I am Pope to use no weapon but that
which Christ has given for my defence, his Holy
Cross."   For this the first Pope under whom Christendom had been united for seventy years was sincerely resolved to do his duty as he understood it.
His understanding was that of a pious Humanist
whose dearest wish, next to the establishment of the
peace of the Church, was to ennoble religion and
worship by the services of literature and art.   He
did this with a zeal born of the pleasure in being

connoisseur and patron, which was his strongest and most active passion.

During the many years when he had accomplished with dignity the hard task of living as a poor man among intimates whose wealth gave wide range to their cultured tastes, he had been distinguished for his beautifully written and bound manuscripts, and was wont to say in familiar moments, " If I were rich I would indulge in two extravagances—building and the collection of books." The literati of Florence were accustomed to gather every morning at a certain corner in front of the palace of the Republic, to discuss the literary and other gossip of the day. And after he had done his duty of waiting on his master, the Archbishop, Maestro Tommaso would ride down the street clad in his blue gown, give his mule to the two servants who followed him on foot, and join the group. Whenever the subject of the arrangement of a library was suggested among them, his opinion was received as that of a leading expert. His plan for a library, made for Cosimo de' Medici's foundation of San Marco, was used by almost all those large-minded patrons who followed that new example by founding public libraries. It was natural, therefore, that as Pope he should collect the scattered manuscripts that were in the Papal buildings and become the real founder of the Vatican library. His agents were seeking manuscripts in all likely places, and he offered the enormous reward of five thousand florins for a copy of the Hebrew Gospel of Matthew. His chief delight was to handle and arrange these volumes, and his particular favorites were magnificently bound in crimson velvet with silver clasps.   They included the presentation copies of the translations from the Greek he suggested and nobly rewarded.   He delighted to be hailed as a new Mæcenas by the wandering knight-errants of learning, who were finding that the pen was as mighty as the sword to win fortune for the skilful wielder of it.   The Curia was almost swamped by the swarm of secretaries who wore the livery of the Church, but loved the shrine of the Muses.   As Nicholas pathetically remarked when he was accused of neglecting some modest talent unknown at his very doors, " Why, I reward even the bad poets, if they only come and ask."

Many of these secretaries of Nicholas were heathen. Not that they attacked the truths of Christianity or refused the offices of the Church, but that the ideals of the New Testament had little influence over their thoughts, desires, or conversation, and the classic authors a great deal.   It was a rationalistic circle, much more interested in the relation of human thought and feeling to the world than in the relation of the soul to God, secretly given to free thought, and more or less openly to free living.   They displayed a respect for the Church as a great institution of society ; and doubtless they tried to preserve such a measure of regard for religion in their hearts as might be a comfort at death, without being too troublesome while they were engaged in living.

Both their heathenism and the form of their Christianity led this circle and their correspondents to take up the invective against the monks which two generations of Humanists had carried on.   Petrarch, indeed, had been on very good terms with all the orders of monks, and was pleased with their praise of his book " On the Solitary Life." But Boccaccio not only made monks the comic heroes of the very worst of his tales, but wrote against them as ambitious pretenders who opposed learning and dishonored the house of God. In the second generation Bruni, the Chancellor of Florence, took up the conflict in his tractate " Against Hypocrisy," and draws such a picture that there is little difficulty in recognizing a caricature of the Franciscan Brothers of the Strict Observance, the begging friars, with their distinguished folks' preacher, Bernardino of Siena. Filelfo continued the attack, and gives a satiric picture of the preaching of the revivalist monks.

Poggio was therefore taking up the quarrel of his class in his lifelong enmity against the Strict Franciscans. And there was added the hatred of a curialist of the opposition party, who had felt the pressure of their overwhelming influence during the latter part of the administration of Eugenius IV. His letters and pamphlets against them are written in his most brilliant and reckless style. He says they are recruited among idle boys, who, having learned nothing and being too lazy to earn their living, go into the order to live without working. They put on a coarse and dirty gown, hang down their heads, look pale and thin, and think they have proved their holiness and humility, but are leading astray silly women, constantly begging privileges and immunities for their order, and hunting bishoprics and cardinals' hats for themselves. Since Bernardino has won such ap-

plause, every stupid idiot in the order wants to imitate him.   They scream and whisper, stamp and
pound the pulpit, and in the end are bathed in perspiration, while their hearers remain stupider than
before.   " Why," he asks, " do they always call the
Redeemer *Jesus*, and not, as other people do, Jesus
Christ? Why do they call themselves Jesusites
[Jesuits] and not, like others, Christians?   It is because
they want, by this trick of a new fashion of speech,
to appear to be a chosen and peculiar band, but really
they are filled with ambitions and all uncleanness."

That such bitter attacks did not mean separation
from the Church, or even war with all monks, is
illuminating for those Protestant readers, who find
it difficult to understand that, within certain fixed
limits of doctrine and certain practical rules of obedience, the liveliest discussion and the freest personal criticism have always been possible in the Roman
Catholic Church.   Poggio himself had intimate
friends among the monks.   His eldest son, though
to his father's great grief, became a preacher of the
strictest order of St. Francis.   He signed his will in
the cloister of San Croce, desired to be buried there,
and left money to furnish a new chapel and for a
hundred masses to be said by the monks for his soul.

It must not be supposed that the monks were silent under such attacks.   We have seen how Bernardino denounced Beccadelli; and a score of pulpits
thundered in reply to Poggio against the immorali-
ties and indecencies of the Humanist writings, charg-
ing that darker heathenism and heresy, denials of
God and the soul, were behind.

One strange outcome of this conflict between those who quoted the classics and practised worldliness, and those who quoted the New Testament and practised other worldliness, was the appearance of men who sympathized with both and spent their lives halting between two opinions. Such a one was Girolamo Agliotti, of the Benedictine cloister of Arezzo, in whom the zeitgeist was so powerful that when he heard the " Gospel of Christ or the letters of Paul or Augustine read, felt them so little that he was inclined to doubt whether there ever had been a Paul or a Christ or an Augustine." " He was much more stirred by Virgil than by the Psalms, and preferred Livy and Quintilian to Ezekiel." In this desperate condition he met Traversari, the Humanistic General of the Camaldolites, and his sympathy allayed the strife of the boy's spirit and gave him peace in the resolve to take the dress of his order. But his fellows regarded the study of anything but the Bible and the lives of the saints as worse than a waste of time for a monk, and he was sent out of the cloister by his abbot. He spent his years in projecting books for which he could never find a patron; wrote one on the " Education of a Monk," but seems to have pleased neither party; and, though the Pope finally gave him the abbacy of the little cloister from which he had been driven, he made no career commensurable with his ambitions or even his talents.

But Alberto da Sarteano, a begging friar who brought the fruits of classic learning to his order, found better service and reward. He was the most distinguished disciple and successor of Bernardino, their great preacher.   He had spent some time in his youth in Florence, and was a friend of the circle of literati centred about Niccoli.   Thence he went to the great schoolmaster Guarino to perfect himself in Greek and Latin eloquence.   They became sworn friends.   When the monk, a year later, preached at a provincial assembly of his order in Latin sprinkled with his new Greek, the teacher, always pleased with his pupils' efforts, was delighted.   Alberto soon laid aside his Latin and his oratory to learn the art by which Bernardino roused the common people to great crises of religious excitement and enthusiasm. Henceforth he became a pillar of his order.   But in the midst of his " trumpet preaching " he was still willing, as his old master wrote with joy, to exhort his hearers to the duty of study, and to support the truths of religion not only by quotation from the Bible, but also from the orators and poets.   No doubt this roused criticism and suspicion, just as Wesley's habit of reading Shakespeare did three centuries later.   But in so distinguished and zealous a servant of the strictest observance of the order, things could be pardoned that would have been unbearable scandal in a weaker vessel.   He was even able to maintain, in spite of one or two half-playful controversies, a friendly correspondence with Poggio. And on his mission journeys the monk was keeping a sharp and sometimes successful outlook for rare books on behalf of the very Humanist who was pouring out the vials of his bitterest satire on the barefoot preachers.

Coming events cast their shadows before, and such

a figure was a prophecy of those Jesusites (Jesuits) who a century later, leading the Catholic Counter-reformation by polished preaching to the higher classes and the creation of a new system of Catholic education, prepared novices for entrance into their order by a long and laborious training in every department of classic and philosophic learning.

Nicholas spent large sums in filling his court with Humanists, replacing by them the monks, the traditional servants of the Papacy. But it was in the arts that he used the bulk of those huge treasures which were raising the Church from the poverty of the schism. We catch a glimpse of the stream flowing quietly from all parts of the world in the flood of gold poured out before the altar of St. Peter by the thronging jubilee pilgrims of 1450—a sum so great that it amazed all beholders. The shops of the goldsmiths as far as Paris were filled with orders for the Papal court, and the ceremonials gleamed with wrought metal and precious stones, fine fabrics, splendid tapestries and embroideries. He bade painters cover the walls of the Vatican with frescoes, and was fortunate in the service of Fra Angelico; whose epitaph bids the passer-by praise him, not because he was a second Apelles, but because he gave all the rewards of his work to Christ's poor. The restless energy of Nicholas turned to every kind of building. The aqueduct was repaired and the fountains of the city increased and adorned; new bridges were built and old ones put in order. The walls were completed and made defensible, and new fortifications rose in the weaker cities of the patrimonium. The palace of the senators was enlarged and adorned, and a new one built for the magistrates. The ruined churches and basilicas were restored. For that part of the city which was called the Leonina, and centred in the Cathedral of St. Peter, the Pope formed a plan more magnificent than anything since the days of the Roman Emperors. Three great arcaded streets, a huge forum, a Papal palace as large as Nero's Golden House, and a basilica that dwarfed the Pantheon were the figures of this dream of marble magnificence. The first step toward realizing it was to destroy a little basilica which for more than a thousand years had preserved the graves of that Probus and his wife who had been the friend of Ambrose and Symmachus. For it is a strange contradiction in the life of Nicholas that no one was ever a more ruthless plunderer and destroyer of old buildings to get space or stone than this son of Humanism in the Chair of St. Peter.

The realization of his other ideal, the rule of peace by peace, was perhaps impossible without a renunciation of traditional Papal rights which would have appeared the most violent of revolutions. The people of Rome were a feeble folk, both in war and peace—filled with great enthusiasms, but hysterical. Nicholas shrank from the tyranny they needed. And yet it was his fate to provoke conspiracy. Stefano Porcaro, a member of one of the lesser noble families, was a man of distinction, largely acquainted among the leaders of the Humanists, and a correspondent of the Florentine circle, who had filled several offices of State at home and abroad. Moved either by enthusiasm or ambition, he bound a body of men by oath to fire the Vatican, fall upon the Pope and cardinals during the celebration of mass, capture or kill them, and proclaim the Republic, with himself as Tribune. The chiefs of this last important plot to restore the ancient Republic ended on the gallows, and it had no result except to embitter Nicholas and increase his constitutional timidity; but it is interesting as a type of a class of conspiracies, all appealing to the example of antiquity and choosing the Church as a convenient place for assassinations, which are scattered through the fifteenth century of Italian history. Everywhere the power of the citizens was decayed and the chartered liberties of the cities of Italy usurped by tyrants who knew no law save of their own making. As early as Boccaccio Humanism had begun to adorn the maxim that the murder of a tyrant is the praise of God. And when Humanism had become the mode it was natural that, since law had perished, envy, discontent, or devotion should frequently imitate the examples of Brutus or Catiline.

But Nicholas's love of peace was disturbed by something far more tragic than a masquerading conspiracy. In the height of his splendid pontificate the fall of Constantinople resounded through Europe. Christendom ought not to have been surprised, because embassy after embassy had sought help, but a great shock of wrath and fear ran through the nations of the West. For a hundred years the walls of Constantinople had stood as a bulwark against Asia. And

K

when it fell the imaginations of men saw the ruthless Turk swarming up the Danube, down the Rhine, and along the Mediterranean to conquer Europe.   The Papacy, as from " the watch-tower of Christendom," sounded the alarm, and the call for a crusade went to every bishopric of Europe.   But even fear, so long as it remained vague and distant, could not unite the Christian world to common action.   Only a meagre response came.   The folks' preacher Capistrano wrote from Germany to the Pope : " All princes and lords say with one voice, ' Why should we set our lives and our children's bread in hazard against the Turk, while the chief priest lets the treasure he ought to spend on the defence of the Holy Faith be wasted on towers and walls, chalk and stone ? ' "   And it came to pass that the talented, once simple-living and merry Tommaso of Sarzana, sickened of all his splendors and artistic pleasures, and died, glad to be released from the heavy burden of an office he had taken with great anticipations.

He called his cardinals around his bed and, after the fashion of antiquity, delivered to them a stately speech, the apology for his pontificate. Even through the rhetoric of his biographer we may see the real feeling of the honest ecclesiastic and the *mens sibi conscia recti* of the dying Humanist.   He told them he had found the Holy Church rent by war and crushed with poverty.   He had healed her schisms, paid her debts, won back her lost cities and secured them by fortresses.   He had made her magnificent with splendid buildings, adorned her by the noblest forms of art, and given her great store of books and carpets, garments and silver utensils. And he had gathered all these treasures, not by greed, simony, or avarice, but rather had used a magnanimous liberality in building, in book-collecting, in rewarding men of science. All these treasures came from the divine grace of the Creator and the continuous peace of the Church.

It is perhaps the most characteristic thing in Nicholas's life that this perfectly true eulogy—and criticism—of his pontificate should have been uttered by himself.

PERIOD II.

CHAPTER XIII.

CALIXTUS III., THE OLD SPANIARD, HIS FAMILY
PRIDE AND HIS ZEAL AGAINST THE INFIDEL
—PIUS II., THE CULTURED MAN OF THE
WORLD WHO DIED A CRUSADER—PAUL II.,
THE SPLENDOR-LOVING VENETIAN NEPOT.

T the death of Nicholas at least two of the
prominent candidates, Domenico Capranica and Bessarion, the learned Greek
convert, were distinguished Humanists.
But the "rhythm of the Papacy" prevailed. The Spaniard, Alfonso Borgia, seventy-
seven years old, a learned canonist, took the title of
Calixtus III.; and the Vatican became at once the
hospital of an infirm old man, filled, as in Eugenius's
days, with monks. Two interests roused the Pope
from the weakness of age—the love of his nephews
and his zeal for the Turkish war.

Two of his sisters' sons, one only twenty-two
years old, were made cardinals, against the protest
of the best of the College; a third became standard-
bearer of the Church, Duke of Spoleto, Regent of
Terracina, and was loaded with riches. A host of
Spanish poor relations and hungry adventurers flocked

to Rome and filled the streets with Spanish dress
and speech. The police courts fell into their hands,
and the swaggering adherents of the Bullshead (the
weapon of the Borgias) terrorized the citizens and
made the name of the " Catalans " hated. One of
these lusty young voluptuaries thus foisted into the
highest offices of the Church was to become Alexander VI. and the father of Cæsar Borgia.

Into the Turkish war the old man flung himself
with the passionate zeal of a Spaniard. The two
hundred thousand florins left in the treasury were
expended on a fleet. To add to this sum he sold
the jewels and vessels of the Church, and even
ordered the silver clasps to be taken from Nicholas's
books and sent to the melting-pot. Many of the
precious Greek manuscripts he gave to a philistine
cardinal, whose household lost or destroyed them.
By his orders every church bell in Europe rang three
times a day, and a swarm of barefoot monks spread
everywhere, calling on all Christians to take the
Cross. But the defeat of Mohammed at Belgrade in
1456 by the Regent of Hungary relieved the immediate pressure of danger, and Calixtus had small
satisfaction of his crusade, except to know that his
squadron of sixteen triremes was afloat and ready.
Then the hand of death came upon him, and he died at
eighty, after a pontificate of three years (August, 1458).

The Cardinal Enea Sylvio Piccolimini was elected,
and took the title of Pius II. He was the son of a
Sienese nobleman who had been educated in the
High School of Siena and under Francesco Filelfo at
Florence. He began his career as a prelate's secre-

tary at the age of twenty-seven in the service of
Cardinal Capranica, one of the leaders of the anti-
papal party of the Council of Basle, from which he
passed in quick succession to the households of several other prelates.   At the age of thirty he found
himself, in company with Tommaso of Sarzana
(Nicholas V.), in the service of Cardinal Albergati.
He travelled on several diplomatic missions, and
finally, after the split of the Council at Basle, became
a secretary in the Curia of the Antipope, Felix V.
(1440).   In 1442 the clever arrangement and neat
style of a letter fom Felix to the German King attracted the attention of a German prelate, and finding that its author was present with the embassy, he
urged the King to offer him a position as royal secretary. . Enea was rejoiced, because he had regarded with dismay the increasing poverty of the
Antipope, who was saved from simony because no
one would buy his Church appointments.   And besides, he reflected with apprehension that if Eugenius
won in the schism his career was ruined.   The service of neutral Germany seemed to him, as he wrote
to a friend, secure for the present and most promising for the future.

He commended himself to his new master, and
it was only a short time before he became one of
the four deputies of the King to a Council of
representatives of the German priests and bishops
to discuss the schism.   A double embassy carried
their conclusions to the Council at Basle and to
Eugenius IV. at Rome.   Enea Sylvio was the
ambassador of the second message.   He used the

audience with the Pope to make his own peace, and
became a secret tool of Papal politics to return the
German Church to obedience.   In the Papal court he
met his old comrade, Tommaso of Sarzana, who at
first refused his hand, and, even when informed of
Enea's secret conversion, would have little to do
with him.   It was not long after the secretary's return that the King sold his obedience in a secret
agreement for two hundred and twenty-one thousand
ducats.   In the spring of 1446 the German princes
despatched an embassy to the Pope to insist upon
the rights of the German bishops.   Frederick asked
that one of the Papal embassy then with him should
return at once to Rome.   And the Bishop of Bologna, once Tommaso of Sarzana, started.   Hard on
his heels the King sent also his secretary, Enea
Sylvio.   The two had a miserable time crossing the
Carinthian Alps, for the torrents had destroyed the
bridges; and once, when they were eating together
at a little inn, the Bishop is said to have jokingly
urged the secretary to order something else, with the
words, " Why should we be economical, since we
are both to become Popes? "   One other long journey across the Alps they made, not together, for
untimely sickness, first of one and then of the other,
separated them ; and then, their work being done, and
Germany in obedience, they received their reward—
the Bishop of Bologna a cardinal's hat; Enea Sylvio
the promise of the Bishopric of Trieste as soon as its
sickly incumbent had finished dying.   Henceforth
his rise was rapid, although not as rapid as his old
acquaintance, Tommaso, who in one year became

bishop, cardinal, and Pope; for it took him eleven years to make the same career.

Pius's past embarrassed him when he ascended the Papal throne, not simply because he had been the secretary of an Antipope, but also because he had lived so openly the life of a man of the world that his literary fame was largely based on a highly colored novel and a series of letters describing his social experiences in a style more interesting than edifying. He issued a retraction, in which he confessed his sins and compared himself to Paul and Augustine. He never had a trace of the persecuting bitterness or missionary zeal of the Apostle, or one flame of the mighty passion of Augustine either for sin or righteousness. But his confession and repentance seem to have been honest. From the time when he received ordination at forty, an age shown by experience to be more apt for moral breakdown than for moral reform, he began to purge and live cleanly. And there are plain evidences that, as this literary adventurer began to make his career, he was sobered and rendered thoughtful by the responsibilities of his position.

When this wandering secretary, who made his living by being a rhetorician and stylist, mounted the Papal throne, what a thrill must have spread through all the hungry Humanists of every court, whose ambitions had previously been bounded by the chance of some little bishopric! Nicholas V. had, after all, been only an adopted son of Humanism. He had made his doctor's degree in theology. But if Pius set an enormous reward on a lost manuscript, every one thought it would be, not a Hebrew Gospel, but the vanished Livy. They were mistaken. He had risen, to use the phrase of Tacitus, "*quod par negoties neque supra erat.*" But it was evident that he felt some measure of the truth behind his rhetoric when, in an oration over the coffin of the Doge of Venice, he once said: "The divine gift of ruling cannot be learned from the philosophers. It is only to be found in those depths of the soul into which man does not descend without God."

With the exception of Filelfo, most of the Humanists he had known in his youth were dead, and his old teacher made himself impossible by his greediness for favors. After all, Pius was rather a writer and speaker than a scholar. It was his own saying that poets and orators must be extraordinary or they are worth nothing, and he did not relish opening the crib for every limping Pegasus. He seemed to be aware that his own good wine needed no bush. A confidence not disappointed; for his writings are perhaps more read and quoted than any of his generation. He was a patron of the arts, and his court was visited by copyists, miniature-painters, goldsmiths, painters, and architects. His birthplace of Corsignano he called Pienza and decorated with a cathedral and stately palace, strangely out of proportion to the little town of a thousand inhabitants. But a cry of disappointment went up when it was seen that Pius was to imitate Nicholas only in his love of peace, and, while he banished the monks of Calixtus, was to inherit his zeal for the crusade. The old Filelfo voiced the feelings of the Humanists when, having insulted the Pope during life in a most false and scandalous anonymous invective, he wrote at his death a " Gratulatio de Morte Pius II.," which held him up to view as an ungrateful and envious foe of poets and scholars.

Scarcely was Pius consecrated when he announced the plan of a Peace Congress of all Christian princes. But it met with little success, and meantime the victorious arms of Mohammed, recovering from the check at Belgrade, were pushed forward up the Danube and along the coasts of the Mediterranean. The Hungarians, the bulwark of Christendom by land, as Venice and Genoa were by sea, were weakened by war with the Emperor. The efforts of Pius's ambassador, Cardinal Carvajal, brought peace, and finally, in 1463, roused Venice and Hungary to the attack. But the allies engaged to their support did not appear in arms, and the zeal of the Doge began to cool. Pius himself took the Cross, and, sick unto death, was carried in boat and litter across Italy to the seaport of Ancona. The journey took a month, and before he reached the goal he found the roads crowded with volunteers from all parts of Europe, undisciplined and unarmed, often starving and desperate. This wild mass, finding no ships or organization at Ancona, slowly dispersed, to every one's relief. At last, nearly a month late, the Venetian sails hove in sight. The Pope watched them from his window, but in the morning he was too ill to see the Doge, and the next day he died. The crusade died with him. A medal shows the Pope seated in the bow of a ship, holding in one hand the standard of the Cross, and raising the other in prayer. The inscription runs, " Let God arise, and let his enemies be scattered." The image has impressed itself on the memory and imagination of men, and has linked together Urban the inspirer and Pius the martyr of the War of the Cross against the Crescent.

But it was a different age from the days of Urban. Europe was incapable of large united action. The feudal system was dying, and the throes of its agony filled the world with misery and disaster. It was only as against foes who spoke another tongue that the sense of nationality was strong, and every land was given up to strife which to the common sense of the time did not appear civil, but only the natural defence of inherited rights. No sooner was the Hundred Years' War of France and England ended, in 1453, than the French Crown and its great vassals began a civil struggle, while in England the houses of York and Lancaster flew at each other's throats. Meantime, Aragon and Castile were fighting in Spain, and the German cities and princes were plunging into ceaseless feuds that wasted the strength of the Empire for nothing. Not even the fear and hatred of the Turk could bring Europe to concord. The jealousies of factions enabled him to gain a foothold in Europe, even as the jealousy of nations now permits him to sterilize his dominions with a feeble tyranny. Hungary, Poland, Genoa, and Venice held him at bay. Had they been backed by a small part of the men-at-arms of France, the bowmen of England, the *landsknechts* of Germany, the burghers of Flanders and Switzerland, and the money of Italy, he would soon have been sent back whence he came.

It was a subtle and real prophecy of the dark days when Italy was to be trampled by the feet of foreign armies, making her riches and beauty the prize of war, that, of nineteen cardinals assembled for an election, six were Frenchmen and six Spaniards. The Italian party was strong, and the Cardinal of San Marco, Pietro Barbo, was elected at the first ballot. Nicholas and Pius had been " new men" who, having chosen to serve the Church, had risen without the aid of family connection, by sheer force of ability. But Pietro Barbo was one of the many nephews of a Pope who attained to the tiara. He was the son of the sister of Eugenius IV., and, following the custom of the sons of the merchant nobles of Venice, was in readiness to embark for a trading voyage to the East, when, at the age of thirteen, he heard of the election of his uncle to the Papacy. He at once went to him in Ferrara, studied, took holy orders, and at the age of twenty-two became a cardinal. He was a man of very moderate intellectual abilities, but inherited the dignified bearing and personal beauty of his family. So entirely conscious was he of his advantages in this respect that nothing but the protest of the cardinals prevented him from taking the name of Formosus and induced him to finally adopt the title of Paul II. Both before and after election he signed the new capitulation, in which the cardinals renewed their constant attempt to make the Church an oligarchy instead of a monarchy. By this agreement the Pope was pledged to carry on the war against the Turk, to reform the Curia, to call a Council in three years, to restrict the College to twenty-four members, to name none under thirty years old, none untrained in theology or jurisprudence, and not more than one of his own relatives. The agreement disappeared after Paul's coronation. Instead of it he presented a new agreement in conclave, covered it with his hand, and bade the cardinals sign. Only one refused, the old Carvajal, though Bessarion made a long resistance.

The successor of Pius and Nicholas was not without some pretensions as a patron of art, but on very different ground. His taste was rather that of the noble Venetian merchant whose family had acquired in the Oriental trade the love of plate, silks, and jewels. He had a new tiara made with two hundred thousand florins' worth of precious stones in it, and was fond of displaying a superb emerald on his finger. He found a good opportunity of increasing his collections in the death of Scarampo, the executioner of Vitelleschi, who had succeeded him as commissioned Judge Lynch in the Papal States. Eugenius had rewarded the ruthless peacemaker with a cardinal's hat by the same creation which gave it to his nephew, and the two had hated each other ever since. When the Cardinal died, leaving to his nephews a treasure specially rich in plate and jewels, his old enemy, now Pope, reversed the will and confiscated the estate; and all Rome rejoiced at this posthumous plundering of the great plunderer.

The Pope was as generous as he was splendor-loving. He presented his cardinals with purple mantles and scarlet saddle-cloths, insured each one whose income fell below four thousand gold florins an addition of one hundred florins a month, gave great feasts to the city officers, and strange carnival sports—races of buffaloes, asses, old men, and Jews—to the people. In fact, except that he held himself aloof from foreign politics and cared nothing for the game of diplomacy, his court differed little from that of any other rich prince of his time who understood the art of enjoying life and keeping his people content by flattery and justice.   He regulated the misuse of ecclesiastical funds and stopped a good deal of indirect bribery and simony.   He made an earnest effort to check the incessant murders which arose from the vendetta or custom of the avenger of blood—feuds bitter and more constant than the old family quarrels of Kentucky.   He tried to regulate taxes, and destroyed the robber nest of Count Eversus, bandit and counterfeiter, who had long terrorized a part of the patrimonium.   It was as a matter of practical politics that he came into conflict with the Humanists of the court and city.   The College of Abbreviators (cabinet secretaries of the Papacy) had been filled by Nicholas with his friends.   And as the easily triumphant candidate of the aristocratic ecclesiastical party, himself a nepot and supported by the younger and more splendor-loving of the cardinals, Paul had no intention of continuing to pay salaries to seventy Humanists whom he regarded as learned fossils wasting the patronage he wished to divide among those who had been useful to him.

The displaced, losing the comfortable positions they had expected to hold for life, raised a great outcry, but made little by it.   And when their leader, Platina, sent a letter to the Pope, threatening to appeal to a Council, he was cast into a hard imprisonment that soon brought him to his knees.

It was similar practical politics that led Paul to suspend the Roman Academy. The younger poets and scholars were formed into an Academy whose members took Greek and Roman names and celebrated the birthdays of Rome and Romulus; at which ceremonies Professor Pomponius Leto was Pontifex Maximus. But Paul was mindful of Stefano Porcari, with his dangerous enthusiasm for the liberty and glory of antiquity, and his police suddenly swooped down upon the Academy and lodged twenty members in jail. Some of them paid on the rack for their meetings; but even the torture disclosed nothing more serious than the boasting of a drunkard. An accusation of heresy was not pressed very hard, and in the end Pomponius resumed his lectures, and the accused heretic became librarian of the Vatican and historiographer of the Popes.

While the Pope thus absorbed himself in ruling and enjoying Rome, the Turk was conquering. The fall of Negroponte woke Italy to a pressing danger, and united the five great powers, Venice, Naples, Florence, Milan, and the Pope, in a league against the common foe of Christendom. The signing of the league was among the last things Paul did. Toward the end of July, 1471, he took supper in the garden by his titular church. In the morning they found him dead in his bed. He had given the red hat to three of his nephews, but he gave none of them an influence or duty in the government greater than his abilities warranted; for Paul was a ruler who needed no favorites and suffered no counsellors.

PERIOD II.

CHAPTER XIV.

THE NEW LEARNING CROSSES THE ALPS—ITS SPREAD IN FRANCE—THE FORERUNNERS OF GERMAN HUMANISM.

DURING this generation (1440–71), in which Humanism had furnished two Popes and become the ruling spirit of Italian society, it was making the first faulty visible beginnings of spreading beyond the Alps; but not deliberately, for Humanism showed at first a very provincial spirit, and nothing could exceed the scorn with which the Italian man of letters spoke of all the other nations of the world except his own. Petrarch displayed, when he went to Cologne, a naïve astonishment at finding "a well-built city, good manners, dignified men, and beautiful and pure women." Paris was a centre of classic learning, where lectures were given on the Latin poets; a city of bibliophiles, which Richard of Bury (born 1281) named the "Paradise of the World" because of its rich book market; but Petrarch called Frenchmen a nation of barbarians, and said one must not look for orators or poets outside of Italy. Boccaccio called the Spaniards half-barbarians.

Poggio could not endure the manners of the Londoners, and wrote sarcastic letters on the intolerable length of their feasts, at which he could only keep awake by going out and dashing cold water on his eyes. In the same spirit, Enea Sylvio, during the days of his German secretaryship, made merry over the gluttony and drunkenness of the Germans, who had no intellectual life. He caricatured the nation in the person of a certain count who had his boys waked in the middle of the night and poured wine down their throats because they must be thirsty; and when it made them sick fell into a passion and accused his wife of infidelity. But the New Learning which these scornful writers so brilliantly advanced and defended began almost immediately to spread among the transalpine peoples they despised.

The first faint beginnings of this spread of the New Learning were perceived in France, which had preserved a stronger intellectual life than any other nation except Italy. Scarcely was Petrarch dead before the stirrings of the movement of which he was the apostle began to appear in the land on whose borders he had spent so much of his life. Jean de Montreuil (1354–1418), whose learning and Latin style raised him to the position of Chancellor of Charles VI., was a great reader and admirer of Petrarch. He found a living model and teacher in Salutato. Jean styled him the "Father of Latin Eloquence," maintained a correspondence with him, and expressed his admiration by sending presents to his wife showing the skill of French workmen in the fine arts. His great friend was Nicholas of Cleman-

L

ges, who formed his swinging Latin style on Cicero
and Quintilian so successfully that the Italians wondered to find a Frenchman so accomplished in eloquence and poetry.   He was Papal secretary during
the years of the schism, and when he lost that position lived from the income of Church benefices.   In
the later years of his life he lectured on theology and
eloquence in Paris.   Neither of these men knew
Greek, nor did any Frenchman among their contemporaries.   And it was not until 1430, probably after
the death of both, that we find the first notice of the
study of that tongue at Paris—the record of a small
salary paid to certain masters who taught Greek and
Hebrew.   This first beginning seems to have come
to nothing, and it was 1456 before an Italian who
had been in Greece was installed as teacher of rhetoric and the Greek tongue.   The study does not seem
to have amounted to very much, for a whole generation later we are told by the most competent of
judges that the instruction in Greek was imperfect
and unsatisfactory.   But the impulse which found
expression in such men as Jean of Montreuil and
Nicholas of Clemanges did not die.   In the face of
the Sorbonne, the centre of traditional learning and
reactionary orthodoxy, there flourished at Paris a
little coterie of lovers and promoters of the New
Learning.

During these thirty years (1440–71) a generation
of German-speaking men, whom we may call, for the
sake of clearness, the "Forerunners of German
Humanism," must have been doing a quiet but
mighty work of preparation in their native land.   At

the end of the period (1471), when they were dead or growing old, Humanism was still an exotic in Germany. But by their labors the soil had been so well prepared that before another generation had passed, their successors, the Older German Humanists, were confessedly able to wrest the palm of scholarship from Italy and carry it to the North.

The exact methods of this preparation would be hard to trace and tedious to describe in detail. It is better to suggest by a few striking examples the processes by which the New Learning began to establish itself in Germany.

At the beginning of the fifteenth century the unity of Europe was broken. The national sentiment had everywhere rejected the old idea of the organization of Christendom into one great civil institution. Before the middle of the century the strength of this sentiment was demonstrated. The party of Conciliar Reform used it at Constance to defeat the Papalists by the plan of voting, not as a whole, but in nations. And the Papalists in turn skilfully used it to defeat the reform of the Curia by the granting of national concordats. It was made absolutely plain by the supineness with which Europe allowed Constantinople to fall before the Turk.

But in spite of this change, three agencies operated mightily to preserve a sort of unity of Christendom. The Holy Roman Empire had broken down. Sigismund was only in name the head of Europe. But the institution which had been incorporated into the creation of Charles the Great, the Holy Church Catholic and Roman, survived. In the beginning of

the fifteenth century, corrupted as it was, weakened
by a hundred years of misrule, and shattered by the
conflict of two colleges of cardinals for its leadership,
it still kept intact its hierarchical organization and a
sense of unity.   It was only by virtue of his title of
"Defender of the Church" that Sigismund could
appear at Constance presiding over the nations.   In
such assemblies Humanism began to spread by contagion, and German prelates who had met the young
Humanistic secretaries of their Italian brothers, or
been impressed at some banquet by the elegance of
their Latin citations, acquired a taste for the new
letters.   This influence first appears plainly in the
Council of Basle.   The Cardinal Cesarini, one of the
noblest men of the times and president of the Council,
was a distinguished representative of the New Learning.   His graceful speaking and good style came out
of the study of Cicero, Augustine, and Lactantius.
The same strain of the eloquence of antiquity appeared in the speeches of some of the scholars of
Vittorino da Feltre.   Traversari of Florence broke
down, indeed, in his first speech, and had to pull his
manuscript out of his long sleeves; but he got himself in hand later, and even sprinkled his speeches
with quotations in Greek.   The bitterest ecclesiastical politician, who had no understanding whatever of
the breadth and purity of Cesarini's love for the
Church, was impressed by the strength of his style
of speaking.   And the most zealous monk saw a certain usefulness in Greek, after all, when Traversari
used it in defence of Papal authority.   That the good
old Bishop of Chiemsee should be impressed with

Enea Sylvio's style, and advise the King to give him a place as secretary, is not surprising. And it followed as a matter of course that the brilliant Italian became the centre of a little circle of German imitators.

This coterie met strong opposition. The works of Enea and Poggio and the rest which found the quickest circulation were those in which the new style was devoted to the service of the goddess of lubricity. And the conservatives at once began to attack poetry as the servant of vice, and good Latin as the sure mark of a desire to exchange honest old German manners and morals for Italian falseness and wickedness. Enea was not slow to answer "the asses who thought little of poetry, the oxen who despised the Muses, the swine who turned their backs on the Humanities." And it did not take much such fighting to show some defenders of righteousness that they must have as good weapons as their opponents, or lose. And so there arose a curious relation, half fascination and half repulsion, between the Humanists of Italy and this generation which we have called the "Forerunners of German Humanism." It cannot be better shown than in the story of the acquaintance of Gregor von Heimburg and Enea Sylvio.

Gregor was at the Council of Basle as a young doctor of canon law. He was called in 1435 to the service of the city of Nuremberg, and remained a servant of princes and cities until his death in 1472. He became a great patron of classic learning, and delivered an oration in the castle at Vienna on the "Study of the Humanities." A circle of learned

friends gathered around him, clergymen and jurists.
Enea Sylvio, then Bishop of Trieste, addressed him
in a letter as one who had brought " Latium to Germany, even as of old Greece had been brought to
Latium." But Gregor had a rough straightforward-
ness of speech, a sturdy faithfulness of opinion, that,
in spite of this flattery, brought him into deadly conflict with his old friend the Italian. It was in 1459,
when Enea was presiding as Pius II. over the
Peace Congress at Mantua, that Gregor was presented as the representative of several German
princes. His first appearance at the Papal reception
was surprising, for he failed to remove his hat, and
his speech was filled with ill-concealed sarcasms
against the finished style of the Pope, who knew so
well how to express the changes of opinions through
which he had passed in a career now so brilliantly
crowned. At the close of his address, in which he
carelessly showed the curialists by his learned allu-
sions how rhetorically he might have spoken had he
not chosen the blunt speech that was not of kings'
courts, but of loyal hearts, he excused himself for not
removing his hat. He had catarrh and wanted to
keep his voice from getting husky. And this German who could be classic, but chose to be " barbarous," became the leader of the opposition which made
Pius's plans for enlisting the Congress in the crusade
a failure. The next year, when Gregor, in the
name of his master, the Duke of Austria, fastened on
the doors of the chief churches of North Italy an
appeal from the Pope to a General Council, Pius
promptly excommunicated him. He found shelter

in the service of several German princes, like himself in rebellion against the head of the Church, but it was not till after Pius's death that the ban was removed. This experience was the cause and result of a reaction in Gregor against Humanistic rhetoric. "The best sign of a noble spirit," he said, "is not to make the style of this or that author our own, but rather, as the fruit of our study of them, to develop our own individual talent. The bee who collects honey is not a good model for the orator. Rather, like the silkworm, which spins silk out of its vitals, he must be able to make speech out of himself."

Besides the Church another great agency was still active to preserve the unity of Europe. Money knows no country and trade no boundaries, and by them the nations were drawn together in a sort of commercial confederation. Florence had been for years the centre of European finance, and Venice the great market where Europe and Asia exchanged products. But the free cities of the North had already gained riches and skill in commerce; and in particular Augsburg, the centre of trade between Italy and Germany, was rapidly acquiring the wealth and culture which made the daughters of its patricians matches for princes. The greatest family of their prince merchants, the Fuggers, had laid, by commerce and mining, the foundations of that fortune which made them the Rothschilds of their age. The exigencies of this commerce led the merchants to the South. So Sigismund Gossembrot, a rich patrician of Augsburg, brought back a taste for classic literature, and, like his fellow-townsman, the leading physician, Hermann Schedel, gathered a library and patronized the arts.   Gossembrot sent his two sons to the school of Guarino, that they might learn the Humanities.   But such a taste for foreign rationalism did not remain unrebuked.   Conrad Säldner, for twenty-five years professor of theology at the University of Vienna, became involved in public correspondence with Gossembrot, reproaching him with neglecting the learned men of Germany to honor a lot of half-baked poets who knew nothing of the good old seven liberal arts.   " Who are Bruni, Vergerio, Barbaro, Valla, Poggio? " he asked.   " I never heard of one of them, except Poggio, and I never heard anything that was good of him."   As for Guarino, whom Gossembrot hailed as a man raised up of God, the old theologian gave his solemn word that he had never heard the name mentioned in Austria, Swabia, Bavaria, Hungary, or Bohemia. But even the bitter truth in Säldner's reproaches against the " poets " could not prevail before the New Learning.   Honest old Mrs. Partington and her broom have always been helpless against the tide. Italian letters and art began to become the mode in Germany.   And so it was that the Pfalzgraf Frederick, a just and generous prince, having married Clara Dettin, the daughter of an Augsburg patrician, made his court a home of the Muses, and as the liberal patron of the University of Heidelberg was soon to do much for the spread of the New Learning.

In one marked particular trade made a free circuit from North to South.   But this time Germany sent out the current. In the early sixties two workmen from the shop of Faust and Schoeffer in Mayence carried their hand-press to Italy to seek their fortune. They found a patron in Torquemada, the learned Spaniard, then abbot of one of the monasteries of the little mountain town of Subiaco, near Rome, where they issued the first book printed south of the Alps—the Latin grammar of Donatus. The new invention met with scant favor at first from the wealthy connoisseurs, to whom a printed book seemed to exhale that odor of Philistinism which still hangs faintly around the type-written letter. And so the first adventurers of the press made no fortunes; they only unlocked the treasures of learning for the common people and helped to give arms against tyrants to every friend of truth and liberty in Europe.

But Germany was not only a part of the invisible monarchy, the Church, and united by her merchants to the confederacy of commerce. She was also by her universities a member of the republic of letters. The universities of the middle ages formed one body, speaking one language, for all lectures were given and all theses written in Latin. Students passed freely from one to the other, and nothing could, therefore, influence the universities of one land without in time influencing those of other lands. The new spirit and method of study were carried from Italy to Germany, just as the new method of German criticism in this century was brought from Germany to England and America, by the students and younger professors. So when Peter Luder, a wandering scholar, a *bemoostes Haupt*, who had been a long

time acquiring a somewhat mythical degree from
some university whose name was not mentioned,
drifted back from Italy to Heidelberg in 1456, he
found things partly ready for him. It was not so
much that the Faculty of Arts had just purchased
fifty-six volumes of Latin classics and the works of
Petrarch as that the students had an inkling of some
new method in the air of learning. The professors
would not give the disreputable-looking man, whose
antecedents were unknown, any recognition. But
the Pfalzgraf granted him a small pension and the
right to lecture on the Humanities. Nobody came
to his course on Seneca. And so he struck another
note. One side of the writing of the Humanists, the
pagan feeling that whatever pleases is permitted, was
no new thing. It belongs to human nature, and the
rediscovery of classic literature only gave it free rein.
It had found expression already in poems which,
though written years before the birth of Petrarch,
" foreshadowed the mental and moral attitude which
Europe was destined to assume when Italy through
Humanism gave its tone to the Renascence." These
were the songs of the wandering scholars, some of
whose lineal descendants, more decently phrased, are
still to be found in the German *Commercebücher*.
The spirit of Horace and Ovid had long ruled among
their lyrics, and when Luder announced a course on
Ovid's " Art of Love " he found hearers. It is little to
be wondered at, however, that the faculty turned the
cold shoulder on so scandalous a colleague, and after
borrowing from everybody who would lend him a
couple of florins, the poor apostle of poetry wandered

off to other universities, turning up successively at Erfurt, Leipzig, Padua, and Basle. It was at Leipzig that he seems to have had the most success. For, though in his introduction to the course of three lessons that was to free his hearers from " kitchen Latin " he put an accusative instead of a dative, a band of young ne'er-do-weels with tastes for the New Learning gathered round him half in joke. Among them was Hartmann Schedel, nephew of the learned physician of Augsburg.

But of course such vagabonds of Humanism as Luder were only signs, not causes, of the times. And a movement whose sources are too deep to be traced was stirring in German education. In sixty years, from 1348 to 1409, German states and cities had founded seven universities. A century later a similar movement began, in 1456, that founded eight new universities in twenty years. Still more remarkable was the activity in the founding and development of city schools, which began in the middle of the century, until Schlettstadt, Deventer, Münster, Emmerich, Alkmaar, Zwölle, had flourishing high schools. The two largest of these were Schlettstadt and Deventer, one in the southern Rhine country and the other in the lowlands; for the stream of learning seems to have followed that river from the Alps to its mouth. Under Hegius, Deventer rose to two thousand scholars. The first master of Schlettstadt, which increased to nine hundred scholars, was Ludwig Dringenberg, an old-fashioned Latinist, capable of breaking several rules of syntax in a single line, but a hard-working teacher with the knack of making his scholars love learning, and withal a conservative with an open mind. A man of piety as well as wit, he took alarm, perhaps at such phenomena of the spirit of the times as Luder's lectures on the "Art of Love," and proposed to abandon letters as unholy and enter a convent. He wrote to Gossembrot, the learned Augsburg merchant, about it, and was won by the answer to work for a quarter of a century more, until his death. It was among the boys of such new schools that the New Learning found its adherents.

This influence of the breath of a new spirit, whose stirrings were faintly felt to the remotest confines of the European republic of learning, can be seen in two churchmen of similar name and not dissimilar character and labors, Johann Wessel (about 1420–89) and Johann of Wesel (year of birth unknown, died an old man in 1481). Johann Wessel was educated at the city school of Zwölle, where as a poor scholar he probably received the care of the inmates of the neighboring convent of the Brothers of the Common Life.[1] He entered the University of Cologne, where he found some monks who had fled from Greece before the Turk. From them he took private lessons in Greek, and, probably from learned Jews, lessons in Hebrew. From Cologne he went to Paris, where he stayed some sixteen years without official position, but regarded as one of the ornaments of the University. He entered into correspondence with Cardinal

[1] The common statement that the reform in *methods* of education owed much to them, and especially to the influence of Thomas à Kempis, rests on entirely insufficient evidence and does not accord with his work or character.

Bessarion, and visited Rome in 1471. Sixtus IV., whom he had known in France as cardinal, is said to have told him to ask any favor he would. To the surprise of the court, he asked, not a bishopric or other office, but a manuscript of the Greek and Hebrew Scriptures from the Vatican library. For Wessel cared more for the Bible than for anything else in the world, and declared that the Gospel was the source of religion and theology. It was this desire to return to the historical origins of Christianity, which he had gained from Humanism, joined to a sense of the value of the individual soul, doubtless strengthened by his boyish intimacy with the Brothers of the Common Life at Zwölle, which suggested his criticism not only of the abuses of the Church, but of the prevalent ideas of religion. His writings maintain that religion consists, not in outward ceremonies, but in faith. He emphasized the inward marks of membership in the true Church of God, the desire for holiness, love to one's neighbor, obedience to Christ. For the Church, like religion, rests on the Gospel, and therefore both Pope and Council can err. Only as the Pope teaches and commends the truth and law of the Gospel is he to be obeyed. For, after all, he is only the defender of order. In matters of faith he has no authority. These ideas, which he had doubtless been communicating orally during the thirty years of his brilliant academic life, he committed to writing during his last ten years, which he spent in retirement at his native place. The writings were passed around among the large circle of friends, admirers, and scholars with whom he stood in correspondence. Such a private circulation aroused no special hostility on the part of the orthodox party, who read little, and it was not till after his death that his tractate against absolution and indulgences was attacked as heretical.

Very different was the fate of Johann of Wesel, who first appears (1445–56) as a professor of philosophy and theology at the University of Erfurt, where his influence was so great that fifty years later young Martin Luther wrote that he found his ideas and writings still ruling the University. While in this position he wrote, among other things, a tractate against indulgences, which seems to have excited little attention at the time. He was called in 1460 to become preacher in a city of the Upper Rhine, and there his views, similar to those of Wessel, began to make trouble for him. The words of the preacher were heard by those who read little, and his nervous phrases, meant for the common people, made his meaning plain and offensive to the dullest and most jealous supporter of things as they were or ideas as they had been. It was a scandal to the orthodox when he said, for instance, in preaching against putting undue confidence in outward ceremonies, that " if Peter advised fasting, he only did it to help the sale of his fish," or that " consecrated oil [used in the unction of the dying] is no better than the oil one eats at the table." So it came to pass that in 1479 he was called before an ecclesiastical court to answer a charge of heresy. He appeared leaning on a staff and supported by two monks. He stood manfully at first, asserting that " if every one should fall away from Christ, I alone will honor Christ and be a Christian "; but in the end he confessed his errors, submitted to the judgment of the Church, and asked for mercy. Two years afterward he died in prison. Forty years later a court met within a few miles of the same place, and the refusal of another professor to recant his errors began in Europe a hundred years of religious war.

Thus through trade, the Church, and the institutions of learning those first influences of Humanism came in by which Germany was being prepared for the rapid growth of the next thirty years. These agencies were of course at work in other lands; but in all those matters Germany had especially intimate relations with Italy. Her people were converted late in European history by Papal missionaries, and her metropolitans were canonically dependent on the Pope. Her emperors were kings of Rome, and when crowned at Aachen were expected to go to Italy to receive two more crowns. Over the Brenner Pass across Tyrol poured the steady stream of an old-established traffic between the free cities of North and South. And yet there is another reason which can be imagined for the rapid assimilation of Humanism by Germany and the quick moulding of the new impulse into a new German Humanism with an original national genius. The Germans, with all their love of home, have always been ready to seek and to use foreign things. They have never been seamen and so they have not been given, like the French, Spaniards, and English, to exploration; but they are the greatest travellers in Europe. More Germans visit

Switzerland and Rome than any other people, and the increase of travel promises to make them in a short time the most numerous foreign visitors to Paris.   This pleasure of travel finds expression in the folk-songs that voice the energy, curiosity, and poetic feeling which make the *Wanderlust*.   And it may be that the creation by German speech of this unique word gives the key to the rapid assimilation of Italian Humanism by the German race.

PERIOD II.

CHAPTER XV.

THE MAN OF THE RENASCENCE ON THE THRONE OF ST. PETER—SIXTUS IV., THE TERRIBLE.

T the death of Paul II. a new generation of Popes began. Christendom had been reunited at the death-bed of Eugenius, and the policy of his successors had moved within certain fixed limits. Nicholas, the doctor of theology, who loved literature and the arts, Calixtus, the friend of the monks, Pius, the classical secretary and accomplished diplomat, had agreed in limiting the activities of their pontificates within ecclesiastical lines; for their crusading zeal belonged to the duties which for generations men had assigned to the Papacy.

Paul II., the splendor-loving nepot, though a transition character, resembled the generation he closed in that his interest in material things was confined to the patrimonium. He displayed little thought of gaining new cities or territories, and kept aloof from all ambitious mingling in the politics of Italy or the diplomacy of Europe. But these four were succeeded by a line of Pontiffs who involved the Church in foreign politics and brought on the closing catastrophy of the Renascence Papacy, the sack of Rome by the Lutheran army of an orthodox Catholic emperor.

These seven men are perhaps more visibly the product of their times than the wearers of the tiara of any age of Papal history. In spite of their marked individuality, they show an unmistakable community of traits. They were completely dominated by the ideals of contemporary Italian society; they drew their income as successors of St. Peter; they used the stately ceremonials of their office, and believed in the doctrines of the Church after their fashion; but their interest centred on their power as Italian princes, and their virtues and vices were those of their class. They were men of the Renascence on the throne of the Papacy, and the office was to them only a means to accomplish personal ends. Of the seven the character of Leo X. was the least incongruous with his title of Vicar of Christ, but the epigram of Sarpi upon him is fair: " He would have been a perfect Pope if he had combined with his many fine qualities some knowledge of the affairs of religion and a greater inclination to piety, for neither of which he manifested much concern."

In order to understand the policy of these Popes, or do justice to their characters, it is needful to perceive the animating motive of their age. It was the passionate desire for a distinction entirely personal. We have seen how in the writings of Petrarch the self-consciousness of the individual appears. The thirst for distinction became a means and an effect of its development, and from the pressure of political and social circumstances, the influence of the classic writers, and the process by which every class of characters moulded by the spirit of an age tends to produce the extremest type possible, a new passion was trained on the hearts of men—the modern desire for fame. We do not know the names of the architects of the mediæval cathedrals, and they took no precautions against that forgetfulness. When Froissart wrote his account of the great knights of his day he addressed it to their peers, and rightly assumed their entire indifference to the opinion of the mass of men, peasants and burghers. But in Italy, by the second generation of the fifteenth century there existed a common desire for admiration which had no reference to tradition, was unlimited by class feeling, and appealed to the age and to posterity. Among the ancient Romans, where it sought its models, this love of fame had been modified by the pressure of a great legal system, working by its own momentum, and the presence of institutions too venerable to remain unfelt. Even Julius rejoiced that he was a *Roman;* and the ideal of the judgment-seat of Cæsar awed at times the worst of the emperors. But the corruption of politics in most of the smaller states of Italy had gone so far in the fifteenth century that the very idea of the commonwealth was lost, liberty only the war-cry of a faction, and law looked on as the will of those in power. Whole sections of the Italian people were manifestly incapable of any stable government except tyranny.

Amid this environment the love of fame produced strange results. In many otherwise noble and gentle natures the sense of duty seems to have atrophied, and, as a consequence of the paralysis of conscience, the ideal of religion became in many minds divorced from morality in a way difficult for us to understand. There arose an ambition which, positing purely personal ends, disregarded, apparently without a pang, every question of the right or wrong of its means: and this, not under the impulse of passion, but as a calm and reasonable assumption. Such an undefined ambition produced among the best of the men it dominated a many-sided development of personal skill, a power and an independence of character seldom matched. In the worst it bred a shameless and bestial egotism.

Francesco Sforza, one of the models of Italian ambition in the fifteenth century, is also one of its most favorable representatives. He was the illegitimate son of that peasant Jacopo Attendolo, nicknamed Sforza, or " the Stubborn Fellow," who, at twelve years of age, joined a company of free-lances and became the most distinguished soldier of the day. The boy was brought up in arms according to three precepts: " Let other men's wives alone ; strike none of your followers ; never ride a hard-mouthed horse." At the death of his father, drowned in leading his men through a river, Francesco was twenty-three. He called together the soldiers, swore them to himself, and with their aid secured the inheritance of all his father's castles. The Queen of Naples took him into service, and in twenty-two victorious battles he proved himself the first soldier of Italy. In 1441 he was leader of the army of Venice against Filippo

Maria Visconti, Duke of Milan. The Duke's generals had Sforza penned up in a position where he could neither fight nor retreat and ruin seemed near. One night the curtain of his tent was raised, and a messenger appeared to offer him the hand of the Duke's daughter. The crafty tyrant feared lest too complete a victory should deliver him, helpless, into the power of his own mercenaries. Sforza accepted, and when revolution followed the death of Filippo, entered the service of the Republic of Milan. For Venice would not consent to recognize the new sister Republic, except under hard conditions, and Milan needed soldiers. He won two great victories, and then entered into agreement with the Venetians to make peace, on condition of their aid in becoming Duke of Milan. The city, divided into bitter factions which had been fighting to the death ever since the Republic was proclaimed, made no long resistance. Their burghers would not fight, except with each other; and though Venice fell away from Sforza and offered help, a sudden mob killed the ambassador and opened the gates. In February, 1450, the illegitimate son of a peasant became ruler of one of the great states of Italy. Pius II. wrote that when Sforza came to the Congress of Princes in Mantua, nine years later, he was the most admired man in Italy: "Calm and affable in conversation, princely in his whole bearing, with a combination of bodily and intellectual gifts unrivalled in our time, unconquered on the battle-field." Such a man, whose power rested on no institutions and recognized no laws, a mercenary soldier who had made a brilliant career by strength, skill, and unblushing treachery, was for Italy the glass of fashion and the mould of form.

When the Conclave met after the death of Paul II., in August, 1471, they chose Francesco della Rovere, who took the title of Sixtus IV. He was born of poor parents in 1414, became a Franciscan monk early in life, had been professor successively at Bologna, Pavia, Siena, Florence, and Perugia, rose to be General of his order in 1464, and by the favor of Bessarion, the learned Greek, was made cardinal in 1467.

The influence to which he owed his election was made plain by the fact that Cardinal Borgia, the nephew of Calixtus III., Orsini, of the great Roman family, and Gonzaga, of the noble house of Mantua, were promoted and rewarded as soon as he became Pope. But the new Pope kept his best rewards, not for the people who made him, but for those he made. At the first consistory he began to give red hats to his nephews, six of whom became Princes of the Church. The two first in whose favor he broke the Capitulation of the Conclave, which all the Popes for forty years had signed and promptly broken, were Giuliano Rovere and Pietro Riario. Giuliano was already Bishop of Carpentras, and he was made in addition Archbishop of Bologna, Bishop of Lausanne, Coutance, Viviers, and Mende, in Savoy and France, and of Ostia and Velletri in Italy, Abbot of Nonantola, Grottoferrata, and a few other places. Pietro Riario, also a young man in the twenties, called the son of the Pope's sister, but generally reported to be his own son, was provided for even more thoroughly.

He lost no time in using his good fortune, plunged into every kind of debauchery, and displayed a luxury that made even Rome wonder. When the young daughter of the King of Naples came to Rome on her way to her husband, the Duke of Ferrara, Pietro received her in his palace. Every wall was covered with costly tapestry; nothing but was of gold or silver, silk or satin. And the great banquet he gave matched the feasts of Lucullus. The host sat by the side of the Princess in his purple gown, while under the command of a seneschal, who changed his dress four times during the feast, a host of attendants bore in on huge platters every beast of the field and bird of the air cooked whole, from peacocks in their feathers to a roasted bear in his skin with a staff in his mouth. There were huge castles of confectionery and ships of sweetmeats, tasted by the guests and then broken and flung to the crowd that filled the place in front of the palace. And a whole flock of singers and musicians made merry for the feast of this young monk of St. Francis who was a prince of the Church. But in two years it was over. The nepot died at twenty-eight, worn out by excesses. He had spent two hundred thousand florins and left a great mass of debts. An unknown satirist hung on his grave an epitaph bidding "every wickedness and all scoundrels depart now from Italy, for the accursed pest of the Southland is dead."

But plenty of brothers and cousins were left to rejoice the heart of Sixtus. Not all of these went into the Church, and the Pope began to carve out positions for them by politics and war. One was married to a daughter of the King of Naples in exchange for some feudal rights which the owner owed the Chair of St. Peter. Another was married to the daughter of the Duke of Milan and made Captain-general of the Church. It was through this Girolamo that the Pope became involved in bloody politics that made all Italy hate him. Giuliano and Lorenzo de' Medici, grandsons of Cosimo, were rulers of Florence without the name. And some fanatic lovers of liberty and haters of the house of Medici were ready tools of the ambition of Girolamo and Sixtus; for the Medici stood against their plans to conquer great possessions for the house of Riario in Romagna. A conspiracy was planned in the Vatican itself, and the two brothers were attacked by assassins in the cathedral at Florence at the very moment of the elevation of the host. Giuliano was killed on the spot. Lorenzo escaped into the sacristy, slightly wounded. But there was no rising of the people for "liberty," as the conspirators expected. Rather, the whole city shouted the cry of the house of Medici and strung up every one concerned in a row along the windows of the Palace of Justice, among them the Archbishop of Pisa. Sixtus was furious at the failure. When the news came, Girolamo insulted the Florentine ambassador in Rome by bursting into his palace and dragging him to the Vatican under arrest. And the Pope excommunicated the Medici and the Signory of Florence, because the people of the city had laid violent hands on clergymen, to the great insult of the Christian religion. He followed this by the interdict and war. The Florentines compelled

their clergy to say mass, and appealed to a Council
and the world. France and the leading states of
Italy entered into league with the Republic, and the
ambassadors of the Emperor protested to the Pope;
but the fighting went on, and only the sudden landing of the Turk in Italy forced Sixtus to peace.

An expedition from Rhodes had seized Otranto
on the 21st of August, and fear drove all the states
of Italy, France, Hungary, and the Emperor into a
great league against the infidel. It was needless, for
Mohammed II., the conqueror of Constantinople, died
in 1481, and two of his sons began to fight for his
throne. Sixtus, disregarding the chance of laming
the foe of Christendom, allowed the allied fleet of
Italy and Spain to break up, and plunged once more
into his plans for the house of Rovere. He renewed
the attempt to increase his power in the Romagna,
and induced the Venetians to join him in trying to
conquer Ferrara, promising the city to them, but
plotting to keep it for his nephew. But all the rest
of Italy rallied to the side of Hercules, the Duke,
and the great faction of the Colonna rose in Rome
against the Pope, because he favored their foes, the
Orsini. The disappointed Sixtus, checkmated at his
own game, made peace within the year. But it was
scarcely a year later when a frightful civil feud broke
out between the Orsini, backed by Girolamo Riario,
and the Colonna. The streets of Rome were filled
with murder and plundering, while the fields of the
Campagna were wasted with fire and sword. Already
Rome had seen the Lateran filled with lounging soldiers, who played cards and dice in the sacristy, on

the top of the chest in which were packed the relics of the saints and the vessels of the mass. And now, when his nephew had sworn to lay every castle of his foes level with the ground, the Vicar of Christ, in the robes of his office, publicly blessed the cannons of civil war. The death of the head of the Colonna marked the triumph of the successor of St. Peter. One annalist reports that his mother opened the coffin in which the body, scarred with torture, was borne to her, lifted by the hair the head which had fallen under the axe, and cried aloud: " Behold the faithfulness of Pope Sixtus. He promised me the life of my son."

It must not be imagined that in all these wars to make his family rich and powerful Sixtus was a feeble old man, used as a tool by greedy nepots. On the contrary, the will and craft of it were more his than theirs. Everywhere the big tyrants were trying to swallow up the little ones, who through all Italy had overthrown the liberties of the cities; and Sixtus saw in the office of the Pope the chance to establish the power and riches of the della Rovere.

Like all the other heads of dynasties in his day, he sought to find glory in the patronage of letters and art. The ex-university professor was a strong supporter of the Roman Academy, persecuted by his predecessor; Pomponius Leto, its head, became one of the most distinguished men of Rome. Even before he made his nephews cardinals Sixtus began to build a library. When it was finished he appointed as librarian that Platina, the historian, who had been tortured by Paul to wring out the supposed secrets of the Academy. He loved to collect books, for which his favorite binding was ornamented by niello-work. For he was a great patron of the workers in gold, silver, and bronze, though he was equally fond of the art of the decorator of majolica. He built largely on bridges, aqueducts, walls, and palaces, and some of his churches are among the ornaments of Rome. Most noted of all is the Sistine Chapel, for whose decoration he employed all the great masters of Tuscany. For though he himself liked the pictures of Cosimo Rosselli because he used plenty of gold in his coloring, he called to his court all the best artists of the day.

How much the remark of that crafty tyrant, Ferrante of Naples, that narrow and crooked streets gave great chances for insurrection, had to do with his plan for Haussmannizing Rome[1] is hard to say. At all events, his building rules for the city made and kept them wider, let in light by tearing down balconies, and began to cure the worst of their filth by laying pavements. He would not let the city of the della Rovere be inferior to the residences of the other great families of the day.

But though he widened the streets of Rome, he did not improve what went on in them. The intensity which Paul II. showed in policing the city Sixtus used only in political wars. There was continual riot and bloodshed in Rome. In January, 1483, there died the Papal Chamberlain, one of the richest and most learned of the cardinals. For more than

---

[1] Baron Haussmann straightened the streets of Paris under Napoleon III. for looks and artillery.

thirty years he had lived in Rome, a patron of árt and letters, adorning the city with many buildings, and leading a life of stately hospitality, surrounded by his illegitimate children, who passed for the sons of his brother. When he was dying one of the noble family into which his daughter was married came into the palace by way of the church which was next to it, packed up thirty thousand florins worth of silver plate, and went off to Venice with his plunder. The next day, when the body was being carried by the clergy of one church to San Agostino, which he had rebuilt, the bearers and the monks who were to receive the dead fought with the torches and candlesticks of the procession over the gold brocade which covered the bier. Swords were drawn on both sides, and with great difficulty the body was hastily gotten into the sacristy while the fight went on. When the trouble was over the corpse was found to be stripped of its costly rings and every ornament worth carrying away.

In the midst of his splendor and craft death came to Sixtus without warning—popular report said from a fever brought on by wrath that the peace which had been made between Venice and the powers of Italy had left his plans out of the reckoning. Rome had suffered frightfully under his rule, and the Church was filled with threats of appeal to a Council, before which even Sixtus trembled. He knew his administration could not bear investigation, for it had been the foundation principle of his finance that " the Pope needed only pen, ink, and paper to have any sum of money he wanted."

At the news of his death the city rose in wrath and joy. The house of Girolamo Riario was plundered of everything movable, and everything breakable, down to the marble door-posts, was destroyed. The magazines of the Genoese who had been partners of the Pope in wheat speculations were sacked, and others of his rich friends suffered from the mob. The Papal army, besieging a small city, broke up in panic, abandoning its camp-train. The banished Cardinal Colonna came back with two thousand armed partisans and filled the city with yet wilder confusion.

PERIOD II.

CHAPTER XVI.

INNOCENT VIII., THE SULTAN'S JAILER—ALEXAN-
DER VI., THE HANDSOME SPANISH NEPOT—
THE FRENCH INVASION.

HEN the disorder had become wearisome
even to those who took part in it, the
Conclave met on the 26th of August,
1484, and by the skilful bribery and wire-
pulling of Cardinal Giuliano della Rovere,
Sixtus's ablest nephew, the Genoese Cardinal of
Molfetta was elected. He took the name of Innocent VIII., apparently on the principle of *lucus a non
lucendo*, for the stately and handsome man, being in
Rome, had done as the Romans did. A satirist con-
gratulated the city that, after being depopulated by
the wars and slaughter of Sixtus, it was now to have
for ruler one who might indeed be called the father
of his people.

Giuliano della Rovere, the power behind the throne,
was not long in leading the new Pope into the paths
of his predecessor, and the Papacy backed the bloody
war of the feudal barons of Naples against their
King. Florence and Milan stood by the King;
Genoa and Venice were allies of the Pope. But in

less than a year the opposition among the cardinals, headed by Borgia, the defeated candidate for the throne, forced the Pope to make peace, and his allies the barons died by dozens in the hands of the executioners.

Meantime the Papal rule had broken down completely, so far as any of the real purposes of government were concerned. Rome was full of murder and violence. The ambassador of the Emperor was stripped to his shirt just outside the gates. It was notorious that gold would do anything in the Curia. Innocent made at a stroke fifty-two new secretaryships, which he sold for twenty-five hundred florins apiece. He used up in retail trade three hundred other new offices. Occasionally a few poor vagabond criminals were hung by night, but public trials were a farce and no one who had money need suffer. An innkeeper who killed both his daughters got free for eight hundred florins. The vice-chamberlain, being asked why so few people were punished when crime was so common, answered with a fine smile, "God does not wish the death of the sinner, but that he should live and pay."

The clergy set the worst example. Their houses were filled with concubines.[1] The sacred vessels of the churches were continually being stolen, and a wide-spread conspiracy to sell forged Papal bulls was discovered among the curial secretaries. Wickedness was unabashed, for the rulers set the example of law-

[1] One diarist tells us that when the Papal vicar issued an edict forbidding this, the Pope compelled its recall at once: "Propter quod talis effecta est vita sacerdotum ut vix reperiatur qui concubinam non retineat vel Saltem meretricem."

lessness. The cardinals led in the dance. Their houses were flanked by towers and raised on arches, that the steep steps might be defended by their hundreds of armed retainers. The store-rooms were well stocked with powder and lead for the arquebuses. When the princes of the Church went abroad they ruffled it in silks and jewels, even wearing swords by their sides, and were followed by a train of swaggering fellows who stopped at nothing. The Pope's son tried to storm the house of a burgher in broad daylight in order to carry off his wife. One day he burst into the Vatican in a rage. Cardinal Riario had won forty thousand florins from him the night before, and he accused him of cheating in play. The Pope ordered Riario to return the money, but the wily Cardinal answered that he had already paid it over to the master builder of his new palace.

Roderigo Borgia, the richest man in the College, stately and with a most persuasive manner, whose dark eyes were said to fascinate the women " as a magnet draws iron," lived for gallantry. His palace, the finest in Rome, was splendidly furnished. The entrance-hall was hung with tapestries representing historical scenes. It opened into a little room, also superbly hung, where stood a bed covered with red satin under an alcove painted blue with stars. In this room stood the great sideboard on whose shelves and cornice were displayed the gold and silver plate, a large collection of heavy and elaborate pieces. Two little rooms opened off this, one being in satin, with Turkish carpets on the floors, and a bed covered with Alexandrian velvet. The other and richer one had the bed covered with gold brocade, and a velvet-covered table in the middle surrounded by elaborately carved chairs. Ascanio Sforza, on the other hand, was the sportsman of the College, and astonished Rome by the size of his stable, his huge pack of hounds, and the variety of his superb falcons. A supper he gave to the Prince of Capua was said to have been like the feast in a fairy tale. Giuliano della Rovere, while he did not despise gallantry and patronized art richly, was the politician of the College. He did not scruple to seize a courier of the Duke of Milan, in order to take away his papers by force, and exercised such power that the ambassadors complained: "One Pope was enough for them; two were too many."

Under these circumstances it is not to be wondered at that a sudden alarm of the Pope's death threw the whole city into confusion. The shops were closed and barricades sprang up everywhere. The cardinals went to the Vatican and immediately started an inventory. They found eight hundred thousand florins in one chest and three hundred thousand in another. Then the Pope recovered from his swoon. When he heard what had been going on he remarked, "I shall have the pleasure of going to the funerals of these gentlemen of the College of Cardinals before I die."

There were three great public excitements during the rule of Innocent. The first was the finding of the so-called daughter of Cicero. Workmen digging in the Campagna opened a Roman grave, and in the beautiful sarcophagus, covered by some preserving

N

fluid, lay the corpse of a young girl, her long black
hair gathered into a golden net.   She looked as if
just dead.   And all Rome was filled with excitement
when the body was brought to the Capitol.   That
enthusiasm for antiquity which was now the universal social mode seemed to be boundless.   For fear of
the scandal which might spread from some open confession of heathenism, the Pope had the body secretly
buried again in the night.

Another great excitement was the entry of Prince
Djem.   This son of Mohammed, the conqueror of
Constantinople, fled from his brother, the Sultan, to
ask shelter from the Knights of Rhodes.   They held
him as a pledge of peace, and exacted from the Sultan thirty-five thousand florins a year for holding him
in prison.   They sent him to France for safer keeping.   Innocent brought him from France, and on the
13th of March, 1489, he entered Rome beside the
Pope's son, with a long train of Moslems and Christians riding two and two behind.   The precious prisoner lived for years in the Pope's care, while his
brother with one hand paid tribute to the Pope for
keeping him, and with the other hired assassins to
put him out of the way.   A letter of Andrea Man-
tegna, the painter, describes this strange inmate of
the Vatican: "The brother of the Sultan lives here
in the palace.   Sometimes he comes to dine where
I am painting, and for a barbarian he behaves very
well.   His bearing is full of a majestic pride.   He
does not uncover his head, so that everybody else
keeps on his hat before him.   He eats five times a
day, and sleeps just as often. •Before eating he

drinks sugared water.   His walk is that of an elephant, his movements as elegant as those of a big Venetian wine-cask.   His servants praise him much and
brag about his riding.   It may be true, but I have
never seen him mount.   His eyes are often half
closed.   He is of a very cruel nature, and they say
he has killed four people.   One day he thrashed an
interpreter so hard that they had to carry the man
to the river to bring him to.   He troubles himself
about nothing, and acts as if he did not understand
anything that is said or done.   He sleeps in clothes,
receives his visitors like a tailor with his legs crossed,
and wears thirty thousand ells of linen on his head.
His trousers are so wide that he could hide inside
them.   His pronunciation is horrible, especially when
he is angry."

It was in thankfulness for taking such good care
of Djem that the Sultan, having already paid one
hundred and twenty thousand ducats for three years,
sent an embassy in May, 1492, to bring the holy
lance which had killed Christ as a further gift.   Rome
had celebrated in January the fall of Granada, by
which the Moslem had been driven out of Spain, and
they hailed this relic with a festival as splendid.
Bishops received the iron lance-head in a superb
crystal reliquary from the Turkish ambassadors, two
cardinals received it from the bishops, the Pope received it from the cardinals, and in long procession
the whole city moved to St. Peter's, where the Pope
blessed the people, while Cardinal Borgia, standing
beside him, held the relic in the air.

It was less than two months after when death

drew near to Innocent.   A Jewish physician offered
to cure him by giving him a drink made of the blood
of three boys.   They were hired for a florin apiece,
and the drink was mixed.   But the boys and the
Pope died together.

Three candidates made an open bid for the Papal
crown in the conclave.   Giuliano della Rovere, the
nephew of Sixtus, was backed by the French King
with two hundred thousand and by Genoa with one
hundred thousand florins. ، Ascanio Sforza, the great
hunter, brother of the Duke of Milan, backed himself.   But Roderigo Borgia, who supported Sforza
to defeat della Rovere, came out a winner.   It was
well known in Rome that he did it by bidding
highest.   Only five cardinals out of twenty-three
refused the bribe; and it was noted that three of
them afterward obtained the Papacy.   The gossips
even knew the price of each vote.   Borgia sent to
Sforza's house four horse-loads of gold, gave him his
own palace with all it contained, and made him vice-
chancellor.   He was the most costly.   The others
tapered down to the ninety-five-year-old Patriarch
of Venice, who only got five thousand florins.

Alexander VI., the new Pope, was a man of imposing appearance, great practical skill in affairs,
persuasive and quick in argument.   His crowning
was hailed by the poets.   They called him Divus
Alexander.   And one wrote: "Rome was made
great by Cæsar, but now Alexander makes it far
greater.   The first was a man, the second is a god."
Within a year of his crowning the first gold came to
Rome from the New World, and the Pope drew a

line from pole to pole, dividing all the new West between Spain and Portugal.

Alexander was the handsomest Pope since Paul II., and had always exercised a peculiar power over women. The first notice we have of his life is a letter from Pius II., written when the Cardinal was twenty-nine, to rebuke him for a garden-party he attended in Siena, which had become the scandal of the city and was a "disgrace to the order and office of the clergy." In the days of Paul, Sixtus, and Innocent, Borgia had forgotten even the need of concealment. His mistress, Vannozza, daughter of a lesser noble of Rome, had borne him four children, Juan, Cæsar, Jofré, and Lucrezia, who were openly acknowledged. But Vannozza was now fifty years old, and scarcely was Alexander Pope when all Rome was full of the name of Julia Farnese, a young married noblewoman, eighteen years old, whose relation to the Pope was become so notorious that the King of Naples could write of it to his ambassador in Spain. In 1492 she bore a daughter, and in September, 1493, her brother was made a cardinal. Before the end of the year the Pope and his son Cæsar were splendidly entertained by the Farnesi at their castle near Rome.

But as compared with Innocent and Sixtus, Alexander promised to be a good ruler. He did not seem one to be feared. This is how an eye-witness describes him in a festal procession: "He sits on a snow-white horse, with clear brow and a dignity which constantly compels respect. How wonderful is the mild tranquillity of his mien, how faultless the nobility of his countenance, his look how generous! And how his stature and bearing of easy beauty, and the air of boundless health around him, increase the veneration he inspires!" Nor did the new Pope display the inactivity of Innocent. When he was crowned he found that two hundred and twenty murders had been committed in two months. He reformed the courts, reëstablished peace, and compelled order. His foreign politics were not notably dangerous. The great catastrophe which was to come upon Italy could not be laid at his door. It was the Duke of Milan who called the French King over the Alps.

In order to understand the invasion which opens the last act of the drama of the Renascence Papacy, we must glance for a moment at .the political condition of Italy. There were in the peninsula five great powers: Florence, Milan, and Venice in the north, the States of the Church in the centre, and Naples in the south. Naples was a kingdom, Venice an oligarchy. Milan and Florence had both lost their liberties; the first was called a duchy and the second was nominally a republic, but really under the rule of Piero de' Medici, the great-grandson of Cosimo. A number of the smaller cities of Italy also constituted independent states under the rule of tyrants. Outside of Naples the municipality was, by inheritance from the ancient days, the central point of Italian government. Each one of these city states, large and small, was anxious to cheat or conquer its neighbors. And as a consequence there reigned a petty local jealousy and a besotted local pride. And so when Lodovico Sforza, Duke of Milan, called the French to his help in 1494, almost all Italy was glad; for each state hoped to gain some advantage over its neighbors from the presence of the foreigner, and the common people hoped that some fortune might free them from the tyrants. Lodovico called them because he was afraid. He had imprisoned his nephew, the rightful Duke, and was killing him by slow poison. The wife of his victim was calling on her father, the King of Naples, to avenge her wrongs, and Lodovico needed a strong ally. His efforts to bring in the invader were seconded by Cardinal Giuliano della Rovere, nephew of Sixtus IV., now living in France for fear of Alexander.

It was not hard to rouse an enthusiasm for the adventure in Charles VIII., the French King, an ambitious boy of twenty-two, ugly, almost deformed in body, of violent but weak will, surrounded by flatterers as incapable as himself. Against the advice of his barons he decided to lead an army into Italy to reassert his claim to the throne of Naples, which sixty years before had been held by the younger branch of his family. And in the end of August he crossed the Alps with about forty thousand men. He halted at the first town and plunged into such a debauch that he had to wait a month before he was fit to go on. And thus, with long feasts and short marches, he made his way along the whole length of the Italian peninsula until he reached Naples, in the end of February. There was almost no fighting. After the French had stormed two small towns and put the whole population to the sword, all opposition ceased.

But in the midst of his feasting and triumph bad news came to the conqueror. The Pope, Venice, the Duke of Milan, the King of Spain, and the Emperor had leagued against him and his retreat was cut off. In idle recklessness he revelled two months longer in the gardens of Naples, and started his long retreat, with only twelve thousand men, about the end of May. It took him six weeks to get to the north, and in the passes of the Apennines he only saved his artillery by five days of the most extraordinary labor, in which the generals labored like the common soldiers. But it was not until he was over the mountains and safely down into the great plain of the Po that the army of the League, outnumbering him three to one, barred his way at the town of Fornovo (July 6, 1495). The battle was won in less than an hour, and the little French force made its way up the Po and over the Alps without another sword-stroke.

PERIOD II.

CHAPTER XVII.

SAVONAROLA AND FREEDOM.

N the whole story of this dallying march to the end of Italy and back with a handful of soldiers there are only two Italians recorded who faced the boy invader like men. These were the friar of San Marco, and his friend, Piero de' Capponi, one of the syndics of the city of Florence. It was on the King's downward journey that Savonarola came into his presence as ambassador of Florence. "O most Christian King," he said, "thou art an instrument in the hand of the Lord to relieve the woes of Italy and reform the prostrate Church, as for many years I have foretold. But if thou be not just and merciful, if thou respect not the liberties of the city of Florence, the hand of the Lord shall smite thee with terrible scourges. These things say I unto thee in the name of the Lord." And the King and all his men of war did honor to the monk. An alliance was made, and the gates of the city opened to the army of France. Charles rode through the narrow streets with levelled lance, the symbol of a conqueror; but he soon found his mistake; for when he demanded too large a subsidy in exchange for his alliance, the City Council demurred.   Disputes arose, and Charles bade his secretary read his ultimatum to the assembled syndics.   They refused to accept it, and the King cried out in anger, " Then I will sound my trumpets." Capponi sprang forward, snatched the paper from the hands of the secretary, and tore it in fragments, crying out, " And we will ring our bells!" And Charles made a fair treaty with the only state in Italy he was forced to respect.

In order to understand how this monk and his friends had become leaders of the only free city in Italy, we must go back some thirteen years to the time (1481) when Brother Savonarola came from a Dominican monastery of Bologna to San Marco in Florence.   He was twenty-nine years old, the grandson of a distinguished court physician and university professor of Ferrara, whose son had degenerated into a mere courtier.   He had been a teacher of novices and was assigned the same duty at San Marco.   His homilies soon stirred the spirits of the young men under his care, and he was invited to preach a course of Lenten sermons in the Church of San Lorenzo.   Like all his previous attempts to preach in public, these sermons were notable failures. At the last ones he only had an audience of twenty-five, including women and children.   And similar ill success followed another effort two years later.   The reigning preacher of the day was a certain Fra Mariano, whom all Florence flocked to hear.   The literati praised him for his musical voice, chosen words, and harmonious cadences, his lines from Plato, Aristotle, and the poets. Savonarola was abrupt and unstudied in voice and manner, and preached from the Bible, which the learned Florentines of the age would not read because the Latin of Jerome was bad. It was just after this disappointment that he thought he beheld the heavens opened and all the future calamities of the Church passing before his eyes, while a divine voice charged him to announce them to the people. From that moment he felt elected to a mission to cry to all nations, " Repent and return to the Lord."

The next year he was sent as Lenten preacher to San Gemignano, a little town among the Sienese hills.

The sending of mission preachers has been as common in the Roman Catholic Church as the modern Protestant use of evangelists, and at no time have they met with more astonishing success than during the last half of the fifteenth century in Italy. We have the names of more than twenty men who mightily stirred the cities in which they preached. Robert of Lecce, for instance, in 1448 had fifteen thousand hearers in the city of Perugia, who listened to him four hours amid sighs, tears, and outcries of repentance. The whole city made a renunciation of worldly pleasures, symbolized by a " burning of vanities." Debtors were released, blood foes were forgiven, and the entire population apparently converted from evil to good.

Some such effect as this Savonarola produced in San Gemignano when he first preached on the theme of his life—the triple assertion which formed the background of all his subsequent utterances: (1) The Church will be scourged; (2) she will be regenerated; (3) and that speedily. He did not yet announce this as a direct revelation of God to him, but supported it by reason and the Scriptures. The audiences were moved almost to ecstasy.

In 1486 he was sent to Brescia. He preached on the Book of Revelation, and declared that the wrath of the Lord was coming. The streets should be filled with blood and fire. Let them repent, for the just shall find mercy. A generation later, at the horrible sack of Brescia by the French, the people recalled his words. For three years he preached throughout Lombardy, and his fame filled all Italy.

In 1489 he was summoned back to Florence, and began to expound the Apocalypse in the convent garden, standing by a rose-bush whose scions were tended by his brethren for four hundred years. His audiences grew until he had to preach in the church. His three theses of judgment, regeneration, and that speedily, roused an extraordinary excitement, and the city began to be divided into the friends and foes of Savonarola. He published treatises on philosophical subjects to defend himself against the charge of ignorance, and to commend the teachings of the Church he wrote tractates on " Humility," " Prayer," " The Love of Jesus," " The Widowed Life." By these writings, as well as by his sermons, it is plain that his best equipment for his work was his knowledge of the Bible. He knew the Bible thoroughly (and it must be remembered he had neither a vernacular version nor a concordance), and by his method of exegesis he could find in it proofs for everything, big and little. Here are specimens written on the margin of two of his Bibles that have survived. They are from the opening verses of Genesis. The interpretations are arranged under six heads. The division of the waters means spiritually, the movement of the passions and of errors possessing the intellect; allegorically in the Old Testament, the Gentiles separated from the chosen people; allegorically in the New Testament, tribulations separating many from the Church; morally, the struggle of the passions against duty; anagogically, joy of the blessed when freed from tribulation.

The fifth day (birds, fishes) means spiritually, the contemplation of higher and of lower things; allegorically in the Old Testament, the Maccabees (who always wavered); allegorically in the New Testament, the contemplative and active life; morally, the contemplation of things divine and of things human; anagogically, angels and men admitted into the angelic choir.

Of course it was not such exegesis which crowded the great church when he preached and stirred his hearers to enthusiasm. This sort of thing appears in all his sermons, but it is shot through and through with sudden flashes of invective against gambling, against usury, against the temptation of the clergy, appeals to abandon worldly things, and praises of Jesus Christ. It was when he launched out into these discharges that his eyes flashed and his wonderful voice rolled. Especially did he sway the hearts of his hearers when he spoke of his visions.

For the power in the man seems to have been his conviction that he was directly inspired of God. He felt that he must preach these things, for he writes how, having determined not to mention his visions in a certain sermon, he agonized all night, and at dawn heard a voice say, " Fool, dost thou not see it is God's will? "   " Whereupon I preached a *terrible* sermon."   He spared neither high nor low, and being invited to preach before the Signory, rebuked tyrants and bad rulers in terms that many present applied at once to Lorenzo the Magnificent, grandson of Cosimo, the uncrowned King of Florence.   With Lorenzo, Savonarola refused all intercourse, would not pay the customary visit to the patron of the monastery even when he was elected prior, and distributed among the poor the great sum of money Lorenzo sent to the convent, saying in the pulpit, " No good dog stops barking because a bone is flung to him."

Soon after death came to Lorenzo, and he sent for Savonarola to hear his last confession.   " I know no honest friar but this one," he said.   With great agitation he spoke of the sins that tormented him —the sack of the city of Volterra, the robbery of the funds of the institute for giving dowries to poor girls, through which many had been driven on to the streets, and the bloody vengeance for the Pazzi conspiracy.   Savonarola said many times, " God is good, God is merciful"; and when Lorenzo was through and calmer, continued, " But three things are needful."   " What things, father? "   " First, a great and living faith in God's mercy."   " I have it."

" Second, you must give back your ill-gotten wealth."
Lorenzo nodded assent. " Lastly, you must restore
liberty to the people of Florence." The dying man
turned his face to the wall ; and looking sternly at
him for a little, the friar left him unabsolved.

It was in this mood that Savonarola saw two visions
which, in medals and engravings, were spread through
Italy. The first was a sword suspended over a great
city, and on the sword, " Gladius Domini super ter-
ram cito et velociter." The second was a black cross
rising from the city of Rome and stretching its arms
over all the earth ; on it was written, " Crux Iræ
Dei " ; while from Jerusalem rose a shining golden
cross, on which was " Crux Misericordiæ Dei."

Scarcely was Piero de' Medici firmly established
in the seat of his father, Lorenzo, than he procured
from the Superior an order for Savonarola to preach
in other cities. It was to checkmate such designs
that Savonarola and his friends obtained a Papal brief
erecting the convent of San Marco into an independent congregation, subject only to its own prior and,
of course, to the Pope. Savonarola's first step was to
reform his own house. He reduced living expenses
and founded schools for painting, sculpture, architec-
ture, and manuscript-making. He provided that the
brethren apt to teach should go out regularly on missions. Each was to be attended by a lay brother, who
worked for his support, that he might be not kept
from speaking the truth for fear of checking alms.
He revived in the monastery the study of theology, philosophy, Greek, Hebrew, and the Eastern

tongues.   Under his rule the number of friars increased so greatly that the building was not large enough to hold them.

And now the true genius of Savonarola's oratory began to appear.   More and more plainly he spoke, as one to whom God had given a secret word.   He was instant in threatening, prophesying, declaring visions of judgment.   " The princes of Italy," he said, " are like men taking the back of a whale for an island and building on it a great and wicked city of oppression and blood.   The whale plunges and Babylon is destroyed."   " Woe," he cried, " unto the Church!   Once she had chalices of wood and prelates of gold.   Now she has chalices of gold and prelates of wood."   It was a series of sermons on Noah's ark, where he explained each of the ten planks with minute allegorical interpretation, that he accompanied with prophecies of a new Cyrus who should come in triumph to scourge and free Italy. In September he began to preach on the deluge, and on the 21st he found the Duomo filled with a crowd that had waited from early morning.   Like the note of some strange trumpet his voice rang out the words of his text, " Lo I will bring waters upon the earth," and all stood trembling while for many minutes he smote them with his stern eloquence. For the night before news had reached Florence that the army of France was pouring down the slopes of the Alps.   We have seen how supinely the princes of Italy had watched this gathering storm.   No one prepared and it came to the people like an earthquake.   Savonarola had warned them and called them to be ready, and to Savonarola, as to a prophet of God, the hearts of all turned in the hour of fear.

Piero de' Medici was no man for the situation. After a feeble attempt to fight, he went to Charles, then hemmed into a position of the greatest military peril, and in a cowardly interview surrendered the fortresses of his quadrilateral without a blow. When the news reached Florence the streets filled, and all day a great mass of armed men drifted aimlessly through the city. After sixty years of tyranny, the folk were up, and no man knew where their wrath would carry them. Then Savonarola entered the pulpit, not now in the garb of the prophet of woe, but with the gentle words of the Gospel, and he stayed the storm till the Signory had resolved that the Republic must "shake off this baby government and care for itself." It was decided to arm the citizens, to secretly fill every cloister with soldiers, and then to send an embassy to offer peace to the French. Savonarola, the one man whom Charles respected and who had "the entire love of the people," headed the embassy. And when the King was gone at his commanding request,[1] Savonarola, "lover of liberty and hater of disorder," was a tower of strength to distracted Florence. "Woe to thee, Florence, if thou desirest a head to dominate and oppress all the rest. The sole form of government suited to our needs is a civil and general government."

---

[1] "Hearken now to the voice of God's servant. Pursue thy journey without delay. Seek not to bring ruin on this city and thereby rouse the anger of the Lord against thee."

o

And he suggested as the best plan a grand Council after the model of Venice.

"A grand Council." It was the word that solved the problem. The people caught it as it fell from the pulpit, and the foundation of the government was laid. By the time Charles left Italy (July, 1495) the building of the new city was complete, and in all the plan the master word came from the sermons of the Prior of San Marco. It was not an entirely wise government, nor what we should call a free government, but it is considered by many of her historians the best Florence ever had. Its unwisdom and lack of freedom are plain in the war with the people of Pisa, long ruined and insulted by the yoke of Florence. This foolish and cruel war to crush a sister city was never rebuked by Savonarola, and it caused the fall of the new Republic. But it is possible to recognize that there was a very narrow and intolerant strain in the puritan patriot without forgetting that when the sword of her tyrants sank in terror the voice of Savonarola awed the invader of Italy, and in the cathedral of her only free city rang through perilous days the praise of liberty.

PERIOD III.

FROM THE FRENCH INVASION TO THE SACK OF ROME (1494–1527).

PERIOD III.

CHAPTER XVIII.

THE HOUSEHOLD OF ALEXANDER VI.—THE PROPHET OF RIGHTEOUSNESS AND THE VICAR OF CHRIST.

HE year 1496 found Pope Alexander VI. living peacefully in the Vatican with his blooming family gathered around him. Juan, who was Duke of Gandia in Spain, where he had left his newly married wife, lived in the Vatican. Lucrezia, Alexander's daughter, was married to a natural son of the younger line of the great Milanese house of Sforza. They lived in a palace of their own. The sixteen-year-old son, Jofré, married to a daughter of the King of Naples, resided in the palace of a cardinal. Cæsar, who had gone into the Church, was only a bishop, and lived alone not far off.

It was a gay life with which these brides of sixteen filled the Vatican quarter. They went to high mass at St. Peter's, and crowded the cardinals so as to be close to their father when he said prayers for the world. The Pope himself was not much given to the pleasures of the table, and the cardinals used to invent excuses to escape his dinners of a single course. But he went often to the splendid festivals of his daughters, and frequently received them in the Vatican, with the glittering cavalcade of young cardinals and courtiers who danced attendance upon them. Rome had become used to seeing the head of a celibate clergy living thus, but the public talk of the city said that the life of the Pope and his children was much worse than it looked, and the ambassadors of foreign princes reported terrible things of it in their letters home. The Cardinal of Gurk, who had withdrawn to Perugia, told the ambassador of Florence: "When I think of the life of the Pope and of some of the cardinals, the idea of living at Rome fills me with horror. If God does not reform his Church I will none of such a life."

The satirists found plenty of material. Hear Pontano, a contemporary Neapolitan poet:

"Can you tell me the name of that remarkable old man, more decorated than a relique-box, smelling of musk like a civet-cat, and stepping gingerly as a young dancer, who hums a song and keeps turning his head and winking as he walks? It is a cardinal just landed from Valencia, who has only one thought in his head—to please the ladies. Hear him sing his love adventures. And how he ogles the windows! How he smiles and bows gracefully! Beautiful little grayhead, you will die younger than on the day you were born."

In sterner strain wrote Baptista Mantuanus:

> "You who would live well depart from Rome,
> For all things are permitted there except to be good."

Already Alexander had become involved in controversy with Savonarola. Just as the French left Italy a Papal letter invited the friar to Rome. It was called forth by his strictures on the clergy, the advice of Cardinal Sforza, brother of the Duke of Milan, whose plans were blocked by the Republic of Florence, and the furious attacks of the Arrabbiati party of city politics. The letter was couched in tones of affection, but Savonarola feared a snare. He answered that his health was broken, his life guarded against assassination even at home by armed men, his presence necessary to the city. He begged to be excused, and the Pope sent a message that he need not come at present. But scarcely a month was past when a second letter arrived, forbidding Savonarola to preach, revoking the order which had made San Marco an independent congregation, and referring it to the Congregation of Lombardy. For the desire of the Pope to aid his new politics by reinstating the Medici at Florence was now added to his other motives for silencing this "pestilent fellow." Savonarola protested, but obeyed the inhibition from preaching.

He spent the next few months in writing letters and planning the reform of the carnival. There were two evil carnival habits common in the city. The boys of Florence had a way of forming gangs, which blocked the streets with long poles and levied toll on all who passed, spending the money in debauchery. The game of "stones" followed the bonfires at night. It was so brutal that several players were killed each year. People are very tenacious of such customs; only a few years ago the law suppressing the brutal eel-pulling raised the barricades in the Dutch cities. And the Signory had in vain tried to stop this beastly sport of " stones." The friar undertook to try. He formed the youth of Florence into bands, ordered and drilled, and bade them collect alms for the poor. He wrote new songs for them to sing, and asked his friend, the poet Bienveni, to write more. He devised a great procession of the whole city, and while working good the boys forgot to do evil.

Meantime the Pope had changed his policy. At the request of the Florentine government he removed the inhibition from Savonarola. He had given the friar's sermons to a bishop who was a Dominican and therefore free from the intense jealousy of the monk against a member of a rival order. He reported that the friar respected the dogmas and authority of the Church, speaking only against simony and corruption, and counselled the Pope to make friends, even, if necessary, by offering the cardinal's purple. And so a Dominican was secretly sent to Florence to offer the red hat to Savonarola, on condition that he should change the tone of his sermons.

This was in the winter of 1496, and in Lent of that year Savonarola, protesting that he believed all that is believed by the Roman Church and submitted to her authority, was again swinging the lash of his terrible invective on the sins of Italy. An extraordinary effect followed his words. Everywhere he was hailed as a prophet of God or an emissary of the devil. And in Florence, while the Signory treated him as the first citizen of the Republic, the Arrabbiati laid daily plots to assassinate him as the most dangerous opponent of their treason.

There was no enemy more bitter against the Republic and its first citizen than the Pope. But he was too busy during the summer to attend to the friar or the plots of the Medici to reconquer Florence. For another plan was on foot. Italy was divided into two parties: on the one side a league of Venice, Milan, Rome, Spain, the Emperor, and England; on the other Florence, Savoy, with other small states, and France. And out of the desperate political disorder the Pope proposed to draw lasting gain to his house. The first thing was to resume the system of Sixtus IV., to crush the small rulers in the patrimonium, who had grown again from vassals to tyrants. He began with the Orsini, the richest and most powerful; declared them rebels,—which was true enough, for they were in the pay of France,—confiscated their lands and gave them to his son, the Duke of Gandia, who in October, 1496, became Standard-bearer of the Church. But it was an empty triumph. On the 23d of January the Orsini defeated the Papal troops in hopeless panic, and Gandia, wounded, fled to the walls of Rome, where he remained the rest of the winter.

Meantime at Florence, during Lent, the boys were going from house to house to collect " vanities," and when the last day had arrived a vast pile was arranged in the piazza on a scaffold pyramid sixty feet high and two hundred and fifty feet around the base. Then, amid hymns and the ringing of bells, the pile was fired and went up in smoke. Perhaps no act of

Savonarola has been so much discussed as this comparatively unimportant burning of the "vanities." There was nothing new in it. The Florentine pile was only one of many others before and after. Perhaps, also, it was more valuable. When Lippi made a practice of using the notorious features of his mistress in pictures of the Madonna for chapels, and Bartolommeo painted for a church a picture which had to be removed, by the advice of those who heard the confessions of the worshippers in it, there must have been a number of burnable pictures in Florence of considerable artistic value. But it is not probable that the pile contained many works of art that decent people would not willingly let die. Jerome Savonarola was a puritan, but he was no more a philistine than John Milton. The man who had for disciples and friends Bartolommeo, the Della Robbia, Lorenzo di Credi, Botticelli, and Michael Angelo would not wantonly have destroyed innocent beauty. Nor would that friar have burned any treasures of learning who, in the year of the "vanities," stripped his convent of its last remaining lands and had it assume a heavy debt, in order to save the library of the Medici from being dispersed at public sale.

It was in the early spring of 1497 that Cardinal Cæsar, the Duke of Gandia, and Giovanni Sforza, of Pesaro, two sons and a son-in-law of the Pope, stood before the altar of St. Peter to receive the palms from the hand of their father. But there was no peace in their hearts one with another. Already Sforza was a worn-out tool of Borgian ambition, and they were secretly trying to force him to consent to divorce, that the hand of Lucrezia might again be used in their game. During Holy Week, on pretence of going to service in a distant church, he flung himself on a swift horse and rode through the gates to refuge in his own city of Pesaro.

And now the Pope turned his attention to Florence. Piero de' Medici had been living in Rome, as most pretenders have lived, in gambling and debauchery, loaded with debts, pledging everything he could find a pawnbroker to take, and already looked at askance by the money-lenders. When he marched to Florence in April the Pope gave him good wishes. He arrived before the city at daybreak, with the hope that his partisans would rise and open the gates. But no one stirred, except to sight the culverins, and he withdrew as swiftly as he had come.

Within a month a Papal bull excommunicated Savonarola because he had refused to obey a command to unite his convent with the Roman Congregation. But scarcely was it sent when something happened at Rome which shook the nerves even of Alexander. Foiled in his attempt to make his son, the Duke of Gandia, great at the expense of the Orsini, Alexander had created him hereditary ruler of Beneventum, Terracina, and Pontecorvo, nominally as a vassal of the Church, really as an independent prince. A week later, on the 14th of June, the new Prince and his younger brother, Cæsar, took supper with their mother in a vineyard, and at the close of the feast rode off together. Gandia soon left the party, attended by one servant. In the morning he had not returned, and his servant was picked up senseless

and dying in the street.   They found a coal-seller on
the banks of the river who said that the night before
he watched two men who came cautiously down to
the Tiber and looked around.   They went back
among the houses.   Again they came out and
looked.   They gave a signal.   Then came a rider on
a white horse.   Behind him was a body with head
and arms hanging on one side, the feet on the other.
He rode to the edge, and the servants threw it in.
The cloak floated, and the masked man stooped for
. a large stone, threw it, and sank the cloak.   Then all
went away.   The police asked why he had not reported the facts to them.   He answered, " I did not
think it worth while ; I have seen in my time a good
hundred bodies thrown into the river there."   All
night and morning they dragged the river, and at
midday drew out the eldest son of the Pope, pierced
with nine wounds.

Alexander almost went mad with grief.   He shut
himself into his room and would not be comforted.
From Wednesday evening until Saturday morning
he neither ate, drank, nor slept.   On the 19th
he called a consistory, and in an address filled
with penitence and zeal announced the appointment of a commission of six cardinals to draft
a plan for the reform of the Church.   They drew up
a great bull for reform, of which two copies still survive in the Vatican archives.   Its introduction announced that the wholesome ancient rules by which
councils and Popes had checked sensuality and avarice were broken through.   " An unbearable dissoluteness has come into the Church.   We propose,
therefore, to begin reform with the Roman court,

which ought to be an example of virtuous living to all the Church." Excellent provisions followed for regulating the scandalous worldliness and luxury among the cardinals. No cardinal was to draw more than six thousand florins yearly from benefices, or have more than eighty servants and thirty horses in his court; nor were his heirs permitted to spend more than fifteen hundred florins on his funeral. Cardinals were to be forbidden to gamble at cards, to give great public hunts, to attend the performances of profane comedies, to employ clowns, jugglers, or bands of musicians. Simony, with all its attendant evils, was most sternly forbidden.

It was while the Pope was in this mood that the excommunicated Savonarola wrote him a letter of condolence. "The Lord in his mercy," he concluded, "passeth over all our sins. I announce things of which I am assured. But let your Beatitude turn a favoring eye on the work of faith, for which I labor without ceasing, and give ear no longer to the impious. Thus the Lord will bestow on you joy instead of grief, inasmuch as all my predictions are true, and none that resisteth the Lord can ever know peace. Charity moveth me to write these things, Most Blessed Father, and the hope that your Beatitude may receive true consolation from God; for the thunders of his wrath will ere long be heard, and blessed will be those that have put their trust in him. May the Lord of all mercy console your Holiness in your tribulation."

The epigramist wrote differently of this "fisher of men who drew out in his nets his own son."

The search of the police could not clear up the

mystery of the murder.   Many writers suspect that their failure was due to suggestions from the highest authority not to look too far.   Whether this be true or not, the historian is not called upon to make good their lack of energy.   The dark question, Who murdered the Duke of Gandia? is useful to him only to bring into his pages some touch of the perennial interest of a strong detective story.   But it is of the greatest historical significance that within a few months Rome and Italy came to believe that an illegitimate son of the Vicar of Christ had killed his brother out of jealousy, and that the father was unwilling to punish the murder.   This much only is certain, that Cæsar Borgia soon displayed in his open deeds a jealous ambition, daring and cowardly, which was quite capable of fratricide, and that through all his career he remained the darling of his father's heart.

The Pope's contrition lasted but for a little.   That fatal paternal passion which Balzac has pictured in Père Goriot seems to have replaced in his old age the lust that had ruled him down to its very threshold, and before the summer was over he was discussing plans by which Cæsar, laying down the purple, was to become a prince like his dead brother. It was said that the first step suggested was that his brother Jofré's wife, his adultery with whom was suspected by all Rome, should be divorced and married to him.   If this plan was entertained, it was soon abandoned, but the divorce of Lucrezia was accomplished at the end of December, 1497, by what all Italy called open perjury.

Meantime Savonarola, fearing to draw the interdict upon Florence, was silent, while the government was using every effort to have his excommunication annulled. But the wrath of Alexander was implacable. So far from restoring Savonarola, he even threatened to demand that he be surrendered for punishment at Rome. Then Savonarola's patience was exhausted, and on Christmas day, after six months' silence, he said mass and gave communion to a vast congregation. Soon after he announced that he would preach, beginning on Septuagesima Sunday (February 11, 1498). The Vicar of the Archbishop forbade any one to attend the sermon on penalty of being denied confession, the sacrament, and burial in consecrated ground. But the Signory sent him word that it would be well for him to keep quiet. The preacher discussed the authority of the Pope, and, again protesting his orthodoxy and his Catholicity, asserted the right of every honest conscience to resist unjust commands. "When I reflect," he cried, "on the life led by priests, I am constrained to weep. O my brethren and my children, shed tears for the woes of the Church, so that the Lord may call the priests to repentance, for it is plain that terrible chastisement awaits them. The tonsure is the seat of all iniquity. It begins in Rome, where the clergy, who make mock of Christ and the saints, are worse than Turks and Moors. Not only do they refuse to suffer for the Lord's sake, but men traffic with the sacraments. At this day there is a trade in benefices, which are sold to the highest bidder! Think ye that Jesus Christ will any longer permit this? Woe, woe to Italy and to Rome! Come, come, O priests! Come, my brethren, let us do our best to revive a little the love of God! 'O father, we shall be cast into prison; we shall be done to death.' So let it be. They may kill me as they please, but they will never tear Christ from my heart. I am ready to die for my God. Thou hast been in Rome and dost know the life of these priests. Tell me, wouldst thou hold them to be pillars of the Church, or temporal lords? Have they not courtiers and grooms and horses and dogs? Are not their mansions full of tapestries and silks, of perfumes and lackeys? Seemeth it to thee that this is the Church of God? Their vainglory filleth the world, and their avarice is equally vast. They do all things for gold. O Lord, Lord, smite them with thy sword!"

This was war to the death, and the monk felt himself called of God to it. The last day of carnival he gave the sacrament to a great crowd and went up into a high pulpit in the open square. Holding the host on high, he prayed, "O Lord, if my deeds be not sincere, if my words be not inspired by thee, strike me dead on the instant." Never had the results of his preaching been greater. Each new discourse was printed and carried over all Italy and the world. The wrath of the Pope was intense. The Florentine ambassador wrote from Rome how he had burst out in a fury before many of the cardinals, threatening to ruin the Republic and the friar together. Every enemy of the city was up in arms against her, and civil discord was threatening within. The friar was as much hated as loved. The Compagnacci, the lewd fellows of the baser sort who disliked puritan laws and wanted back again the old debaucheries of the carnival; the Arrabbiati, who wanted to overthrow the Republic and set up an oligarchy of their own faction; the Greys, or adherents of the Medici, were united in only one thing, their dislike of Savonarola and his followers, who were called the Piagnoni or Snivellers. Their puritan inquisition was doubtless very irksome to all who did not share their exalted zeal. And so on the 17th of March a new Signory inhibited Savonarola from preaching. He obeyed, but turned to his last resort, the General Council, threatened by many reformers, feared by every Pope for two generations.

The theory of Conciliar Supremacy, victorious at Constance, promulgated with greater emphasis and clearness at Basle, had been buried when the discredited remnant of that Council broke up in 1449. But its spectre would not down, and rose threateningly amid the triumphs and feasts of the autocratic Papacy. It was doubtless held by the great body of the French clergy as a part of Gallicanism or the local independence of the national Church under its own hierarchy, which had been established by the Pragmatic Sanction of 1438. Even in Germany, whose princes weakly surrendered the concordats of Constance and Basle in the Vienna concordat of 1448, there were still many defenders of the idea that the Pope was not the absolute monarch of the visible Kingdom of God, but the constitutional ruler of the Church. Every Pope since Nicholas V. had taken pains directly or indirectly to

P

deny the doctrine of Conciliar Supremacy and evade the decrees of the Church which provided for the regular assembly of a General Council. Pius II. expressly forbade any appeal from his authority to a General Council. Almost every reformer that we have mentioned, and many others, had reiterated the demand and longing for a common meeting of Christendom to reform the Church. Every conclave of cardinals had before the election of another Vicar of Christ renewed the demand or agreement that the decisions of former conclaves and councils in regard to the calling of a new General Council for the reform of the Church in head and members should be carried out. And every Pope had broken the agreement or evaded the demand. In 1482 a Dominican, Andreas, Bishop of Crain in Epirus, having first vainly tried to persuade Sixtus IV. to summon a Council, posted on the doors of the cathedral of Basle a letter to the Pope and a call to Christendom to meet in General Council for the reform of the Church in head and members. He was arrested and imprisoned for life. The banished Cardinal Giuliano della Rovere had been trying for several years to call Europe to a General Council to hear his complaints against Alexander VI. Savonarola himself had often hinted in vague and veiled terms of a General Council, and written of it privately to the King of France, and it was therefore no new or heretical idea that he now determined to realize.

He made copies of a letter to the princes of Europe, which had been ready for some time, and prepared to send them by trusty messengers to the rulers of France, Germany, Spain, England, and Hungary. They began:

"The moment of vengeance has arrived. The Lord commands me to reveal new secrets and to make known to the world the peril which threatens the bark of St. Peter. . . . Now I hereby testify, in the word of the Lord, that this Alexander is no Pope, nor can be held as one; inasmuch as, leaving aside the mortal sin of simony, . . . and likewise putting aside his other manifest vices, I declare that he is no Christian and believes in no God, the which surpasses the height of all infidelity." These charges he offered to prove, not by argument and evidences alone, but by signs and portents given by God to attest his truth. Most of these letters were never sent, but one of his messengers on the road to France was robbed by Milanese bandits, and his despatches sold to the Duke, who sent them to the Pope.

And at the very moment when he was betrayed to his worst enemy abroad, Savonarola fell into the power of his cruel foes at home. The Franciscans had from the beginning opposed his work. And a certain friar, Francesco of Puglia, of that order, after denouncing him in the pulpit as a heretic and a false prophet, challenged him to the ordeal by fire. Domenico, who had taken Savonarola's place as preacher, at once accepted the challenge in his master's stead. It was a glorious opportunity for the friar's enemies, and, though the Franciscan tried to draw back, and Savonarola at first rebuked his friend's zeal, the keen politicians soon gave such official recognition to the affair that one side or the other had to publicly submit and withdraw. The whole city fell into a fever of excitement, and after a long discussion it was finally decided in the City Council that the trial by fire should take place as the easiest way of quieting the uproar; though one speaker sarcastically suggested that the trial be by water, as less dangerous, for if the friar could go through it without getting wet, he would certainly join in asking his pardon. Savonarola had tried to prevent the trial, but when it was determined he felt assured that his champion would walk through unharmed. The same enthusiasm spread to his followers, and the brethren of San Marco addressed a letter to the Pope, saying that three hundred of them, besides many laymen, were willing to pass through the fire in defence of their master's doctrines. The Franciscan champion, a substitute for the original, had asserted from the first that if he entered the flames he should perish, and when the day arrived, and all Florence waited for the spectacle, he did not come. After hours had been passed in unprofitable discussion, darkness fell on a wearied and disappointed city. The champion of San Marco had been ready and eager for the trial, but the enemies of Savonarola spread abroad the report that he had balked the multitude of their miracle or their tragedy. It was a crime unforgivable by the Florentines, and Savonarola was delivered into the hands of his enemies.

The afternoon of the next day a mob stormed the convent. They found no easy task, for some lay brethren had concealed arms in the cellar a few days before. Savonarola wanted to bear all things, and

calling the brethren to the choir, intoned the chant
"Salvum fac populum tuum Domine." But there
was a stern resistance in many parts of the building.
A young German monk wrested a weapon from the
hands of one of the mob and laid about him mightily,
chanting at every stroke, "Salvum fac populum tuum
Domine." When they broke into the sacristy, the
praying monks beat them out again with the heavy
crucifixes and candlesticks. The steps of the choir
were stained with blood, and the church rang to the
shots of the arquebuse which two brethren had
planted by the side of the great crucifix on top of
the altar. In the midst of it all the police arrested
Savonarola by order of the Signory.

He was put to the torture. Just what he said we
do not know, for it is evident that the published confessions were, like the published confessions of Joan of
Arc, garbled. But we know enough to believe that,
like Joan of Arc, he admitted that his voices and visions
were false. And in this he denied his own belief.
For he had always thought he was a prophet, for which
all the people at one time held him. It does not
appear, however, that there was anything in his predictions more supernatural than in those of Joan of
Arc, and his voices and visions were like those of
many men of his time. Columbus heard a voice
from heaven bidding him sail on. That most engaging gossip and man of science, Cardano, had the
most implicit faith in his most extraordinary dreams,
and believed himself, like Socrates, to be directed by
a demon. Benevento Cellini tells us his father had
"a certain touch of prophecy, which was doubtless

a divine gift," and that amiable scoundrel himself, when shut up in prison with nothing else to do, had vivid and splendid visions of the glory of God. And visions are recorded in more than one biography of our own century. Savonarola's confessions, that through all his desires to reform the Church there was the hope of " doing great things in Italy and beyond the borders," " of preaching things at the Council of which I might be proud," of thinking himself " higher than any cardinal or Pope if he had reformed the Church," were probably true enough. For the last infirmity is found as commonly as elsewhere in the noblest minds which labor with perfect honesty for pure religion.

The failure of the miracle caused his downfall. The false confession that he had deceived the people by his visions brought death. For the multitude had not followed him to learn truth, but to hear politics. His rapid and violent reformations had in the popular heart no roots of true religion. The Florentines were, after all, only better in degree than the rest of the Italians. They lacked the first national quality of patience, and would bear no yoke except the yoke that tyranny held firm upon their shoulders. Even the monks of San Marco wrote to the Pope asking forgiveness for having followed Savonarola. " The fineness of his doctrine; the rectitude of his life, the holiness of his manners; his pretended devotion, and the good results he obtained by purging the city of immorality, usury, and every species of vice; the different events which confirmed his prophecies in a manner beyond all human power and imagination, and which were so numerous and of such a nature that we could never have been able to renounce our faith in him unless he himself had made retraction declaring that his words were not inspired by God "—these were the things they alleged in excuse for having been his friends.

Savonarola's cup of bitterness was almost full, but he still had to endure more tortures at a fresh trial before two Papal commissioners, who were sent, according to the talk of Rome, with instructions to put him to death, "even if he were another John the Baptist." On the 28th of May, 1498, with two of his brethren, he was degraded and unfrocked by his Bishop, handed over to the secular arm as heretic and schismatic by the Papal commissioners, and hanged and burned by the Signory of Florence.

PERIOD III.

CHAPTER XIX.

THE FALL OF THE HOUSE OF BORGIA.

N order to understand the subsequent history of the family of Borgia, which had bought the Papacy, we must remember that such family histories were common enough in Italy during the last half of the fifteenth century. The spectacle of Alexander and Cæsar ruling in the name of Jesus of Nazareth over his disciples is not an isolated phenomenon. The Church did not breed this disease within herself. Rather the weakness brought on by her own corruption was unable to resist the contagion of the times. Just as the della Rovere (Sixtus IV., Julius II.), terrible, sagacious, magnificent, patrons of art, are a picture of the good tyrant of their generation, so the Borgias are a perfect example of the bad tyrant. For a certain character of wickedness was common enough among the large and small tyrants of the age to form the bearers of it into a distinct type, monstrous, inhuman, incredible, only to be matched in the pages of Suetonius and Tacitus. It is needless to suggest illustrations. John Webster's "Duchess of Malfi" or "White Devil" gives in

248

classic form a clear impression of the type, and it is etched in Browning's little poem, "My Last Duchess."

The insult to humanity in such lives was made more palpable by the smallness of the states they ruled. While the Cæsars filled the streets of Rome with blood and their villas with lust, the cities of the Empire, enjoying the justice of their municipal governments, heard of these crimes as distant rumors. But the tyrants of Italy had raised their power on the ruins of the ancient municipalities, and their movements were talked over by every gossip of the little cities of which they were masters. It does not seem unhistorical to see in the flourishing growth of such a type under such circumstances very strong evidence that the social organism of Italy at the end of the fifteenth century was rotted through and through. When an indictment is drawn against a whole people by historians, the bill of particulars is apt to be made up of special instances of private or public wickedness which have been recorded because they were unusual, or else of vague lamentations by contemporaries over the degeneracy of the times. But the future historian who should regard simply the record of murders and lynchings in the United States for the past ten years, or read only certain extracts from Ruskin or Carlyle, would hardly get a fair view of the morality of the Americans. It is possible to collect many isolated notices which indicate a desperate condition of moral depravity in Italy at the close of the fifteenth century. Venice had eleven thousand courtesans, a proportion which would give over one hundred thousand to New York. In the

year 1459 seven princes received Pius II. at Florence.
All of them were bastards.   Such facts as these seem
to be significant ; but who shall say whether they are
not offset by the abundant evidences of a beautiful
family life, the memories of gracious and gentle women, of noble bishops and pious teachers, the records
of the continuous foundation of hospitals, whose size
and care of the sick filled Luther with astonishment?
As Burckhardt suggests, " The ultimate truth with
respect to the character, the conscience, the guilt of
a people remains forever a secret."   But surely the
political conditions of Italy in the fifteenth century
suggest very strongly that lust and luxury, or something else, had weakened among the people the
fundamental qualities of courage, patience, and self-
sacrifice.   How else could the vile and monstrous
regiment of many of her tyrants have been borne, or
only broken by lawless revolts which made the last
state of the cities worse than the first?

An Italian tyrant of this most evil type was now
Vicar of Christ, and when the friar of San Marco was
dead he had nothing to fear.   With Savonarola in
freedom, Alexander had cause to remember the fate
of John XXIII.   Had a man of the same will, eloquence, and sincerity appeared in the north, farther
from Rome and amid a people of greater patience and
tenacity, he could not have been so silenced.   For the
world was filled with fears and hopes of some great
catastrophe.   On the banks of the Tiber and the
Rhine prophecies were circulated, dark and threatening as the Florentine monk's, of some awful judgment of God upon the degenerate Church.   The

King of France had a medal struck bearing the inscription, "I will destroy Babylon," and the rulers of Spain and Germany threatened schism more than once.

But when Savonarola was gone no man was left to give point to the anger of the world, and the spectre of a General Council being laid, Alexander could devote himself to arranging a marriage for Cæsar. The King of Naples refused with indignation the hand of his daughter, but finally promised the hand of a bastard of his house to the divorced Lucrezia, and they were married in July, 1498. The next month Cæsar publicly laid aside the cardinal's purple, and in December journeyed to France. The money for his costly outfit had been obtained by selling Church offices, confiscating the estates of accused prelates, and by the fines of three hundred people absolved from sudden accusation of heresy. The new King of France, who wanted the help of the Pope for a second invasion of Italy, received him with honor, made him Duke of Valence, and married him to a sister of the King of Navarre. The Pope, Venice, and France formed a league for mutual gain. France was to have Milan; Venice, Cremona; and Cæsar, French troops to conquer the Romagna, suppress its petty tyrants, ancient vassals of the Papacy, and form a principality for himself.

On the 6th of October, 1499, King Louis entered Milan in triumph; and a lot of Italian princelings followed the invading army as jackals follow the lion.

Already the Pope had declared that the lords of Romagna had forfeited their lands for failure to pay tribute, and the plan of the Borgia was openly declared. Cæsar possessed no mean resources for his undertaking. In France he had become reconciled to della Rovere, the only powerful cardinal who still remained in opposition. And the truce was sealed by the marriage of the Cardinal's nephew to a Papal niece. The house of Este, the oldest in Italy, rulers of Ferrara, backed all his undertakings, and the heir of the house was soon to marry his sister Lucrezia. He was in very friendly correspondence with the Gonzaga of Mantua, and two years later they were to betroth their daughter to his son. The King of France gave him troops, including a thousand Swiss mercenaries, and, with his own hired soldiers, he mustered eight thousand men. The treasures of the Church furnished the sinews of war. On the 1st of December he took the town of Imola, and in January his army entered Forli. The gifts of the two hundred thousand pilgrims who came to obtain the blessing of Alexander VI. were timely, for Cæsar's expenses were over eighteen hundred ducats a day, and a further gain was made by levying on all ecclesiastical incomes the " Turkish tenth " for a threatened crusade.

At the end of February the sudden return of the Duke of Milan compelled the French King to recall the troops loaned to Cæsar, and he returned to Rome in triumph. All the cardinals received him as he rode in at the head of his mercenaries, and the city gave in his honor a great spectacle—the triumph of Julius Cæsar. He went at once to kneel at the feet of his father. He was clad, Spanish fashion, in black, and greeted the old man in his own beloved tongue. The Pope was hysterical for joy, weeping and laughing in a breath, to see his family once more united around him. Five months later, as Lucrezia's husband, the young Neapolitan Prince, came out of St. Peter's Church, assassins fell upon him with daggers, left him for dead on the steps, and springing upon the horses of some mounted men waiting in the street, made off. The Prince dragged himself to the Pope and accused Cæsar of the deed. His wife and his sister-in-law tended his sick-bed, and for fear of poison cooked his food themselves. The Pope set a guard of sixteen men for his defence. Cæsar came to see him, and as he went out turned and said, " What does not happen at midday may happen at night." A few days later he came again, drove Lucrezia and Sancia from the room, called in his hangman, and the wounded man was strangled in his bed. There is uncertainty about the details of this story,—accurate details of such occurrences would probably be very difficult to obtain,—but there was no mystery about this murder in the house of Borgia. Alexander acknowledged that the final murderous assault had been made by Cæsar, but said he had great provocation. There is no need to seek, like the common talk of Rome, for strange and dark motives. It may have been the sudden flaming out of personal hatred, or Cæsar may have wanted to use his sister's hand for the third time in his desperate game of ambition.

Whether Alexander's attempts to defend the victim were real or feigned, he accepted the deed when it was done, and turned to the task of gathering gold for Cæsar's army. The next month twelve new cardinals paid ten thousand florins apiece for their red hats. And the winter campaign of Cæsar was so vigorous that in the spring the Pope named him Duke of Romagna, with Imola, Forli, Pesaro, Rimini, Faenza, Cesena, and Fano for his dominions, and thirty-six thousand florins yearly income paid by Florence to purchase peace.

Cæsar became supreme in Rome, and the city trembled before his will. His father smiled on his pleasures enough to be present at a most scandalous banquet, followed by a performance which was called in the diaries and letters of the times "the dance of the fifty courtesans." A Venetian who dared to write a pamphlet on the Pope and his son was found strangled in the Tiber. Alexander expressed his regret to the ambassador, and explained that his son was " a man of good disposition, but constitutionally unable to bear an insult."

It must have been during this year that a letter from a friend in Rome to a certain Sylvius de Sabellis, a refugee at the imperial court, was printed in Germany and spread over the world. It describes the Pope as worse than Mohammed, an Antichrist, than whom no more open enemy of God, opposer of Christ, and subverter of faith and religion could possibly be imagined. " All things are for sale with this Pontifex. One trembles to relate the monstrous lusts, insulting both God and man, which are openly practised in his house. His son Cæsar goes about surrounded, like a Turk, with harlots, and guarded by armed men. At a word from him any one is killed and thrown into the Tiber, or poisoned, and his property, both in and out his house, seized. The thirst and rapine of his servants are satiated with human blood, and for fear of their cruelty the noblest families are leaving, the best citizens are hidden, and, unless we are succored from such ills by the Emperor as soon as possible, needs must that every one take thought to abandon the city and flee."

In June the fishers found a group of dead bodies in the Tiber, among them two young boys of eighteen and fifteen. They were Astorre and Octavian Manfredi, who had surrendered Faenza the year before, on solemn promise of freedom, and been lying in the castle of San Angelo ever since.

Four days later Cæsar marched on another campaign. He took Urbino and Camerino by treachery, plundered the empty palace of the first, and threw the fratricidal tyrant of the second into prison. Every little city trembled before his craft and a will that feared nothing human or divine. Meanwhile, at Rome, Alexander was providing the finances. At this time died the Cardinal Ferrari, who had amassed enormous wealth in the service of the Borgia. The Pope seized his riches, and all Rome said that the white powder of the Borgia had been his death. No one pitied him much, for the satirists decorated his grave with such epigrams as this: " Here lies Ferrarius. The earth has his body, the bull [crest of the Borgias] his goods, hell his soul."

In the midst of his greatest success a sudden danger shook Cæsar's triumph. His mercenary captains, petty tyrants who had sought refuge in his service, formed a conspiracy, revolted under the lead of the Cardinal Orsini, raised twelve thousand men, and utterly defeated Cæsar's troops under the command of two trusty Spanish captains. But Cæsar, who never accomplished very much with the sword in pitched battle, was not at the end of his resources. He skilfully played upon the jealousies and fears of the confederates, and while negotiations were going on his agents were quieting his rebellious cities. One of them, Messer Ramiro, used in this work a desperate cruelty, and in the end of December, when he had successively blotted out all dangerous elements in the cities assigned to him, Cæsar called him to conference at Cesena. Four days later his dead body was found in the market-place, cut in two pieces —a broken tool.

Meantime, at Rome, the nervous Pope was plunging into wild amusements. One night, according to the diary of his master of ceremonies, he watched a procession of indecent masks which halted long before his windows.[1] On others Cardinal Orsini, secret head of the league against the Borgias, joined him, according to reports from the Venetian ambassador, at the gaming-tables in the Vatican, when certain fair ladies sat among the prelates. Alexander was anxiously awaiting news from Cæsar, who was trying to persuade the revolted generals to meet him at Sinigaglia for a conference which should

---

[1] Burchard hated the memory of Alexander VI., but that is no good reason for doubting the accuracy of his unadorned reports of such notorious occurrences as the above.

change the truce into lasting peace. Deluded at last by his solemn pledges, they entered the town on the 31st of December, leaving their troops scattered in detachments at various distances from the walls. The instant they entered the doors of the castle they were seized and disarmed. Two of them were strangled that night, one weeping, and the other begging as a last favor that the Pope would absolve him and bless his soul.

When Alexander received secret word of the success of this treachery all his court marked the sudden merriment of his manner. On the 3d of January Cardinal Orsini was cast into prison, his palace seized, and his eighty-year-old mother driven into the streets, where she wandered long before any one dared to aid her. A quick succession of arrests followed, the house of each man being at once pillaged and its contents of plate and other valuables carried to the Vatican. On the 18th of January Cæsar heard that the Roman enemies were safely in hand, and at once strangled the two remaining prisoners of Sinigaglia, Paolo Orsini and the Duke of Gravina; and on the 22d it was announced in Rome that the Cardinal Orsini had died in prison. In the end of February Cæsar, having finished the reduction of the towns of his duchy, entered Rome. He was the most noted man in Italy. A clever diplomat like Machiavelli wondered at his statecraft, the King of France called the affair of Sinigaglia worthy of a Roman, and Leonardo da Vinci was glad to be in his service as engineer.

On the 29th of March the Venetian ambassador

Q

wrote that eighty new offices had just been created in the Curia and sold immediately for seven hundred and sixty florins apiece. On the 10th of April Cardinal Michiel died, after two days of sudden illness. Before dawn his house was stripped, and three days later the Venetian ambassador, going to the Vatican, found the Pope superintending an inventory of his movable property in the hall. On the 18th of May the Pope's secretary, Troccio, fled from the city. He was overtaken by a ship at Corsica, brought back, and strangled by Micheletto in prison, while Cæsar looked on through a window. He was accused of betraying the Borgias to France. His estate was confiscated. On the 8th of June the body of Jacopo Santa Croce, with the head beside it, lay all day on the bridge of San Angelo. His property was confiscated and his wife and children left penniless. On the 5th of August the Cardinal Monreale, nephew of the Pope, died suddenly. Alexander was his heir, and the Venetian ambassador reported that Rome estimated the estate at one hundred thousand florins, and said, "The Cardinal has also been sent the way that all the other well-fattened ones have gone." These were violent or crafty men, but a great part of their crimes had been committed to serve the Borgias, and it is small wonder that a great fear fell on Rome. No man of prominence could die of the malignant malarial fever which raged that summer that awe-struck gossip did not whisper, "The poison of the Borgias"; and all rich men began to tremble for their lives.

In the midst of triumph, when their feet were on

the necks of their enemies and they had swept all the gains of victory into their own coffers by destroying the servants who knew its secrets, the end suddenly came. On the night of his nephew's death Alexander went with Cæsar to sup in the garden of Cardinal Hadrian of Corneto, and on the 12th of August both fell ill. The next morning Alexander was better and played cards a part of the day. It was only a brief rally for the debauchee of seventy-three. Whether the report is true that the Borgia had drunk by mistake of the poison they had prepared for their rich host, who was also violently ill, cannot now be determined. Most probably they all caught in the night air a malignant malarial fever. At all events, Alexander's cup was full, and on the 18th of August he died. All Rome spoke in joy and horror of his death, of the awful appearance of the swollen corpse, of the little black dog that ran ceaselessly to and fro through the halls of the Vatican the night before he died. The Marquis of Mantua wrote to his wife that Alexander was heard in his last illness to murmur, "I am coming. It is right; only wait a little." The bystanders remembered that he had made a bargain with the devil to give his soul for twelve years of the Papacy, and the bond was four days overdue. The story was widely accepted, and even among those who rejected it the pious everywhere felt with shuddering relief that the Pope must have gone to hell.

Alexander really died after confession, the communion, and extreme unction, and if he called on any one, it was doubtless the Virgin Mary; for he had always considered himself as under her special protection. He had a picture painted of her, with the face of his mistress, the beautiful young Julia Farnese ; and three years before had presented her altar with three hundred florins at a special service of thanksgiving for saving his life when a fireplace fell on him. For Alexander was not an atheist, and in all probability never once thought of himself as an unbeliever.[1]

Cæsar said afterward to Machiavelli that he had made preparations for every possible contingency except that he should be ill when his father died. As it was, he could only be carried by the six Spanish cardinals into the Vatican. From his sick-bed he issued orders to concentrate all his mercenaries at Rome and keep them under arms. He was the first to hear of his father's death, and his trusty hangman, Micheletto, put a dagger to the throat of Cardinal Casanova and compelled the surrender of the key of the Papal treasure. Two chests full of gold pieces were instantly carried off to Cæsar's bedside. Even before he had recovered, he held court, surrounded by his six Spanish cardinals, as if he were a sovereign, and finally promised the College of Cardinals to leave Rome in three days, on condition of keeping the title of General of the Church.

On the 22d of September, 1503, the Conclave

---

[1] In this connection a section from the preface of Richardson's " Clarissa Harlowe " (1749) might be pertinent: " It will be proper to observe, for the sake of such as may apprehend hurt to the morals of youth from the more finely written letters, that the gentlemen, though professed libertines, . . . are not, however, infidels or scoffers." Quoted in " Ten-Minute Sermons."

elected the nephew of Pius II., who took the title of Pius III.   He was broken in health, and died in less than a month.

Meantime Cæsar had come back to press his fortune. But his foes among the Roman nobility demanded his trial, his mercenaries began to fall away to richer lords, and when Pius died Cæsar was only saved from death by the strong walls of San Angelo.   For the Pope's son was so hated that an enemy killed one of his servants to wash in his blood.   He still remained, however, a power to be reckoned with, and the Cardinal della Rovere visited him in the castle, and they made a bargain.   Cæsar was to give the votes of the six Spanish cardinals, and in return to be named Standard-bearer of the Church.   Della Rovere bought the rest of the votes, and was unanimously elected Pope, taking the name of Julius II.

Then the fortunes of Cæsar sank lower and lower. The once haughty nepot begged an interview with the Duke of Urbino, whose inheritance he had seized, stood cap in hand before him, fell on his knees and begged pardon, promised with many excuses to give back all he had stolen from his palace, and even received his chamberlain with a bearing as servile as it had once been proud.   He feared for his life.   Volunteering for the service of Spain, he was carried to Madrid and thrown into prison.   Escaping two years later, he found refuge at the court of his brother-in-law, King of Navarre, and in three months, at the age of thirty-one, fell in petty battle with a rebellious crown vassal.

PERIOD III.

CHAPTER XX.

HUMANISM IN EUROPE FROM THE ACCESSION OF
SIXTUS IV. TO THE DEATH OF ALEXANDER VI.
(1471–1503)—THE FLORENTINE ACADEMY
AND THE OXFORD SCHOOL—FABER STAPU-
LENSIS AND HIS PUPILS AT PARIS—JOHN
REUCHLIN AND THE OLDER HUMANISTS OF
GERMANY—ERASMUS.

HREE chief tendencies are observable in
the history of Italian Humanism. They
can be traced from the first, but become very distinct with each succeeding generation. There were the pagan
Humanists, like Valla and Filelfo—the men who
lived in the moral atmosphere of heathenism and
practised not only the style, but the vices, of antiquity. We have seen in the person of Savonarola a
learned puritanism which desired to take from the
New Learning only what might help to renew religion and purify morals. We must now consider a
middle Humanism, which hoped to make the world
better by uniting the New Testament and the philosophy of antiquity.

The origin of this party is plainly marked in the

visit of Gemistos Platon to the Council of Florence in 1438. He came in the train of the Greek Emperor, to arrange a union between the Greek and Latin Church as the price of help against the Turks. He was a native of Constantinople, eighty-three years old, and reputed the most learned man who spoke the Greek tongue. He did but little for the cause of union, but much for that cause which lay nearest his heart—the inauguration of a new religion, founded on the teaching of Plato, which was to unite East and West, Mohammedan and Christian.[1]

Plato was then almost unknown in Italy, and the charm of the old man's conversation carried away Cosimo de' Medici. He determined to educate Marsiglio Ficino, the six-year-old son of his physician, to become the translator and interpreter of Plato to Western Christendom. Platon published in Italy several works pointing out the superiority of Plato over Aristotle. In these it appeared that Platon's system of the world was antichristian, for his idea of the eternal existence of an abstract, unchangeable necessity seemed to leave no place for miracle, responsibility, or redemption. Such opinions awoke a storm of opposition, and the defenders of Aristotle used to the fullest the charge of heresy against the assailer of the philosophy of all the orthodox. Platon returned to Greece, and died in the middle of the century, nearly a hundred years old. Some ten years later Sigismondo Pandelfo Malatesta, Lord of Rimini and General of Venetian mercenaries against the Turk, brought the bones of Platon to Rimini, and

---

[1] As he is reported to have said in Florence.

buried them in the Church of San Francesco, which was his family tomb.

From Platon proceeded two schools of thought which, despite their common origin, grew to diametrical opposition; even as the hierarchical tendency which formed the Papal system, and the predestination theology which the Protestant Reformers opposed to it, were both justly supported by the authority of Augustine. Pomponius Leto, one of Platon's scholars, became the founder of the Roman Academy and the centre of the neopagans. Under the patronage of Lorenzo, the grandson of Cosimo, the Florentine Academy, led by Marsiglio Ficino, became the centre of true Platonic influences. For Ficino did not stop with the half-Platonism of Platon. In the original he found the spiritual philosophy with which he Platonized the New Testament, but did not destroy it. The great festival of the Florentine Academy on the birthday of Plato was usually held in the beautiful villa Careggi, in whose rooms, opening on one side into the shady porticoes of the court with its gently running fountains, and looking out on the other upon Florence and the Tuscan hills, Lorenzo entertained the little company with a dinner and music, followed by reading and discussion of Plato's works. In the summer heat they sought refuge in the woods, and under the shade of the lofty planes beside the mountain brook discussed the things of the soul while their eyes traversed the vale of the Arno, seeking vainly the gleam of the distant sea.

Ficino lectured on Plato from the pulpit of the

cathedral, "discussing the religious philosophy of our Plato here in the midst of the church, and meditating in the holy places on the holy truth." For to him the ideas of Plato were prophecies in philosophic form of the teaching of Christ, and he found in the life of Socrates types of the life of Jesus; such as the cock he offered before death, the cup he drank, and his last words. At the age of forty he was ordained priest, and though he Platonized the Gospel, there is little doubt that he ardently desired to promote the influence of Christ in the world by training men who, like Him, were followers of truth.

This personal relation to Christ, which grew upon the head of the Florentine Academy in spite of the mystic thinking and allegorizing interpretation that made Jesus teach the theology of Plato, appears very plainly in Giovanni Pico, Prince of Mirandola (1463–94). From his youth he evinced great aptitude for study, and came to Rome at the age of twenty-four, a heralded prodigy of learning. He posted nine hundred theses for discussion, offering in princely fashion to pay the expenses of any disputants who desired to come from a distance. But Innocent VIII. was moved to prohibit the discussion, and a theological commission pronounced thirteen of the propositions heretical. Pico published an apology written in twenty days, marked by wide learning and a superficial subtlety. But he was not declared free from heresy till just before his death. This experience was for the youth the end of licentious and frivolous living. He turned to virtue, burned his

book of wanton verses of love and other like fanta-
sies, and gave himself fervently to the study of Holy
Scripture.   He undertook it under the burden of
profound erudition.   He had read libraries of the old
fathers of the Church; he had mastered all the
cognition of philosophy both of the old teachers and
the new schools; he knew many languages; he was
very learned in all the subtle and cunning disputa-
tions of the Cabala.   He became a master of allegorical interpretation, and found all the philosophy
of Plato in the books of Moses.   He made a cipher
system, apparently somewhat similar to that by
which a Western student has drawn the secret history of the times of Elizabeth from the plays of
Shakespeare.   For by manipulations of the Hebrew
letters of the first word of Genesis he concludes that
Moses meant to say by it, " The Father, in the Son
and by the Son, the beginning and end, or rest, created the supercelestial, the empyrean, and the sub-
lunary sphere, fitly joined together."

That he might be undiverted from his studies he
sold his princedom to his nephew and gave great
part of the price to the poor.   He was content with
mean fare, but retained somewhat of his old state in
the use of silver plate.   He prayed often, and gave
plenteously to relieve the miseries of such needy
people as he came by the knowledge of.   In Holy
Week he scourged himself for the cleansing of his old
offences and in the remembrance of the great benefit
of the passion and death of Christ suffered for our
sake.   To a man accustomed to vice, who sought
discourse with him on the nature of virtue, he said,

" If we had ever before our eyes the painful death of Christ which he suffered for love of us; and then if we would again think upon our own death, we should surely beware of sin "; and the man forsook his evil ways.   Pico once told his nephew, as they walked in an orchard at Ferrara, that when he had finished certain books he meant to give all his substance to the poor, and with the crucifix in hand to walk barefoot about the world, preaching Christ.   When he came to die, in the flower of his youth, the priest, holding up the crucifix, inquired whether he firmly believed it to be the image of him that was very God and very man, together with the other doctrines that belong to the faith of the Church.   Pico answered that he not only believed, but certainly knew it, and said he was glad to die, because death made an end of sin.   He lay then with a pleasant and merry countenance, and in the very pangs of death spoke as though he saw the heavens opened.   He made the poor of the hospital of Florence heir of all his lands.[1]

About the close of the fifteenth century another transalpine land began to feel the impulse of the New Learning.   It was carried to England by men like Linacre, physician to Henry VIII., and Grocyn, who, having studied Greek in Italy, was the first to give good instruction in it at Oxford.   But it was first made widely effective by John Colet.   He was descended on both sides from gentlefolk and inherited

---

[1] In this account of Pico I have borrowed the diction of Sir Thomas More's translation of his " Life " by his nephew, Giovanni Francesco Pico; published in the Tudor Library with an introduction by J. M. Rigg, Esq., of Lincoln's Inn, to which I am also indebted.

a large fortune.   On finishing his course at Oxford he went to Italy in 1493, and came home in 1496. We have no details of his travels and studies.   He returned apparently unimpressed by the arts of Italy, except music, which he loved, and possessed of the spirit which had mastered the Florentine Platonists— the spirit of intense devotion to the Bible and personal loyalty to Christ.   He settled at Oxford, where he began to lecture on the Epistle to the Romans. These expositions were very different from the scholia in isolated texts, or the diffuse discussion of logical distinctions unknown to the writers, which formed the common method of interpretation of the books of the Bible.   His philological remarks are illustrated from his reading, including patristic, classic, and contemporary writings.   But he does not stop short with such comments.   He is continually turning aside into practical applications; no " threads of nine days long drawn from an anti-theme of half an inch," but true parentheses of passionate feeling.   He had a keen historical sense, also, and tries constantly to keep the readers in touch with the personality, the thought, and the feeling of Paul and the Romans, and thus make the sentences vivid and potent.

A man of Colet's power and learning gathered scholars round him, not only hearers, but friends. The most noted of these was Thomas More, born in 1478.   His father, Sir Thomas More, placed him in the household of the Lord Chancellor, the Archbishop Morton.   There his wit soon distinguished him, and his master was wont to say to his guests, " This child here waiting at table will prove a marvellous man." At Morton's wish he was sent to Oxford, where Colet formed such a high opinion of his powers that he was afterward accustomed to speak of him as the one genius in England. More was admitted to the bar in 1500, and began practice in London. He used the right of teaching conferred by his degree to give a course of lectures on Augustine's " City of God " in the Church of St. Lawrence, of which Grocyn was Rector. They attracted much attention and were well attended, and at the age of twenty-five he was sent to Parliament. When the royal grant for the wars was about to be passed in silence, young More, daring to attack it, so rallied the House that the final vote was only a fourth of the amount asked. Because of the King's displeasure, he found it wise to retire from public life. He thought of a monastery, but by the advice of Colet, who came up to London about this time to take the duties of Dean of St. Paul's, he married and remained, as the phrase was, " in the world." He occupied his enforced leisure with study, being chiefly attracted by the life and works of Pico della Mirandola. Thus he remained in obscurity, solacing himself with his family, his books, and his friends, until the accession of Henry VIII. (1509) set him free from fear and idleness.

Of all the transalpine lands, France was the first to begin the study of Greek—an unmistakable sign of the stirring of the spirit of the New Learning. But the first Frenchman who learned enough Greek to do anything with it seems to have been Faber Stapulensis (Jacques Lefèvre d' Étaples), 1455–1536.

Having acquired the title of Doctor at Paris, he went to Italy in 1492, and probably spent two years there, visiting Florence, Rome, and joining in the circle of scholars who gathered round the printing-house of Aldus Manutius in Venice. The knowledge which he brought back he devoted more and more to the study of the Bible, abandoning in its favor the classic authors who had once been his favorites. He was a frail little man, bent over by much study, with a beautiful face, at once earnest and gentle. The scholars who came to learn of him in Paris all loved him, and of the opponents he soon aroused, none seems to have felt anything but respect for the purity and honesty of his life and the natural kindliness of his disposition. For whether among poor begging scholars, or with his friend, the scion of the great house of Briçonnet, whose forefathers had been officers of State and Church for generations, or as court chaplain to the princes of Navarre, Faber bore himself " at manhood's simple level." He was firmly devoted to the system and worship of the Church, by principle opposed to schism, and by nature averse to revolution. But the more he studied the Scripture the more it became evident to him that the preaching of the clergy and the method of training them needed reform, and during the closing years of the fifteenth century, while he was teaching in Paris or making a pious pilgrimage to Rome, his knowledge of the Bible and his convictions that the world and the Church were ignorant of it grew steadily. Very likely he may have already formed the hope of giving the Bible to the people of France in their own tongue. At all events he was forming that clearer method of exegesis which was the inheritance of his spiritual descendants. Afterward, developed by the genius of Calvin, it was the contribution of the French to the Protestant Reformation, of universal influence even upon Anglicans, Lutherans, and Arminians who rejected the characteristic French theology.

But it was in Germany that Humanism was to find its second home. Before the end of the fifteenth century, while the New Learning in France and England was scarcely more than the possession of a little group of scholars at one university, the spirit of Humanism was appearing here and there through the cities, the universities, and the pulpits of the whole north and centre of the German Empire. The "forerunners" had, for the most part, brought it over the Alps as a help in their efforts to promote the better study of theology and the reform of religion. But by the seventies it had become in Germany the educational mode for all active spirits to train the human mind, not according to the narrow rubrics of the scholastic system, but to give it a liberal education. How broad that ideal was may be seen by the book which the Emperor Maximilian (born in 1459 and afterward the idol and patron of the Humanists) caused to be made to describe his education. The pictures of the *Weiss König* show the Prince studying everything, from theology to magic and from fortification to astrology. How prevalent the ideal was is apparent in the single observation that this first generation of German Humanists, men born about the middle of the fifteenth century, found at Oxford, at Paris, and in the universities along the Rhine and the Danube that impulse which the Fore-runners had crossed the Alps to find in the valleys of the Arno and the Tiber.   ·

They were conscious also of a strong national and patriotic feeling, and were worthy successors of Gregor of Heimburg. This patriotic feeling began to appear in a tendency to write in German and speak to the common people. Yet it was not a polemic age. Those of the Older German Humanists who lived over into the sixteenth century were sum-moned to range themselves in two great intellectual wars; but the last third of the fifteenth century was a time of comparatively quiet labor, when the new leaven was slowly leavening the whole lump. This secret process appears plainly in two signs: the suc-cessive creation at the more progressive universities, like Erfurt, Heidelberg, Freiburg, and Basle, of the new chair of "Eloquence and Poetry"; and in the foundation of learned societies, which were either local, uniting the Humanists of a single city, or of wider range, like the two great societies of the Rhine and the Danube. These societies kept alive their common feeling by an extensive learned correspon-dence, and expressed their common purpose by the attempted publication of literary monuments of classic antiquity or the ancient Latin chronicles of Germany.

Among the Older Humanists of Germany the three tendencies which we have observed among the men of the New Learning in Italy make themselves apparent, but not in the same proportion. For, while the pagan tendency ruled almost absolutely at Rome, and perhaps prevailed everywhere in Italy except in Florence, it is much less prominent in Germany. Its best representative is Conrad Celtes (1459–1509). He finished the education he had received at various German universities by six months in Italy, and on his return received from the city of Nuremberg the poet's crown. The next ten years he spent in wandering over Germany, teaching eloquence and poetry, now in one and now in another university, until at last he received a longed-for call to the University of Vienna, where he spent ten years as head of the new College of Mathematics and Poetry. There he died at the age of fifty, worn out by the excesses of an evil life. He wrote occasionally on theological themes, and even made pilgrimages in hope of being cured of disease, but he cared little for religion. He was a true epicurean, bent on enjoying in this life, " which before was nothing, and shall again become nothing," " sleep, wine, friendship, and philosophy." Patriotism was his master passion. His wanderings were partly caused by the wish to see all parts of the fatherland, and he divides his poem " Amores," which seems to have been as promiscuously inspired as the love poetry of Burns, into four books, named, indeed, after four heroines, but arranged " according to the four provinces of Germany." He advises his countrymen not to flock over the Alps, and proudly calls the Italians to come and study in that Germany which had given to letters the glorious discovery of

R

printing, was the seat of the Empire and therefore
the true home of laws, and would soon surpass Italy
in poetry and eloquence.   The great unfinished
work of his life, "Germania Illustrata," an historical
and geographical description of the German Empire,
was the praise of the fatherland; and his pleasure in
it never flagged.

The second tendency of Humanism, the ecclesiastical, whose carriers desired to use the New Learning as a better tool for the reform of morals and
religion, was more powerful in the first generation of
German Humanism than it ever was in Italy.   It is
well represented by three men who lived as friends
in and about the city of Strassburg.   Jacob Wimpheling (1450–1528) was educated at the University
of Erfurt, the first in Germany to establish a chair of
"Eloquence and Poetry."   There he found the New
Learning in full tide, and received from the inscription in a church of the city, "Noli peccare Deus
videt," an ineradicable impression.   Returning to the
University of Heidelberg, he pursued the study of the
classics without direction from the professors; and
when Johann von Dalburg, just returned from Italy,
was made Bishop of Worms (1482), and began to reform the discipline and instruction of the University,
Wimpheling became his right-hand man.   He also
published a defence of the Elector Frederick, whose
efforts to reform the clergy of his state had brought
against him an accusation of disrespect to the Pope.
Soon after Wimpheling became cathedral preacher
at Speyer, where he attacked the sins of the clergy
and people, formed association and correspondence

with all the men of the New Learning within reach,
and plunged into the long debate over the Virgin
Mary, as a defender of the Immaculate Conception.
From these labors he was called to the chair of Eloquence and Poetry at Heidelberg. He relinquished
his work there to fulfil his promise made to an old
friend to retire with him to a hermitage. But the
plan was stopped. His friend was suddenly elected
Bishop of Basle, and Wimpheling was persuaded to
settle in Strassburg to finish an edition of the works
of Gerson and promote the cause of letters and religion in South Germany.

The active persuader to this resolution was Geiler of
Kaisersberg (1445–1510). He was educated at the
new University of Freiburg, where he seems to have
been too much of a dandy, for it is recorded that when
he became a magister he was obliged to solemnly swear
that for two years he would not wear either pointed
shoes or a certain kind of neckwear. When he had
finished his studies at Basle, having learned gravity as
well as theology, he became a preacher at the cathedral, and soon after lectured on theology at Freiburg.
This position he relinquished to become cathedral
preacher at Strassburg. There he gave himself for
the rest of his life to the attempt to reform the
morals of the city. In his sermons, where language
so frank and popular as sometimes to shock even
that rude age is sprinkled with quotations from the
classics, he lashed every sort of sin and every rank
of sinner. The prince neglecting religion and plundering the people; the small tradesman in the City
Council afraid to vote according to his conscience for

fear of losing some one's custom; the young nobles
who stroll into church with falcon on wrist and dogs
at their heels; the big merchants who form trusts to
destroy weak rivals and raise prices; the citizens who
live extravagantly and fail to pay their bills; the
grocers who give short weight; the artisans who glibly
promise work by a certain day and never intend to
keep their word; the luxury of the rich who dine on
bears' claws or beavers' tails and let the sick poor
die in misery and hunger; the bishops who are bishops of purses, not of souls; the priests who heap up
benefices and think only of usury; the canons who
gossip in the cathedral during mass, and wear fine,
clean linen, while the altar-cloth is dirty; the monks
who keep the rule of mixing water with their wine
by pouring a drop of water into a cask, and the penance of flagellation by putting on a heavy jacket and
beating themselves with foxes' tails, or whose young
men give a banquet and a dance for the neighboring
convent in honor of their first celebration of mass—
all these are vigorously painted in his discourses.
He preached little but morality, for he shared in the
opinion that doctrine was not for the laity; but he
was a fervently orthodox Catholic and a stern defender of the rights and privileges of the Church.
It was to aid in this work of reformation that he
stopped Wimpheling on his way to a hermitage, and
secured the appointment of their common friend,
Sebastian Brant (1457–1521), as Chancellor of the city
of Strassburg.   Brant had for some years been professor of Latin and semi-official poet of the city of
Basle, and all three, Geiler in the pulpit, Wimpheling

by his efforts to improve the education of the clergy, and Brant by his satiric writings, began a crusade for the purification of society, the reform of ecclesiastical abuses, and the renewal of religion.

Brant was the poet of the trio. Like his friends, he was warmly devoted to the doctrine of the Immaculate Conception of the Virgin, and plunged hotly into the controversy, which, in spite of the bull of Sixtus IV. forbidding the two parties to accuse each other of heresy because the point was one on which the dogma of the Church was not explicit, had reached a very high degree of bitterness. Brant as a defender of the glory of the Virgin led all the rest in zeal and wrath. The most influential of Brant's writings was his satiric poem of the "Narrenschiff," or "Ship of Fools." It is called a poem, though it is of the kind of poetry which has been described as only a more difficult way of writing prose. It is an inchoate collection of separate pieces of verse, imperfectly held together by the vague image of a ship filled with fools and sailing without chart or compass for the land of Cocagne. Passages from the Bible, from Plutarch, from Latin authors, popular proverbs, sage reflections, sketches of character, are thrown together with no regard to art. He describes all kinds of fools. Book-collectors who never read, adulterers, the proud, those who waste their time in hunting, lovers of money, those who cannot keep a secret, the sick who will not obey their physicians, blasphemers and despisers of the Holy Scriptures, drunkards, gluttons, gamblers, and harlots, the envious, the mockers, the

lazy, the ungrateful—all to whom God or a philosopher might say, " Thou fool," are sketched in a style
which appears now both rude and weak, but which
was very effective in its day.   The book was published at Basle in 1494, and in 1498 it had appeared
from the press of six cities in five original and three
stolen and interpolated editions.   It was received
with a storm of applause by the Humanists, and the
Latin translation of it ran through three editions and
was translated twice into French within two years of
its appearance.   Ten years later it was put into English verse by Alexander Barclay and into English
prose by Henry Watson.   It was preached upon and
imitated until " The Fool " became a stock figure in
the literature of the early fifteenth century.

Between men like this trio of friends and the pagan
Humanists like Celtes stood the Middle Party, who
hoped to demonstrate the reasonableness of virtue and
religion.   The core of the party was composed of men
who, like the Florentine Academy, strove to unite
the mystic philosophy of Greece and the New Testament.   Their best representative is Johann Reuchlin.
He was educated at the city school of Pförzheim, his
birthplace, went to the University of Freiburg, and
afterward to Paris as the companion of the younger
son of his Prince.   Paris was then the chief university of the world, and her degrees conferred a special
distinction.   She had appointed a Greek teacher, the
first north of the Alps, and Reuchlin was able to
make the poor beginnings of a knowledge of that
language.   From Paris he went to Basle in 1475,
where, under the private instructions of a wandering

Greek, he learned enough to write a Greek letter to a friend in Strassburg, who wrote to his fellow-student Brant that he could understand, but could not answer it. Reuchlin's education as a doctor of laws being completed, he entered into the service of Count Eberhard of Würtemberg, an uneducated prince with a love for learning, who kept scholars employed in translating for him the chief works of classic antiquity. Reuchlin was one of the retinue that accompanied Eberhard to Rome, and until the death of the good Prince he served as councillor and ambassador in many affairs of State. He then passed into the service of Philip of the Pfalz, also a patron of the Humanists, for whom he made a third trip to Italy. On his previous journey he had met Marsiglio Ficino and Pico della Mirandola, and on this third trip he completed in Rome the studies in Hebrew which he had begun with a Jewish court physician during an embassy to the Emperor Maximilian. It was in 1502 that he received an appointment as one of the three judges of the Swabian League, a very honorable post which he filled for twelve years.

But while he had been acquiring the reputation as a clever jurist and able statesman which gained this appointment, he had also been earning greater fame as a scholar. His first work, at the age of twenty, was a small Latin lexicon, which in thirty years went through twenty-five editions. A succession of translations from Greek into Latin showed his knowledge of Greek. His comedy of " Henno," written for the students of Heidelberg, showed a clear Latin style and held the boards of student theatricals for many years.   And his work "On the Wonder-working Word" had made known his knowledge of Hebrew and the mystic teaching of the Cabala. For he followed Pico della Mirandola, whom he called the most learned man of the day, in the exposition of the Platonic and rabbinic mysticism, feeling that in it was to be found the best illustration and defence of Christianity.   These labors had in the early nineties brought such renown that the Emperor Maximilian offered to ennoble his family, to make him an imperial Pfalzgraf, with the power of acting as judge on all imperial questions, and, further, of conferring, on his own responsibility, ten doctor's degrees.   Reuchlin refused the title with thanks, in which his younger brother, an honest scholar and clergyman of moderate abilities, joined him.   He preferred not to disturb by material decoration that spiritual dignity which by the beginning of the sixteenth century was conferred upon him by the common consent of all who loved letters; the leadership of the learned men of Germany.   From them he received an affection and admiration whose honesty cannot be hidden even by the overloaded compliment of the reigning epistolary style.   For by the new century the Humanists of Germany were a large and resolute body, conscious of their power, known to one another, and needing only the call of a proper leader to form a closed phalanx that would stand firm against all forces of ignorance, tyranny, and reaction.

Meanwhile, under the influences of a cosmopolitan education, another northern student had come to the

maturity of his powers, whose strength as a scholar
and whose genius as a writer were much greater than
those of Reuchlin. Desiderius Erasmus was born at
Rotterdam eleven years later than Reuchlin, in 1466.
He was educated at the school of Deventer, where
he had some teaching in Greek from Alexander
Hegius. He left at the age of thirteen, knowing
Terence by heart and able to read Horace easily.
The boy was soon after left an orphan, and fell on
evil days; for one of his guardians lost the larger
part of the estate by careless investment, the second
died of the plague, and the third, an ignorant and
fanatic schoolmaster, was possessed with the idea of
forcing Erasmus into a monastery. After two years
of struggle he became an inmate of the Augustinian
house of Steyn. The monks were coarse men, caring nothing for literature, and understanding by religion the discipline of their order, with its vigils and
fasts, which they varied by drinking-bouts. Erasmus's delicate constitution could not endure the fasts,
and his fastidious spirit shrank from the drinking-
bouts; but in spite of every repugnance, the poor lad,
with no friend to turn to, was finally persuaded to
become a monk. He spent six years in the convent.
The example of the monks was bad, and he tells us
he was inclined to great vices; but he studied much,
and gained among all who knew him the report of
a very accomplished writer of verse and prose. It
was this private reputation which led the Bishop of
Cambray, then contemplating a journey to Italy, to
offer Erasmus the post of secretary. He accepted,
and was ordained priest in the following year. The

Bishop deferred his journey, and sent Erasmus to study theology at Paris.   There he settled, with the idea of pursuing his studies and maintaining himself as a private tutor to young gentlemen of fortune. It was thus that he became acquainted with Lord Mountjoy, one of those patrons whose gifts and pensions became afterward a chief source of his income.

After five or six years at Paris, his skill in Latin letter-writing having gained him much reputation among "the men who know," he went to Oxford with introductions to the head of St. Mary's College. In England he fell in at once with the Grecians, of whom Colet was leader.   He met Thomas More, then just of age.   One of those stories which are entirely true even if they never happened shows us at a glance the position of the two men in the little circle of elect spirits in which each moved.   Having conversed brilliantly for some time without knowing each other's names, Erasmus suddenly cried, "You are either More or nobody," to which the other replied, "And you are either Erasmus or the devil." But it was Colet who exercised the greatest influence over Erasmus and in whose society he took the greatest delight.   They had much pleasant intercourse and many discussions, scholarly and grave, but full of fire.   Erasmus has told how Colet's eye would flash and his quiet countenance appear transfigured as they discussed at dinner " why Cain's offering was rejected," or some similar topic.   His whole tone was filled with vehemence as he finally broke in on Erasmus's commonplace praise of the " Aurea Catena " of Aquinas with a denunciation of one who had

" contaminated the whole doctrine of Christ with his own profane philosophy."

It was doubtless the friendship of Colet, Platonist and biblical student, that fixed Erasmus's bent to the study of the New Testament rather than to the classics, and formed in him the determination to revive the " true philosophy of Christ."

When he had returned to his studies at Paris this serious inclination of his mind appeared in the first of his writings, which carried his fame outside the circle of Humanistic students among whom his letters and his praise had been circulated: the " Enchiridion," or " Christian Soldiers' Dagger," printed at Louvain in 1503. It was written at the request of a wife to awaken her husband to a sense of religion, and against " the error that makes religion depend on ceremonies and a more than Judaic observance of bodily acts, while neglecting true piety." It is a skilful mixture of the teaching of the New Testament and the Platonic philosophy. The end of life, he says, is Christ, and that is " no unmeaning word, but love, simplicity, patience, purity, in short, whatever Christ taught." He then refers to the usages of religion, and exhorts to an effort to find their spiritual meaning. " If you worship the bones of Paul locked up in a casket, worship also the spirit of Paul which shines forth from his writings." " For it is not charity to be constant at church, to prostrate yourself before the images of the saints, burn candles, and chant prayers. What Paul calls charity is to edify your neighbor, to rejoice at your brother's welfare and help his misfortune as if it were your own, to instruct the ignorant, to comfort the cast down, to do good in Christ to all to whom you can do good, that, as he gave himself wholly for us, so we also may serve our brothers' need and not our own." He then shows how the life of the monks, " who have set themselves apart for the service of religion," is not lived in this happiness, being " filled with Jewish superstitions and the vices of the world." " And when they are grown gray in the observance of the rules of their order you shall find that they have nothing of the temper of Christ, but are altogether unspiritual and unsocial, peevish, and scarce supportable even to themselves; cold in charity, hot in anger, obstinate in hatred, ready to fight for the most trifling cause, and so far from the perfection of Christ that they have not even the natural virtues of the heathen. Unteachable and sensuous, they turn with disgust from the Scriptures. They never show kindness, but are full of foul suspicion and vain conceit." This attack upon the errors and vices of monasticism did not in the least hinder his intimacy with the Franciscan monk John Vitrarius, who urged its publication. For the noble man, of whom Erasmus has left a pen-picture done with the skill of affection, had suffered from these errors and vices of his fellows. Having endeavored to reform a convent of dissolute nuns, the Suffragan Bishop of Boulogne laid a plot by which eight of the worst lured him into a secret place and would have strangled him with their handkerchiefs had they not been accidentally interrupted. And at the risk of excommunication, and in face of two citations from his Bishop, he had denounced the sale of indulgences and "the silly credulity of those who thought their sins would be pardoned if they put their money in the box."

When the "Enchiridion" was published a witty friend wrote, "There is more religion in the book than in the author"; but the friendship of Vitrarius, who knew the writings of Paul by heart and though "he preached seven times a day never lacked words or learning when his theme was Christ," must have still further increased the concentration of Erasmus's studies upon the aim of promoting "the pure philosophy of Christ." The "Enchiridion" went through many editions with great rapidity. Twenty years after its publication the Archdeacon of Alcor, in Spain, wrote: "There is no other book of our time which can be compared to the 'Enchiridion' for the extent of its circulation. There is not even a country inn that has not a copy of it in Spanish, and this short work has made the name of Erasmus a household word."

Thus at the death of Alexander VI. (1503) a little group of English scholars, represented by Colet, of Frenchmen, represented by Faber Stapulensis, joined in spiritual friendship by the citizen of the world of letters, Erasmus, were bending all the resources of the New Learning to the study of the Bible; while in Germany a large and resolute body of Humanists, spread through the cathedral chapters and universities of the Empire, were giving unanimous homage to John Reuchlin and applauding his labors to promote the study of Greek and Hebrew.

PERIOD III.

CHAPTER XXI.

JULIUS II. AND LEO X.—THE NEPHEW OF SIXTUS IV. AND THE SON OF LORENZO THE MAGNIFICENT BECOME POPES.

ULIUS II., the lifelong foe and now the successor of Alexander VI., had the fiery temper and stern will of the "terrible" Sixtus IV. But his ambition was higher than his uncle's, for though he advanced his nephews and made a great marriage for his natural daughter, his heart's desire was not to enrich his family, but to make the Church State strong among the powers of Italy. There were no luxurious nepots at Rome in his day. He avoided even the appearance of the riotous living of Alexander, and the expenses of his household were only fifteen hundred florins a month. The income of the Church (a single monk brought back twenty-seven thousand florins from the sale of indulgences) was spent in adorning the city of Rome or maintaining his army. His treasury was never allowed to be empty, and so good was his financial management that, in spite of his great outlays in the arts of peace and war, he left his successor a treasure of seven hundred thousand florins.

Julius had to face a difficult situation for one who desired to make the patrimonium a strong and independent state. France had seized Milan and Genoa in the north, Spain had conquered the kingdom of Naples in the south, and these two were ever threatening to renew their long and deadly duel for the spoils of Italy. Venice, the only really strong power in the peninsula, sat aside, secure behind her lagoons, and anxious only to draw her own gain out of the general ruin. He who would play in such a game must be strong, and in one of the first bulls of his reign Julius announced that he felt it his duty to regain the lost lands of the Church. But he waited two years and a half before he moved from Rome, with twenty-two cardinals and a long train of bishops and prelates, to occupy the chief cities of Romagna, Perugia and Bologna. The host was carried in front of the Pope, and only five hundred men-at-arms were at his back. The tyrant of Perugia, stained with every crime, was awed by the cool will of Julius, who came into the city, leaving his little army outside. Instead of murdering or imprisoning the Pope, which Machiavelli despised him for not doing, he entered the Papal service as a mercenary soldier. Then, with a larger army, to which eight thousand French troops were joined, Julius turned against Bologna. The Bentivogli fled, and the Pope entered in triumphal procession under an arch inscribed " To Julius, the Expeller of Tyrants." A still more splendid triumph awaited him in Rome.

But crafty Venice, who had so long drawn profit from her neighbors' misfortunes, was now to suffer.

Spain claimed some conquered cities on the Apulian coast; Austria demanded Friuli; France the return of Brescia, Cremona, and other cities of her Dukedom of Milan; the Empire, Verona; the Florentines were promised Pisa. Ferrara, Mantua, and Urbino followed the Pope. And so in the spring of 1509 the Republic of San Marco saw all Italy and three fourths of Europe in arms against her. It was Julius's vengeance on the Venetians for the four cities of the Church they had seized and their resistance to his appointments of aliens to Venetian benefices. "I tell you," he cried one day, in rage, to the Republic's ambassador, "I will make Venice once more a little fishing-village." "And we, Holy Father," he was answered, "will make you once more a little priest." The League was blessed by the Pope and Venice cursed by the interdict. Two months laid the proud Republic at his feet asking for mercy. Then Julius's heart misgave him. He could not destroy the bulwark of Italy against the Turk, the only state as yet unconquered by the foreigner. In January, 1510, while France and the allies still called for war, the ambassadors of the Republic knelt before the Pope as he sat on the steps of St. Peter's, in the presence of all Rome, and lightly struck them with a rod at every verse of the intoned Miserere. Then they finished the penance by a pilgrimage to the churches of the city. What the Venetian ambassador wrote home was plain to all the world: "At sixty-five years of age the Pope, suffering from gout and other results of the free life of his youth, is still in the fullness of strength and activity, and wishes to be lord and master of the play of the world."

Peace with Venice was followed by war with France, and to carry it on Julius made a Holy League with Spain and Venice to drive the French over the Alps, hoping also for the aid of England and the Empire. The Bishop of Sitten raised twelve thousand Swiss to come down into the plain of the Po for good pay, and Julius put into the field every mercenary he could afford. At the siege of Mirandola he himself was seen in the trenches cheering on the soldiers. He took up his quarters in the kitchen of an old cloister, and when a cannon-ball killed two of his servants while he slept, refused to abandon it. When the town surrendered he could not wait for the gates to open, but mounted by a scaling-ladder over the breach.

It was this spectacle which caused Hutten to write in vitriolic satire, bidding the world look at Julius: " His terrible brow, hiding fierce eyes, with threats of hell-fire blazing in his mouth. Behold him, the author of such destruction and so much crime, born a bitter pest of the human race, whose work and whose recreation is death. Unlike Christ, unlike Peter, what does he do or what is there about him worthy the name of Roman Pontiff? "

By the spring of 1512 the French, in spite of their brilliant victory at Ravenna, had lost every foothold in Italy and were almost overwhelmed by the simultaneous attacks of Spain, Germany, England, and the Netherlands. The Pope had let slip the dogs of war

s

to some purpose, and it is easy to believe that in the pride of his victory he should have wished, as Vasari says, to be painted with a sword in his hand.

Nor was Julius the only Prince of the Church who took the sword.   The Cardinal Ippolito of Este had his brother's eyes put out because his mistress praised their beauty ; and when the Pope's nephew, the young Duke of Urbino, fell upon the Papal favorite, Cardinal Alidosi, and killed him with a dagger in the streets of Ravenna, there were other cardinals who said, " Well done."   Some of those who approved the Papal policy of " thorough " gained by it. In August, 1512, the Spanish commander appeared in Florentine territory by order of the Holy League. He was accompanied by Cardinal Medici.   Prato was stormed and horribly sacked, and the frightened Republic of Florence agreed to receive the Medici once more within her walls.   The government was in their hands within a year.

France had not looked idly on while all Europe was raised against her.   Taking advantage of a temporary disagreement between the Emperor and Julius, she proposed a Council for reform, and in the spring of 1511 a call was issued from a Synod at Lyons for a General Council of the Church, under the protection of the Emperor and the King of France.   It was signed by three cardinals, and claimed the unexpressed support of six others, Frenchmen, Italians, and Spaniards.   The call was fastened on the doors of the chief cathedrals of Italy and spread through Europe.   But only eighteen prelates met in Pisa, and even this poor assembly began almost immediately to dissolve, as its members sought, one by one, to make their peace with a Pope who was too strong for them.

For Julius had met this move of French politicians, using the desire for the revival of religion to checkmate a hostile Pope and keep the patronage of the French national Church in their own hands, by a skilful counter-move. In the summer he called a General Council to meet at the Lateran the following spring. On the 21st of April, 1512, the Council of Pisa, now transferred for the sake of French protection to Milan, suspended Julius from the Papacy. Ten days later the Pope opened the Council of the Lateran with a solemn procession closed by a company of men-at-arms and nine cannons. There were almost none except Italian prelates present, but England, Spain, and Germany were soon to declare their allegiance to the decrees. The tone of them was given in the sermons and orations which opened the first sessions.

Egidius of Viterbo, General of the Augustinians, spoke on the need of the reform of the Church. He declared the defeat of Ravenna a sign from heaven to turn the Church from the sword with which she had just suffered defeat to her own weapons, piety, prayer, the breastplate of faith and the sword of light. " Hear," he cried, " O thou Head and Defender of the city of Rome, hear into what a deep sea of evils the Church thou hast founded by thy blood is fallen! Dost thou behold how the earth has drunk up this year more blood than rain? Help us! Raise the Church! The people, men and women of

every age—yea, the entire world—are praying and beseeching; the fathers, the Senate, the Pope himself,
beseech you to preserve the Church, the city of
Rome, these temples and altars, and to endow this
Lateran Synod with the aid of the Holy Ghost for the
healing of all Christendom.   We beseech thee, teach
the Christian princes to make peace among themselves, and to turn their swords against Mohammed,
the open enemy of Christ, that the love of the Church
may not only survive these storms and waves, but,
through the merits of the Holy Cross and the power
of the Holy Ghost, may be cleared of every stain
and brought back again to its early purity and glory."

The next preacher spoke of the unity of the Church,
which consisted in the oneness of the members with
each other and their subordination to the head, the
Vicar of Christ; whence arose the plain duty of
the Council to punish all schismatics who refused to
obey this head of the whole body.

The third sermon, by the General of the Dominicans, was on the Catholic doctrine of the Church and
her synods.   Its conclusion condemned the opposition Council as from hell—no heavenly Jerusalem,
but rather an earthly Babel, full of strife and confusion of tongues.   The doctrine of Conciliar Supremacy
was denounced as an innovation no older than Constance and Basle, and the preacher exhorted the
Pope to gird on his two swords of spiritual and temporal power and set himself to the work of destroying heresy and schism.

All these utterances were emphasized and summarized in the address of the Apostolic Notary,

Marcello of Venice, who (December, 1512) praised the Pope for having borne heat and cold, sleeplessness, illness, peril, to defeat his enemies in a holy war, to free Bologna, to conquer Reggio, Parma, and Piacenza, to drive the Frenchmen from Italy. And he prophesied that Julius would gain even greater glory in the works of peace, the reform and glorification of the Church, now threatened by foes from without and stained by sin and treachery within. "The Pope," he concluded, "must be physician, helmsman, cultivator, in short, all in all, like a second God on earth."

In this spirit the Council condemned all acts of the schismatics at Pisa and Milan, laid France under the interdict, condemned the Conciliar theory of the constitution of the Church, suspended the Pragmatic Sanction, and summoned the clergy of France to answer for their conduct within sixty days. Julius had not only founded by arms a Papal monarchy in Italy, but secured the regular indorsement of the Church for the theory and practice of that absolute Papal Supremacy which the last two Councils had denied.

During the years when he was thus bringing his plans to triumph Julius was active in enlarging and adorning his palace and cathedral. He determined early in his pontificate to cover his rooms with mural paintings, to complete the decoration of the chapel of his uncle, to build a superb tomb for himself, and to rebuild St. Peter's on its present gigantic scale. For these works three of the greatest artists of our race were at his command. Neither

Alexander, Cæsar, nor Napoleon had such power to adorn their achievements as the Pope to whom it was given to immortalize his conquest of rebellious vassals and his triumphant manipulation of the squabbling politics of Italy by the genius of Michael Angelo, Raphael, and Bramante.

There is no reason to suspect in Julius any artistic ability. The learning which supplied the young Raphael with the information for the wonderful presentation of the ideals of the Platonized Christianity of the Florentine Academy in the pictures of the Stanza della Segnatura was certainly not his. But there was a certain largeness and power about him which encouraged great conceptions, and he had been dowered with that first quality of a strong ruler, the ability to recognize a servant of distinction and to use genius without hampering it. He laid the corner-stone of a new St. Peter's, in spite of the opposition of all his counsellors, and inspired such restless energy into the work on all his architectural plans that he was said to demand of his contractors, not to build, but to make buildings grow. With ruthless haste he destroyed the monuments and pillars of the old Basilica to make room for his new creation, as if he felt himself to be racing with death, which overtook him on the 16th of February, 1513.

On the 6th of March, 1513, Giovanni de' Medici was elected Pope, and assumed the name of Leo X. His appearance was not in his favor. His legs were very weak and his body very heavy, and when saying mass he was compelled to constantly wipe the perspiration from his hands and neck; but he had a sweet voice and charming manner. He was thirty-seven years old, and this youngest of the Popes had a precocious ecclesiastical career from the start, for he was an abbot and an archbishop at seven, and a cardinal at fourteen. He had been educated under the care of his father, Lorenzo the Magnificent, in the midst of the best thinkers, writers, and artists of Italy, and his hereditary love of music, literature, and art was guided by refined tastes. It was to these he had always turned for his pleasures, and when he said to his brother, " The Papacy is ours; let us enjoy it," he was thinking of the measureless opportunities to patronize the arts which were now in his hands.

The first act of his government made this plain. So superb an inaugural procession had never been seen. He spent on it one hundred thousand florins. And all Rome was adorned to match. Festal decorations in every street and house showed the joy of the city and the wealth of the resident prelates. Some of these were erected to honor the Pope, and bore figures of the apostles or ecclesiastical mottoes; but more were to please the new Mæcenas, the patron of classic art and literature. Whoever had a beautiful bit of old marble, a statue of Venus or Apollo, or the head of an emperor, placed it in front of his palace. Agostino Chigi, the rich Papal banker, had erected a huge arch covered with mythological devices. It had this reference to the two preceding Popes (Alexander and Julius): " Venus held rule before; then came Mars; but now Pallas Athena mounts the throne"; and on the other side of the street his neighbor put out the statue of Venus with this inscription: "Mars fuit; est Pallas; Venus semper ero." For the mode of Rome was classic, not to say heathen. A poet handed the Pope an elegy on the death of a friend, in which he called on the dead "to beg the King of Heaven and all the Gods to give Leo the years which the Fates had cut from his life." Another litterateur tells us how he made a funeral mound beside the sea for a drowned friend, and called thrice on his manes with a loud voice; and in a time of pestilence a Greek actually offered a public sacrifice in the Colosseum to appease the demons of death.

Leo wanted peace and the arts, but war was forced upon him. Spain and France had already begun their long struggle for the possession of Italy and the leadership of the world, and Leo was drawn into it. The league of Spain, England, the Empire, and the Pope attacked Venice and France, and in the battle of Novara (June 6, 1513) France was driven once more out of Italy. But the Pope longed to make for his brother Giuliano a powerful principality in Central Italy, and the French King was willing to meet him half way. The schism begun under Julius was healed by the return of the French prelates to obedience and the hand of a royal princess offered to the Pope's brother. But Leo wanted two strings to his bow, and at the very hour he was negotiating with France he was considering a new secret league with Spain and his old allies; for it was said of him that the only thing to which he ever remained true was his own maxim that " to have made a treaty

with one side was the best of all reasons for beginning negotiations with the other."

It was in the midst of these intrigues that Francis
I., a beautiful and talented young prince, full of ro-
mantic dreams of knightly glory, came to the French
throne.   He married his aunt to Giuliano de' Medici,
and the Pope spent one hundred and fifty thousand
florins for presents to the bride and her entry into
Rome.   (This was more than double the estimated
yearly income of the richest merchant banker in
Italy.)   But when the Pope asked that a principality
be formed for his brother out of four cities on the
southern border of Milan, the King sharply refused;
he wanted them for himself.   And Leo joined the
old league of everybody against France.   The
French army crossed the Alps by a forced march,
and in September, 1515, a two days' fight at Marignano made the young King master of North Italy.
The Swiss, in spite of all the efforts of the Cardinal
of Sitten, were terribly defeated by the French artillery, their hereditary formation in solid squares shown
to be useless in the new warfare, and their reputation as the first soldiers of Europe destroyed.   Leo
and Francis met in Bologna.   The young conqueror
kissed the Pope's foot and the two embraced.   Their
treaty recognized all Francis's claims to the Duchy
of Milan, placed the States of the Church under his
protection, and divided the liberties of the French
Church, secured by the Pragmatic Sanction, between
the King, who was to name the bishops, and the
Pope, who was to draw the first year's income of all
vacancies.

After the battle of Marignano a solemn peace was signed between France, Spain, and the Empire; and the Pope seized the opportunity to create his nephew Lorenzo Duke of Urbino, at the cost of the nephew of Julius, who was driven into exile.   But the powers really agreed on only one thing, suspicion of the Pope, who had deceived each in turn; and when the exiled Duke of Urbino suddenly reëntered his dominions with five thousand mercenaries, all stood by to watch Leo get out of the difficulty as best he could.   Money was scarce, and it was only by contracting huge debts at enormous interest that he could put an army into the field to defend his nepot.

And in the midst of this struggle internal troubles came upon him.   A conspiracy to murder the Pope was formed among the cardinals.   Its chief was Petrucci, son of the famous tyrant of Siena.   The Pope had permitted the Cardinal's brother to be driven from Siena in favor of a cousin who stood closer to his plans and likings.   The young Cardinal kept a costly hunting retinue of dogs and horses, which was limited by the loss of the family lands.   He swore vengeance against Leo, and at first meditated killing him on a hunting-party.   He even carried a dagger into the consistory, hid under his cardinal's robe.   But he finally determined, in counsel with Cardinal Sauli, to poison the Pope by means of a physician recommended to him in the temporary absence of his own.   The plot was betrayed by the capture of letters of Petrucci written to his secretary, and it appeared that three other cardinals besides the active conspirators had known of the plot and kept silence. Riario, Dean of the College, of which he had been a member forty years, was disappointed over his defeat by Medici in the last election. Hadrian of Corneto had been told by a fortune-teller that Leo would die young and an old man of unknown origin named Hadrian would succeed. Soderini was angry because his brother Gonfalonier, of the Republic, had been driven from Florence by the Medici. The plot was betrayed and Petrucci condemned to death. The announcement of the sentence raised such a storm of indignation in the consistory that the dispute was heard in the streets outside. Nevertheless he was strangled in prison. Sauli was deposed. Hadrian fled to Venice and was deposed for contumacy. The other two were heavily fined. Afterward the Pope said high mass under armed guard to protect him against the dagger of a cardinal.

He also named thirty-nine new cardinals, and the five hundred thousand florins thus brought in were used to end the war of Urbino. After offering in vain ten thousand ducats to one captain for the surrender of the Duke, alive or dead, Leo finally did succeed in bribing all his generals to desert him, and the Duke was compelled to give up the struggle in consideration of the return of his personal property. Lorenzo de' Medici, thus settled on a ducal throne, was then married to a princess of France, and in 1517 the Pope, with one nepot ruler of Florence, another of Urbino, and the College of Cardinals filled with his friends, held the balance of power in the strife of the young kings of Spain and France so soon to break out, first in rivalry for the throne of the German Empire, and then in war for the possession of Italy.

Meanwhile the Council of the Lateran had been moving in the matter of the so long desired reform of the Church.   Leo proposed to establish it by a bull, but the Council demanded detailed regulations for bishops and all clergy, and Pico della Mirandola sent a memorial suggesting that the Church needed not better laws, but better men.   The bishops of the Council proposed to effect reform by reëstablishing, as against the privileges of the cardinals and monastic orders, the ancient episcopal powers; and when a reform bill was introduced which failed to reëstablish these episcopal rights, they threatened to withdraw from the Council.   The Pope had to act constantly as mediator, and several compromises were introduced which attempted to establish reform while still retaining as much as possible of the privileges and patronage which belonged to each class of the clergy represented in the Council. The ancient laws against immorality among the clergy were reiterated with emphasis.   "Ringing resolutions" denouncing simony and abuses in the bestowal of benefices were passed unanimously. Discipline was made easier by the removal of certain exemptions from episcopal control enjoyed by priests.   Bishops were ordered to supervise clerical education and see to it that the preaching in their dioceses was strong and true; and arrangements were made for the holding of regular diocesan synods.   This last decree would have been really influential for reform, but unfortunately it remained almost a dead letter.

In 1516 appeared a book by Pietro Pomponazzi, a distinguished professor of Bologna, to prove that the soul was mortal. And the Council thought it wise, in view of the prevailing heathenism, to solemnly decree that human souls are individual, immortal, and unmaterial.

The closing ceremony in March was a triumph for the Papacy. All the world was returned to obedience, and Cardinal Carvajal, once head of the schismatic Council at Pisa, conducted the mass and closed a Council which had reaffirmed the entire claim of the mediæval Popes, condemned the assertion of Conciliar Supremacy made at Constance, and asserted the absolute Papal Supremacy. They symbolized these decrees by calling all Christendom to a crusade under the lead of the Pope, and laid a tax for its expenses on all lands of the world.

Already a Papal messenger had written to Leo (1516): "In Germany they are only waiting until some fellow once opens his mouth against Rome." He was now sent back as Legate with a paper reform and the demand for a new ecclesiastical tax.

PERIOD III.

CHAPTER XXII.

TRANSALPINE HUMANISM UNDER JULIUS AND LEO
—(1) THE BATTLE OF THE BOOKS ABOUT
JOHN REUCHLIN; (2) THE THREE DISCIPLES
OF THE PHILOSOPHY OF CHRIST; (3) THE
PUPILS OF FABER STAPULENSIS; (4) ULRICH
ZWINGLI.

T is rather a suggestive division of the
history of German Humanism to desig-
nate its three periods as the *Theological*
(the Forerunners, ending 1471), the
Teaching (the Older Humanists), and the
Polemic, which, beginning with the century, was
broken in the middle by the Protestant revolt. And
it implies a characteristic distinction between northern and southern Humanism that across the Alps
the whole Humanistic body should have become so
soon involved in such a serious discussion as the controversy we are about to follow.

The forces of ultra-conservatism and reaction were
as strong in Italy as in Germany, but the Humanists
were less zealous and determined, and when conflict
arose they were much inclined to say, with Laurentius Valla: " Mother Church does not know anything

302

about criticism, but in this matter I think just as Mother Church does." In the north the common temper of scholars was sterner and more serious. Italian Humanism never displayed any efficient interest in the New Testament, and by the middle of the fifteenth century was the contented servant of privileged abuse. But scarcely had the New Learning passed the Alps before we find its adherents turning to biblical studies and attacking traditional privileges in the name of common justice. While the presses of Venice and Rome were pouring out editions of the classics and erotic poems, the presses of the Rhine were busy with biblical and patristic works, satires, and moral treatises.

This contrast between the spirit of Germany and Italy is remarkable even in the sphere of art, where it shows least upon the surface. Certain general contrasts between the works of Dürer and Holbein and those of Raphael and Michael Angelo, all four of whom did their best-known work in the first quarter of the sixteenth century, suggest it. The northerners made cheap prints to go into the houses of the common people, while the Italians were decorating the tombs, the chapels, and the palaces of princes. The Italians were philosophic, moral, and æsthetic; the Germans religious and evangelic. Michael Angelo painted the creation and prophecy, carved a Moses out of Homer and a David who is one of Plutarch's men; but Holbein cut "Thus saith the Lord" into the lines of the Samuel that meets Saul in his little woodcut for Bible illustration. Raphael made some perfectly drawn pictures out of the life of Christ, that are as much like the four gospels as the fighting Pope with his Humanistic cardinals, for whom he did them, was like the Master and his apostles; Dürer put the spirit of the New Testament into his rude woodcuts of him who preached the gospel to the poor. Raphael painted for all ages *das ewig Weibliche;* Dürer drew for the people of his own age the Man of Sorrows. There is probably as much provincialism in Ruskin's phrase of " kicking prettinesses," applied to Raphael's " Transfiguration," as in Pater's reference to " the grim inventions of Albrecht Dürer "; but it may not jar upon the broad and gentle temper of history to suggest that the greater rudeness and fidelity to the New Testament of the Germans were both, perhaps, the outcome of the spirit of their people.

These reflections may illustrate the deepest reason why the whole New Learning of Germany, applauded by all the northern Humanists, became involved in a desperate battle with the party of orthodoxy over the relation of scholarship to the Bible and the Church.

The protagonist was John Reuchlin, and the occasion was the zeal of John Pfefferkorn, a converted Jew and master of the hospital of St. Ursula in Cologne. With the help of the Dominicans of Cologne he published a series of pamphlets against the Jews, very much in the tone and temper of the anti-Catholic publications with which we are familiar in this country. He followed the Emperor to Italy, and as a result of his impassioned appeals Reuchlin, as imperial councillor, received the request for a formal opinion on the question, " Ought all the books of the Jews to be taken away from them and burned ? " He made a most painstaking answer, in which he advised the destruction only of certain blasphemous parodies of Christianity, two of which he cited as disavowed by the better Jews. He defended the rest of their literature as highly useful to science and theology, and guaranteed to the Jews by the laws of the Empire. This opinion, which was sent under seal, was seen in transit by Pfefferkorn, who immediately published a pamphlet entitled " The Hand-glass," in which he caricatured Reuchlin's official opinion, attempted to show him as a poor scholar and a worse Christian, and ended up by calling all patrons of Jewish learning *Ohrenbläser, Stubenstencker, Plippenplapper, Beutelfeger, Hinterschützer, Seitenstecher.* Reuchlin answered with " The Eye-glass," a pamphlet abounding in similar flowers of speech, which bloomed freely over the whole field of contemporary polemics. The original report of Reuchlin was already pigeonholed and forgotten, but the conflict between the Old Learning and the New, so long impending, was begun, and all Germany flamed into literary war, amid which the threats of the heretic's stake gleamed darkly. For the party of reactionary orthodoxy, headed by the Dominicans and the theologians of Cologne, proposed now to extend to Reuchlin the policy of thorough they had wished for the Jews. But the case was appealed to Rome, and while Humanistic cardinals were stirred up by letters to block the efforts of zealous inquisitors, the cross-fire of satires, poems, and pamphlets raged in Germany.

T

All three classes of Humanists rallied around Reuchlin as a common leader. Johann Eck (1486–1543), the young professor of theology at Ingolstadt, attacked a reactionary theologian at Vienna as a fool and a sophist; for which we cannot help feeling there was some ground when we learn that, as Rector of the University, he forbade a young professor to lecture because he had dared to use the classic *tu* instead of the barbarous but customary *vos*. For it was a cause of much horror to the Old School as the Humanists mockingly put it, " Quod simplex socius deberes tibisare unum rectorem universitatis qui est magister noster."

But the most energetic defender of Reuchlin was Ulrich von Hutten, a young representative of the pagan Renascence. He was placed by his father, a South German knight, in a convent at Fulda to be educated, whence he ran away at sixteen to go to the Humanistic University of Erfurt. Then for years he lived the wild and studious life of a wandering student, subsisting by the charity of friends who admired his talents. Italy, the loadstar of all who loved the New Learning, drew him also, and he learned in the South land not only a deeper love of letters, but a deeper hatred of the abuses of the Papacy. Epigrams written at this time, but published later, show it plainly. For instance, here is one:

On the Indulgence of Julius.

" See how the world of the faithful is guided by the merchant Julius, who sells what he does not possess—heaven.

" Offer me at a bargain what you have! How shameless it is to sell what you are most in want of yourself! If the giants came back Jupiter would be done for. Julius would certainly sell them Olympus. But so long as another reigns and thunders above, I shall never take the trouble to bid for property in heaven."

Hutten came back from his travels a bold and fluent satirist, German to the core, and plunged with fresh zeal into the ranks of the Reuchlinists.

They were already a marshaled army with published lists of names. One of their most distinguished muster-rolls was found in the volume printed at Tübingen, 1514, entitled " Clarorum Virorum Epistolæ, Latinæ, Græcæ et Hebriacæ variis temporibus missæ ad Joannem Reuchlin." It was with the aid of Hutten that a little company of the Erfurt Humanists published anonymously a parody entitled " Epistolæ obscurorum virorum ad venerabilem virum M. Ortuinum Gratium variis et locis et temporibus missæ et demum in volumen coactæ." It is a work so characteristic of its age that, by the confession of its best commentators, translation is impossible and paraphrase difficult. Its humor, whose tone has been well compared to that of "Don Quixote," is stained by the filthy jesting, its hatred of ignorant intolerance by the reckless slander universal among scholars of the day, and it is written in a wild but most clever caricature of the dog-Latin of the monks.

The letters and poems in it were supposed to be addressed to Ortuin Gratius, of the theological faculty of Cologne, by a series of friends who bore such names as Eitelnarrabianus, Kukuk, Buntemantellus, Dollenkopfius, Schaffmulius.   They propounded learned questions for discussion, or reported journeys to other universities.   Through them all runs a thread of allusion to Reuchlin and the advance of the New Learning.   They suggest absurd arguments for his discomfiture, or they tell of how his friends at other universities turned the narrator out of the inn as an enemy of the Muses.   One reports that the chief preacher in Würzburg is a dangerous man who announces that he belongs to no school except the school of Christ; that he preaches plainly, without the tricks of rhetoric and logic, and the people like it. He even dared to say, when Brother Jacob announced the sale of indulgences, that if a man bought a hundred indulgences, and did not live well, he will be damned, and the indulgence will not help him in the least.   Another reports a disputation over a passage of prophecy in which his adversary asserted that the light of truth was about to be cast upon the dirty, dark, and senseless theology which had been brought into vogue a few hundred years before by men ignorant of Latin, Greek, and Hebrew.   God was sending new doctors with lights, like Reuchlin and Erasmus, who had just put out a true edition of Jerome, a real theologian; and he was working at the text of the New Testament, which was worth more than to have twenty thousand Scotists and Thomists disputing for a hundred years over ens and essentia.

A single one of these letters will serve as a favorable specimen.   It is from Thomas Langschneider to his old master Gratius, asking an opinion upon a learned question. With many quotations from Aristotle and the Bible, he describes a feast at Leipzig, given, according to custom, by one who had just become master in theology; and after they had enjoyed the roast capons, fish, Malvoisie and Rhine wine, Eimbecker, Torgauer, and Neuburger beer, they began to discuss learned themes. And finally Magister Warmsemmel, a reputable Scotist, and Magister Delitzsch, a doctor of medicine and law, became involved in an insoluble dispute as to whether one who was about to become a doctor of theology (*Magister Noster*) should be called *Magister Nostrandus* or *Noster Magistrandus*. Warmsemmel points out that *magistrare* is a verb, but *nostro*, *nostrare*, is not to be found in any dictionary. To which his antagonist replied that in Horace's "Ars Poetica" the right to make new words was clearly established. The correspondent asks Gratius to decide which was right, and, in closing, inquires how the war comes on with that scoundrel Reuchlin, who, he understands, obstinately refuses to recant. This mildest of all the letters seems like fairly strong sarcasm, but it needed coarse point to touch its victims, for a Dominican prior in the Low Countries was so pleased with this new defence of the labors of his order on behalf of orthodoxy that he ordered a large number of copies to be sent to friends in high rank. History does not record what he said when he discovered his mistake on reading the last letter of the second part, which even the most Bœotian wits could not misunderstand.

The learned farce was received with Homeric laughter. We can well imagine that, even in Cologne, the student body was delighted with it, and if anything was needed to bring youngest Germany to the side of the New Learning, the "Epistolæ Obscurorum Virorum" did it. But as subsequent editions became diffused and coarsened the judicious grieved. Reuchlin thought it vulgar, and tradition says he remonstrated sharply. A young professor of theology at Wittenberg, Martin Luther, though counted among the Reuchlinists, said it was impertinent, and called the author " Hans Sausage." Erasmus, though he liked it at first, finally spoke of it with asperity as an injury to the Humanistic cause.

For Erasmus was working on altogether different lines. Colet and his two younger friends, More and Erasmus, were united in a more or less unconscious coöperation at a common work—reform by the demonstration of a reasonable Christianity; the philosophy of Christ applied to the problems of the world.

With Colet this desire took a more personal and religious form, and as time went on the thoughts of the Dean of St. Paul became more and more centred on Christ. He had arranged Christ's sayings into groups to remember them better and planned a book upon them. His preaching, the most influential in England, dwelt more and more on the blessings and example of Christ. He loved children, quoting the example of our Lord, and bent his learning to write a little Latin grammar for them, that they might "grow to perfect literature and come at last to be great clerks." He gave his whole private fortune to found St. Paul's School for the free education of one hundred and fifty-three boys, with the " intent by this school specially to increase knowledge and worshipping of God and our Lord Jesus Christ, and good Christian life and manners in the children."

With Thomas More, greatest advocate, and finally Lord Chancellor of England, the desire to propagate the philosophy of Christ expressed itself naturally in the direction of social and political reforms. His " Utopia" was a description of an ideal common-wealth, described by an old traveler he met in Antwerp through the introduction of Peter Giles, a well-known merchant of that city. It ridicules the passion for war then ruling the hearts of all Christian princes; skilfully denounces by comparison the crying injustices done to the laboring classes by society and the laws which "confer benefits on the gentry and care to do nothing at all for peasants, colliers, servants, wagoners, and mechanics, without whom no state could exist." He points out that in England only four people in ten could read, and proposes as a better ideal, not an ignorant nation divided into jealous classes of rich and poor, but a true community, comfortable and educated throughout. He suggests as one means of accomplishing this to so repress idleness, restrict luxury, and manage work that the hours of labor should be confined to six a day for each male. He proposed sanitary reform to stop the plagues, and hints at other improvements which have become matters of course to us of these latter days. Through all the work he shows the firm faith that the teachings of Christ and the guidance of reason are workable, fitted, if men would only live by them, to establish a Kingdom of God upon earth.

With Erasmus this desire to propagate the philosophy of Christ turned in the direction of scholarship. Not, indeed, that the acute writer, who had learned from books and letters a thorough knowledge of the world, neglected the idea of political reform. His " Praise of Folly," which ran through seven editions in a few months, was a classic treatment of the theme handled by Brant in the chaotic " Ship of Fools "; and his " Christian Prince," written for the young Charles, afterward Emperor of Germany, is, as has been well suggested, the opposite to " The Prince " of Machiavelli, then lying in manuscript. He bids the Prince secure " the favor of God by making himself useful to the people, for the duties between a prince and his people are neutral." But these were simply the pastimes of a hard worker. The labor of his life was the New Testament in Greek; not the first Greek Testament finished by the New Learning,— for the Complutensian polyglot was ready a few months earlier,—but the first to be put in circulation.

His preface to the great work makes clear his hope to oppose two evils: first, the pagan tendency of the age, which, while straining the human mind to master all subtleties and toiling to overcome all difficulties, neglects, derides, and treats with coldness the philosophy of Christ; second, the tendency of the Old Learning to substitute the schoolmen for the gospels. " What are Albertus, Alexander, Thomas, Ægidius, Ricardus, Occam, compared to Christ or Peter or

Paul or John? If the footprints of Christ be anywhere shown to us, we kneel down and adore. Why do we not rather venerate the living and breathing picture of him in these books? If the vesture of Christ be exhibited, where will we not go to kiss it? Yet his whole wardrobe could not represent him more vividly than these writings. We decorate statues with gold and gems for the love of Christ. These books present us with a living image of his holy mind."

The publication of this New Testament, which was also a sort of commentary, had been much opposed by the party of orthodoxy, and the grounds of opposition are clearly expressed in a letter of Martin Dorpius, of the University of Louvain, which beseeches Erasmus, "by our mutual friendship and your wonted courtesy, to desist from this attempt to supplement the Latin New Testament with a Greek version which amends the Vulgate." Dorpius asserts the folly of such an attempt to correct a version which has in it no errors or mistakes. "For this is the version used and still used by the unanimous Universal Church, and it cannot be that she is mistaken." "How could it be possible that the heretic Greeks could have preserved a truer text than the orthodox Latins?" "Besides," he continues, "there is great harm in your attempt. If you discuss the integrity of the Scriptures many will doubt; for, as Augustine said to Jerome, 'If any error should be admitted to have crept into the Holy Scriptures, what authority would be left to them?' Therefore, I beseech you, limit your corrections to those passages of the New Testament in which you can substitute better words without altering the sense." [1]

In spite of these alarmed remonstrances the book appeared with a dedication, by permission, to the Pope, and was received with acclaim. Letters came to Erasmus from all sides; among them a poem from Philip Melancthon, a young student of Tübingen, who was already known among his fellows as " the second Erasmus."

To this chorus of praise there was strong dissent. The reactionary orthodox party of course objected bitterly, and Erasmus's enemies were loud against him. Edward Lee, an Englishman, attacked him for many errors, among them the omission of the text on " the three that bear witness in heaven "—which must, Lee said, result in a revival of Arianism and schism in the Church.

And there were other objections in a more kindly spirit. Martin Luther, a young professor of theology at Wittenberg, wrote to his friend Spalatin how much he regretted the evident preference of Erasmus for following Jerome in seeking the historical (he calls it the dead) sense of Scripture rather than the spiritual method of Augustine. " The more I study the book, the more I lose my liking for it. Erasmus, with all his learning, is lacking in Christian wisdom. The judgment of a man who attributes anything to the human will is one thing, but the judgment of one who recognizes anything but grace is another."

---

[1] In 1512 Faber Stapulensis had felt obliged to defend himself, in the preface to his commentary on Paul's Epistles, against the charge of temerity because he had dared in comments to add to the text of the Vulgate the sense of the Greek.

"Nevertheless," he continues, " I carefully keep the opinion to myself, lest I should play into the hands of his enemies."

Dr. Eck, the young professor of theology at Ingolstadt and a correspondent of Luther, wrote also to their common friend Spalatin his objections to the *Novum Instrumentum.* They applied not so much to its theology as to its critical method. Erasmus had pointed out that the apostles, quoting from memory, were not always exact in citing the Old Testament. He had also said that their Greek was not classic. Eck objects to the first remark on the Augustinian ground that to admit error destroys authority, and to the second because it attributes negligence or ignorance to the Holy Spirit. In conclusion he hopes that Erasmus would read Augustine more and Jerome less. Spalatin sent this letter to Erasmus, who replied in a friendly tone to the friendly remonstrance. He was publishing a splendid new edition of Jerome for the purpose of showing that the methods and results of his interpretation were not novelties, but had the authority of the father who gave the Church the Vulgate. Of course he could not surrender his deliberate preference, but he hoped that, as Jerome and Augustine had differed without ceasing to be friends, he and Dr. Eck might imitate their holy example.

Faber Stapulensis, who, when Erasmus settled at Basle in 1513, had written him a letter, brief but full of congratulations, praying that his life might be prolonged to enlighten the world with his labors, accused Erasmus of folly, ignorance, and vanity because he had suggested that doubts had been entertained as to the Pauline authority of the Epistle to the Hebrews. Erasmus had criticised points in Faber's commentary on the Pauline Epistles, published in 1512, and the bitterness of this tone was doubtless due to the touchy vanity which is always the weakness of scholars, and which the most distinguished men of the sixteenth century had no shame in displaying. Erasmus himself too often whines like a spoiled child over the injustice of fate or the lack of appreciation of a world which flattered him incessantly.

Faber was by this time a great figure among men of letters. In 1513 Reuchlin had written to him as the "restorer of Aristotle, the glory of whose works is everywhere," begging that he would present to the Sorbonne his defence against the charge of heresy brought by the theologians of Cologne. He had been gathering around him in Paris a little knot of scholars, chief among whom was Guillaume Farel, born of a noble family of Dauphiné in 1489. Faber led these in pious exercises, frequently going with Farel to pray in the churches and make offerings of flowers at the shrines of the saints. His best lectures were upon the Psalms and the Epistles of Paul, on which he published a commentary, in 1502, which emphasizes the doctrine of justification by faith. Though his devotion to the Church and his hatred of schism remained unbroken, there grew upon Faber a conviction of the evilness of the times and a hope of better things. He seems to have shared the conviction of his correspondent, Erasmus, that reason and the Word of God would dispel the reigning darkness; for Farel has told us how earnestly he used to say, "William, the world is to be renewed, and you will see it." Among his favorite scholars was the son of Briçonnet, a great officer of state who, on the death of his wife, took orders and became a cardinal. Guillaume Briçonnet became bishop and abbot while still young, and made his abbey a seat of letters devoted to religion. It was there that Faber finished, in 1509, his commentary on the Psalms.

Bound to this circle of French Humanists and to Erasmus and his friends at Basle by a lively correspondence was a Swiss who at an early age began to win distinction in letters. Ulrich Zwingli had been born in 1484 in the Alpine village of Toggenburg, of which his father was chief magistrate. His uncle, dean of the cathedral of a small city near by, took the boy into his house and directed his education at the newly opened school. At the University of Vienna he fell under the power of the New Learning, and at the age of twenty-three was called to be pastor of the city of Glarus. He displayed power as a preacher, and strove to use in that exercise of his office all his knowledge, even learning the history of Valerius Maximus by heart to furnish historical illustrations. He soon became possessed of the best library in the vicinity, and as learning was scarce, the fame of his scholarship spread. He also made himself much beloved by the charm of his personality, which was heightened by skill in music; and a young friend, inviting him to his magister banquet at Basle, playfully addressed him as "the Apollonian lute-player and recognized Cicero of our age "—a jest only in form, for he was already hailed as " the first to acclimatize Humanistic studies in Switzerland," and Erasmus wrote to him as one " who, with his friends, would raise the Fatherland to a higher grade of education and morals." These great labors and pleasures were broken by sterner duties when Zwingli marched as chaplain with the city company to support the banner of the Pope at Novara (1513) and Marignano (1515). It was just before the last battle that his powerful sermon in the market-place of Monza hindered the main body of the confederates from accepting the bribes of France and deserting the League on the eve of battle.

Amid all these labors there had been growing in him an ever-increasing devotion to the study of the New Testament. The writings of two men were especially influential in directing his thoughts in this direction. He had the works of Pico della Mirandola in the edition published by Wimpheling at Strassburg in 1504. Even as a student at Basle, Zwingli had gotten into trouble by confessing his agreement with some of the condemned theses of Pico, and now, as a man, he busied himself much with his writings. The works of Erasmus were all in his hands as fast as they appeared; the " Enchiridion," the " Praise of Folly," the "Adages," and all the tractates, were his familiar companions; and when he visited Erasmus in Basle in 1515 he could greet him as an old friend and master. Zwingli said afterward that Erasmus first made him aware of the evils which had gathered around the worship of saints and relics, and pointed out the absence of all allusion to such practices in the Bible. It was from these suggestions that Zwingli became sure, about the year 1515, that "Christ is the only Saviour, comfort, and treasure of our poor souls."

Soon after, his outspoken condemnation of the French alliance, which, in his judgment, put the free confederacy in the hands of the French King, so offended some of the magistrates of Glarus, whom he denounced as takers of bribes, that he accepted a call to be preacher at the abbey of Einsiedeln. Since the fifteenth century the wonder-working statue of Einsiedeln had made it the centre of annual pilgrimages from all South Germany. The riches thus brought to the cloister coffers had wrought great inroads in the simple life of the monks. But the officials by whom Zwingli was called had repressed open scandals, and the abbot, while taking little personal interest in religion, was glad to have good sermons, and pleased that the abbey should become, under Zwingli and his friends, a centre of Humanism in Switzerland. It was very straight preaching the pilgrims heard from the new incumbent; not polemic, but the proclamation of positive truths whose acceptance would have closed the shrines and stopped the pilgrimages. The administrator of the cloister was in entire sympathy with the straightforward preaching, and also joined Zwingli in his literary studies, for which he made large purchases of books from Paris, Basle, and the other German presses. An extensive correspondence united the little circle of learned men with the literati of Basle, at whose head was Erasmus, and the circle of Faber Stapulensis, whose comment on the Psalms was one of Zwingli's favorite working books.   But when the New Testament of Erasmus appeared Zwingli turned to it, and we are told by one of his friends that he learned the Greek text of Paul's Epistles by heart.

He was able to be quite a buyer of books, because since his sermon at Monza he received from the Pope a yearly present of fifty florins, which he used, perhaps by Leo's wish, for the increase of his library.

PERIOD III.

CHAPTER XXIII.

THE COURT OF LEO X.—HUMANISM IN ITALY AND SPAIN—THE THREE BOY KINGS.

OR Leo shared his good fortune with generous hand. His life was mirthful and splendid. He ate little himself, fasting three times in the week, but he entertained royally, and his table cost him ninety-six thousand florins, or more than half the yearly income of the estates of the Church and seven times the total yearly salary of all the professors of the University of Rome. But he gave no banquet as splendid as that to which he was invited by his banker, Chigi, in honor of the christening of an illegitimate daughter. At the end of every course of the feast the gold and silver plate was thrown out of the windows into the river—to be caught by nets hidden beneath the water.

These Papal banquets were adorned by poetry. The recital of extempore verses was a common amusement of Leo, and he often joined in the contests himself. A perfect swarm of poets lived on him, and, like Nicholas, he gave even to the bad ones. With the latter he was not above a practical joke;

for a certain Baraballo, who recited atrocious verses to his own unbounded delight, was crowned poet and led in mock triumph through the city mounted on an elephant, the gift of the Portuguese King, whose navigators had brought it round the Cape from India. Leo would not allow the train to approach the Vatican, but his zest in the colossal joke, in which the whole court joined, is marked by the figure of the elephant on the door between two of the rooms decorated by Raphael.

The Pope's favorite amusement was music. He sang well himself, and often joined in the concerts, to which he listened as in a dream of delight. It was at such times that he was most unbounded in his gifts. He took great pleasure also in acting, and his friends and household presented comedies before him, for which Raphael sometimes painted scenes and arranged decorations. These were frequently of a free tone, and the Pope's presence at them often gave offence to the ambassadors and other visitors. Leo applauded and rewarded successful authors and actors, but he had a monk whose piece was a failure severely tossed in a blanket before him. He was very fond of cards also, and his losses and the presents he made amounted to sixty thousand florins a year—more than twelve times the amount Raphael was paid for his work in the four great frescoed rooms of the Vatican, and ten times what Michael Angelo had received for painting the Sistine Chapel.

Of course no finances could stand such a strain as this. Leo had a regular income of between four and five thousand florins. In addition he sold between twenty-five and twenty-six hundred offices, which brought during eight years and a half a total of nearly three million florins. But he left debts amounting to nearly twelve hundred thousand ducats. Under his successor the ordinary expenses of the Roman State were reckoned at three hundred and fifty thousand florins, so that in eight years and a half the Pope spent on the conquest of Urbino, and other personal and family expenses, about four million florins, or an average of seven times the income of Agostino Chigi, who, with seventy thousand florins a year, was reckoned the richest merchant banker of Italy.

For part of this huge shower of gold scattered with liberal hand Leo received an extraordinary return. The age of Augustus is not rendered more illustrious by the writings of the men he patronized than the age of Leo by the works of the masters of the arts of design whom he employed; and in the popular mind he is remembered, not as the Pope under whom Switzerland and Germany broke away from the Papacy, but as the Pope for whom Bramante, Michael Angelo, and Raphael worked. Neither the glory nor the blame can be laid at his door. He found the immortal three in Rome when he ascended the throne, and he only continued to employ them on the designs of Julius II.; and the revolt of Germany and Switzerland was the outcome of European movements working in England, France, and Germany, which we have seen beginning years before.

Another glory of the court of Leo, which, unlike the undimmed pictures of Raphael, has now faded, was the fame of the litterateurs and scholars who surrounded him.   Rome usurped, under his rule, that unquestioned literary supremacy which she had for some years shared with Florence.   His generous patronage made the Eternal City a veritable paradise of the Humanists.   Next to a well-filled purse a skilled pen was the best recommendation to ecclesiastical preferment.   The chief novelists and historians of Rome were bishops or at least apostolic secretaries, and among the cardinals and their friends were many men distinguished for literature.

These Roman lovers of letters and the arts fall naturally into the three classes we have noted before among the Humanists.

It is difficult to label the most distinguished stylist of his day—Pietro Bembo, Leo's secretary, and twenty-five years later cardinal under Paul III.—as anything but a pagan.   His learning was never turned in the direction of the fathers or the Bible, nor were his philosophical discussions directed toward any of the questions of the day in Church or State.   For every exhortation he turns, not to the New Testament, but to the holy character and teachings of a Socrates or a Plato.   It is quite in keeping with all we know of him that he should write to his friend Sadoleto, begging him to hurry up his work on St. Paul's Epistles and turn to Hortensius; for, he adds, "The barbaric style of Paul will ruin your taste. Stop this child's play, which is unworthy of an earnest man."

This Jacopo Sadoleto, Bishop of Carpentras, afterward, like Bembo, cardinal under Paul III., is a good

representative of the Middle Party, whose effort was
to reconcile ancient philosophy and the Bible. He
answered his friend Fregoso, who blamed him for
diverting any time from the study of the Holy Scriptures: " The knowledge of liberal arts and philosophy
must be regarded as a distinguished part of true
wisdom, as steps for those who will mount to God."
" For," he asks, " do you believe you will find in the
nature of things or in any branch of science anything
which escaped the all-embracing knowledge of Plato
or the intellectual sharpness of Aristotle ? " ·But he
finds the stay of his life, not " in the teaching which
we owe to Aristotle and Plato, but to God, the teacher
and Creator of all." " In him alone is the hope of
life." " Only God can help and hold in trouble.
Only in gratitude to him can we lead a happy and
useful life." Out of this double love of philosophy
and religion came his two chief works, " The Praise
of Philosophy " and " The Commentary on the
Epistle of Paul to the Romans." It is probable that
among the cardinals Contarini and Caraffa shared his
views and hopes of a philosophy of Christ. Sannazaro,
the famous Neapolitan, called the Christian Virgil,
who crowned his popular eclogues of love and friendship with a poem on the birth of Christ, over which
he spent twenty years and his best energies, was
much admired by this circle.

We find the representative of that conservative and
strictly orthodox Humanism which desired to use the
New Learning only as a weapon for the defence of
Christianity and the Church in the person of Hadrian
of Corneto. It is a puzzle as yet unsolved by the

writers who have alluded to it (e.g., Janitschek, Gebhardt, Springer, Grimm, *et al.*) why Hadrian of Corneto wrote the book "On True Philosophy," which was published in 1507. He had long been the friend and follower of Rodrigo Borgia, and when his patron had become Pope rose rapidly in the scale of curial promotion until he obtained the red hat. Bramante built him a magnificent palace, and his riches caused the report that Alexander and Cæsar died from changing the cups in an attempt to poison him in his own garden. He mingled in curial politics, had to flee from the wrath of Julius II., and was aware of the plot to assassinate Leo X. In consequence of this complicity he fled from the city, was deposed *in contumaciam*, lived in Venice, and, returning to the conclave at Leo's death, was murdered on the road by his servant. He was the author of a poem on "The Hunt," which was much admired, and a book on "The Method of Speaking Latin," which went through many editions and is called one of the most solid productions of Italian Humanism. It is difficult to understand why such a cardinal should write a book opposing worldly learning and the study of philosophy, except to confess an inner conviction denied in his life. But such is the purpose of his "De Vera Philosophia," a catena of quotations from Ambrose, Jerome, Augustine, and Gregory the Great.

He begins by asserting that the source of faith and knowledge is the Bible—that there can be no true knowledge without faith and that human reason is powerless for divine things. He goes on to demand an implicit faith in the word of Scripture and to limit all knowledge by it : " For what Scripture leaves hidden human presumption may not attempt to understand by conjecture." Scripture is a field on which, if we wish to build, we must dig steadily until we reach the rock which is Christ. None but those who have received God's Spirit understand his Word. Dialectics must be cast aside, and the ornaments of rhetoric are to be despised. " If you ask me the circumference of the earth, I gladly confess I do not know, and it would do me no good to know. The free arts do not deserve the name, for only Christ makes free. The works of the poets, the wisdom of the worldly, the pomp of style, are the devil's food. What has Aristotle to do with Paul, or Plato with Peter? At the last judgment the foolish Plato and his scholars will be summoned, and the proofs of Aristotle will avail him little. Not by the philosophers is true wisdom. Though they count and measure the stars, though they labor at grammar, rhetoric, or music, it is of no avail. They are only truly wise when they believe on Christ. There is no middle ground. Who stands not by Christ stands by the devil. Whoso is not in the kingdom of God is lost. Why shall I speak of physics, ethics, or logic? All that human tongue can say is in Holy Scripture. Its authority is greater than the power of the whole human spirit."

Already, at the beginning of the sixteenth century, there was stirring in Roman Humanism the spirit of the Catholic Reform. For in Sadoleto we see the complete union of letters and religion afterward to be shaped into the elaborate educational system of the Jesuits, while Hadrian's book foretells the fiery zeal of implicit orthodoxy, despising all things in comparison to the fathers, the Church, and the Bible, which was to mount the throne in Paul IV.

This type of prelate, using knowledge in the service of an orthodoxy which loved existing institutions and desired to reform them, appears at this time in two men illustrious in the service of Spain. Both were learned, one in the Old Learning, the other in the New; one thought Humanism dangerous, the other welcomed it; but both were alike in their devotion to the Church and their desire for reform.

Hadrian Dedel was born in Utrecht in 1459. He received his education at Deventer and Louvain, where he studied especially Thomas Aquinas and Peter Lombard. As a young licentiate his lectures and skill in disputation won him a large fame, which led the Grand Duchess Margaret to give him money to take his degree and become professor of theology. The fruit of his studies appeared in a commentary on Peter Lombard and in a collection of scholastic discussions entitled " Questiones Quodlibeticæ "—a love of the Old Learning which he never lost, for in 1515 he wrote advising the destruction of the books of Reuchlin. Hadrian's reputation for learning and piety induced the Emperor Maximilian to appoint him tutor to his grandson Charles. The other grandfather, Ferdinand the Catholic, to whom he was sent as ambassador, appointed him Bishop of Tortosa in 1515. He had won the affection of his pupil in spite of his steady opposition to Charles's desire to spend more time in knightly exercises than upon books. For the young Prince, not being endowed by nature with a pleasing presence, labored hard to attain the perfect horsemanship which he displayed in his stately entries. When Charles succeeded to the throne of Spain he associated Hadrian with Cardinal Ximenes in the management of the affairs of his kingdom, and shortly afterward Leo X. made him a cardinal.

This Cardinal Ximenes, now eighty years old, was one of the ornaments of the College, though his honors and duties kept him from Rome. He displayed that union of patriotism, zeal for the Church, and love of letters which during the next century, the blooming-time of the Spanish race, was to be characteristic of its greatest men.

He was born in 1436, of a noble family of fallen fortunes, and graduated in theology from the University of Salamanca, where he lived for six years as a private tutor. At the age of twenty-two he went to Rome, where his knowledge of canon law enabled him to live as a consistorial advocate. He returned after six years with letters *expectivæ*, which gave him a claim upon the first vacant benefice in the see of Toledo. These letters had frequently been denounced as an abuse, and were suppressed by the Council of Basle, but as the Pope denied its authority, they were still granted. The historic objections to the abuse of the *expectivæ* strengthened the Archbishop of Toledo, who wished to confer the first vacant benefice upon an ecclesiastic of his household, in resisting the Papal grant. He imprisoned Ximenes for six years, vainly endeavoring to wrest from him the surrender of the benefice. At the end of that time, despairing of bending the will of the prisoner, the Archbishop gave him freedom and permitted his induction. Ximenes wisely exchanged his benefice for one in another diocese, where he soon rose to be vicar-general. But, displeased by the care of the details of the episcopal jurisdiction, he joined the strict Franciscans, and dwelt for many years in a hermitage, where he formed the ascetic habits which he practised all his life. From this retreat he was called to be confessor of the Queen, and shortly after was elected provincial of his order for Castile. In his new dignity he kept to the strictest letter of the rule of St. Francis, traveling on foot, and often begging his food. He soon received the appointment to the Archbishopric of Toledo, which made him at once Primate of Spain, head of the nobility, and the richest subject in the kingdom. He gave great offence by refusing to assume the state usual to his office, and still traveling on foot or by a mule, with one attendant. A letter was obtained from the Pope commanding him "outwardly to conform to the dignity of your state of life in your dress, attendants, and everything else relating to the promotion of that respect due to your authority." Henceforth his state was royal, but he always wore a hair shirt under his robes, and he used the monkish scourge so severely on himself that his friends had to procure another letter of remonstrance from the Pope.

He first signalized himself by zeal for the conversion of the Moors, but recently become Spanish subjects under the treaty of Granada. He frequently invited to his palace the Moorish teachers and conferred with them on religion. "To impress his instructions upon their sensual minds, he did not hesitate to make them presents of costly articles of dress, etc., and to do this encumbered his revenues for years. The conversion of some of these alfaquis was quickly followed by the conversion of great numbers of other Moors, so that after laboring only two months Ximenes was able to baptize four thousand people, in December, 1499." [1] He also burned eighty thousand Moorish books in the market-place of Granada, sparing only the works on medicine, and defended his action against those who condemned it as a violation of the treaty of surrender made with the Moors, and the edicts of the Synod of Toledo, by which no Moor was to be forced to embrace Christianity. He felt himself restrained by no treaty against the descendants of renegades who had been converted to Mohammedanism from Christianity during the Moorish dominion. The children of all such though in a remote generation, he seized, carried off, and forcibly received them into the Church. An attempt to thus arrest a Moorish young woman raised a mob which killed the Archbishop's officer. The courage of the Governor allayed the tumult, and Ximenes persuaded the King to offer to the inhabitants of the guilty city the choice of being baptized or suffering the penalties of treason. They chose the former, and thus in about a year Ximenes converted Granada.

His associate in these labors, the Archbishop of

---

[1] "Cardinal Ximenes," by Dr. von Hefele, afterward Roman Catholic Bishop of Rothenburg.

Granada, had caused the Holy Scriptures and other religious works to be translated into Arabic. But Ximenes drawing his attention to the danger likely to arise in the minds of the rude and ignorant from the reading of the Bible, it was decided to withdraw the Arabic Scriptures and circulate only the safer literature of devotion and edification.

Meanwhile the Primate had been turning his energies to the direction of the reform of education, and became the most munificent of the long roll of patrons and founders of schools which adorns the reign of Isabella. His great University of Alcala, begun in 1500, was opened about ten years later. The head college of San Idlefonso had thirty-three professors, one for each year of the life of Christ, 'and twelve chaplains, one for each of the twelve apostles. Ample provision was made for the study of Latin, Greek, and Hebrew according to modern methods, and the whole University was magnificently endowed. Within twenty years it numbered seven thousand students.

It was with the aid of this corps of scholars that Ximenes began the Complutensian polyglot. The ideas which moved him to the work are set forth in its preface: " No translations represent perfectly the sense of the original. The transcripts of the Vulgate differ so much from one another that it is necessary for us to correct the Old Testament by the Hebrew text and the New Testament by the Greek text. Every theologian should be able, also, to drink of that water which springeth up to everlasting life at the fountainhead itself. This is the reason, therefore, why we have ordered the Bible to be printed in the original language with different translations. Our object is to revive the hitherto neglected study of the Sacred Scriptures." Upon this work he is said to have spent one hundred and twenty-five thousand dollars, whose purchasing value was perhaps five times what it is now. It was dedicated to Leo X. The New Testament appeared before Erasmus's, but did not circulate outside of Spain until after his. One of the editors, Zuniga, having sharply attacked the notes of Erasmus and spoken contemptuously of the northern scholar in the presence of Ximenes, the Cardinal said: "God grant that all writers may do their work as well as he has done his. You are bound either to give us something better or not to blame the labors of others." The New Testament volume contains the Vulgate and a Greek text, with a system of notation indicating corresponding words in the two languages. The four volumes of the Old Testament contain the Hebrew, the Septuagint, the Vulgate, the Targum of the Pentateuch, and Latin translations of the Septuagint and the Targum. The work is accompanied by Hebrew, Chaldee, and Greek lexicons and grammars. Only six hundred copies were printed, and it soon became rare; but its influence passed on through the Antwerp and Paris polyglots, until all were replaced by the London polyglot of 1657.

But the work of Ximenes was not confined to missions, education, or patronage of sacred literature. He spent his enormous income freely in public works, churches, convents, and a great aqueduct for

his native town.   It was not long after he became
Primate of Spain that he conceived the idea of a new
crusade, and tried to rouse the kings of Spain, Portugal, and England.   But he was obliged to content
himself with a small crusade, which he led himself
against Oran, a Moorish town of North Africa grown
rich by piracy.   He equipped the expedition of fourteen thousand men at his own expense.   The city
was taken at the first assault, and the inhabitants,
men, women, and children, put to the sword.   The
expedition returned with five hundred thousand
florins and eight thousand captives, having added a
new province to the Spanish crown.

On the death of Ferdinand it was natural, therefore, that Ximenes should be appointed Regent of
Spain until Charles should return from Flanders to
be crowned.   But scarcely had the new King reached
Spain than he retired the great Cardinal from the
service of State, and a few weeks later Ximenes died.
The exact cause of his abrupt dismissal is not known,
but probably the old man of eighty-two was not
flexible to the plans of a new government headed by
an ambitious boy.

For the destinies of Europe were at this time
mingled with the ambitious dreams of three boys,
each anxious to display his skill and the power of his
new kingdom.

The ablest of the three was Charles I., King of
Spain.   His grandfather, Ferdinand, had married
Isabella of Castile, conquered Navarre, expelled the
Moors from Granada, and thus united Spain from the
Pyrenees to the Mediterranean.   And in the partition

of Italy he had added to the possessions of his house the crown of Naples and Sicily, while the discoveries of Columbus and the bull of the Pope made him master of the gold-mines of the New World. Through his paternal grandmother, daughter of Charles the Bold, Charles was heir to the Netherlands, whose cities had succeeded Venice as the centre of European trade, and Burgundy, which is now the northwest corner of France. He was also the heir of his grandfather, the Archduke of Austria. Thus in 1516, at the age of sixteen, he inherited a power greater than any prince since Charlemagne.

England, whose terrible civil War of the Roses closed with the fifteenth century, was ruled by Henry VIII., a beautiful and talented Prince of twenty-five, the patron of More, Erasmus, and Holbein, but self-indulgent and possessed, in spite of his common sense, by a restless thirst for distinction.

France, to which the great vassal duchy of Brittany had just been organically united, was in 1515 inherited by Francis I., at the age of twenty-one. He was an apt pupil of the culture of the Renascence, and not slack in the practice of its vices, from which his two predecessors died. He was a skilful jouster, and aspired to be the first knight of Europe. This desire was flattered in the battle of Marignano, which, as we have seen, resulted in restoring French rule over the duchy of Milan and bartering the liberties and income of the French Church to Leo X.

At the death of Maximilian, King of the Romans (a title borne by the Emperor elect of Germany until he was crowned at Rome), all three of these young kings became candidates for the imperial dignity which gave the honor of the headship of Europe. It was a dignity to which none but a powerful and wealthy prince could venture any longer to aspire, for the office had almost no revenue and little more power to enforce authority than the incumbent could raise from his personal resources. The German Empire was simply a congeries of states and commonwealths, bishoprics, free cities, and dynastic principalities, under an elective head, counselled by a diet of princes and ambassadors, but possessed of no organ of government by which any class of the German body politic, except its jealous and warring princes, could rightly form or express a common purpose. Among the hundreds of members of this loose confederation smaller leagues arose, which, as we have seen in the life of Reuchlin, sometimes maintained common tribunals, sometimes oppressed a weaker member of the Empire. Strife between these dynasties and commonwealths was incessant, nor was it looked upon as civil and unnatural war that Nuremberg should fight with a neighboring city, or a great noble repress with arms the ambition of some usurping bishop. Just before the end of the century, indeed, the Reichstag had endeavored to establish a perpetual land peace, but within ten years a war between the Swabian and the Swiss Leagues desolated South Germany, and another contest over the will of the petty Duke of Baiern-Landshut laid waste the rich provinces of the Rhine.

The choice of the Emperor of this confederation was in the hands of seven electors: the Archbishops of Mainz, Cologne, and Treves, the King of Bohemia, the Duke of Saxony, the Count Palatine of the Rhine, and the Margrave of Brandenburg. These princes knew the value of their votes in this crisis, and the French agents went into Germany followed by a pack-train of gold. When the ambassador protested that such a way to the imperial crown was beneath his King, Francis answered, " If you had to do with people who possessed even a shadow of virtue your counsel would be good ; but in these times whoever wants the Papacy or the Empire, or anything else, can only get it by bribery or force." Henry of England had no chance against his wealthier antagonists. But the Spanish agents were not behind in offering coin and good marriages, which served as well. The bargaining was sharp. The Count Palatine was said to have changed sides six times, and finally wrote that " we cannot do anything better, worthier, more agreeable to Christ, or more wholesome for all Christians than to elect Francis." When the Spanish ambassador told the Archbishop of Mainz that it was a shame to sell himself to France, he replied that Spain could have him by giving more, and, starting at one hundred thousand gulden additional, finally took twenty thousand after three days of chaffering.

To this willingness to sell his vote there was only one exception, Frederick the Wise of Saxony, whose honest patriotism finally brought him from three of the electors the offer of the crown. The Pope urged him to accept, but Frederick was too modest or too wise to do so. For the Pope did not want either of the great competitors to gain the prize. Francis

v

held the key of North Italy in Milan. Charles was King of Naples, and it was Leo's policy to keep the balance of power between them, to play one off against the other and make his profit out of the game. He who had power to crush the other would be too powerful for a safe neighbor to the house of the Medici or the states of the Church.

Charles won the prize, partly because the German people preferred the grandson of Maximilian to an emperor who spoke a foreign tongue; partly, also, because the agents of Francis had put too much weight on the power and wealth of their monarch, his personal strength and skill in arms, his splendid army, and his obedient kingdom. And the electors, who thought little of the Turkish war, but much of their own independence, preferred the weak and silent Charles. So the able, strong-willed, close-mouthed, and zealously pious lad was crowned Emperor of Germany at nineteen, to the wrath of Francis and the despair of the Pope.

PERIOD III.

CHAPTER XXIV.

THE NORTH LOSES PATIENCE WITH THE PAPACY —THE LEADERS OF REVOLT IN GERMANY, SWITZERLAND, FRANCE, AND ENGLAND.

OTH triumphant Emperor and furious Pope were confronted by a force neither was large enough to understand. For, great as Charles was to become in politics and statecraft, he was not one of the rare men, born and not made, who are capable of appreciating or directing the play of those primal social forces whose appearance foretells the change of ancient institutions and the beginning of a new era of history. He could handle skilfully jealous dynastic interests, but he never understood the meaning of patriotism. He could rule well in peace and war as the head of the greatest house in Europe and the God-anointed King of many lands, but he never knew the force of national feeling struggling half unconsciously for liberty. He was a zealous child of the Church, who in his old age turned aside from the glories of earth to prepare his soul for heaven, but he never felt a thrill of the passion for truth which inspires the voices of those who cry in the wilderness.

339

This great man of a narrow type, and the Pope, whose highly cultivated taste was without a touch of creative power, were confronted by a movement whose violence can be compared to nothing else in European history but the Barbarian Invasion and the French Revolution.

The Reformation of Religion in the sixteenth century was a European movement, the result of forces which had been working for generations, and the men who made it were also made by it. It varied almost immediately into separate ecclesiastical institutions and produced different types of theology, but it was not in any sense sectarian. The influence of it is nowhere more visible than in the reform within the ancient Church, known as the Catholic Reaction. This emerged nearly a generation later, at a time beyond the limits of this sketch, but its spiritual source has been briefly indicated in the Humanistic orthodoxy of Spain and Rome. Neither was the Reformation in any sense a national movement. For one hundred years the transalpine world had asked again and again for that "reform of the Church in head and members" which the Council of Constance had left to the Popes. And when Sixtus IV., Innocent VIII., Alexander VI., Julius II., and Leo X. had demonstrated the unwillingness of the Papacy to reform itself, the Council of the Lateran chose that instant to revoke the decrees of Constance and deny the right of the Church to reform the Papacy. The loyalty with which the nations of the north had clung, in spite of almost unbearable rebuffs and disappointments, to the venerable institution of their fathers was exhausted. They were weary of patience. At last they were reluctantly compelled to admit that they were confronted, not by an ecclesiastical theory, but by an intolerable religious situation. They abandoned all hope of reform and ripened rapidly for revolution.

And the men who could give voice and form to this new desire were at hand among the Younger Humanists. They spoke almost simultaneously in four places where we have seen the New Learning firmly established. By 1525 the demand for revolt against the traditional institution of the Papacy, on the ground of the New Testament and the conscience, had been heard from Martin Luther in Germany, from Zwingli in Switzerland, from spiritual descendants of Colet in England, from the friends of Faber Stapulensis in France. And all of these men read the New Testament, on which they based their criticism of existing institutions, in the edition of Erasmus.

Martin Luther was an Augustinian monk who taught theology in the new University of Wittenberg, founded by Frederick the Wise of Saxony. In 1517, when a Dominican by the name of Tetzel came up through Germany selling indulgences for the triple benefit of the Archbishop of Mayence, the banking-house of Fugger in Augsburg, his creditor, and the Papal fund of St. Peter's, Luther was roused, as many men of his day had been, by this abuse of a traditional custom of the Church. Tetzel was forbidden to enter Saxony by the Elector, who had endowed the University by impounding the money gained by a similar

traffic sixteen years before.   But Tetzel approached
as near to the Saxon boundary as he dared and set
up his booth.   Luther, who had already preached
twice to warn the people against buying, published
in October, 1517, ninety-five theses in Latin, intended to provoke an academic disputation upon the
virtue of indulgences.   These theses were addressed
to the learned.   They were heard by the people.
Translated at once, in fourteen days they were read
by all Germany.   Two of the chief prosecutors in
the affair of Reuchlin, which was still dragging its
course through the courts of the Church, immediately
attacked Luther as a heretic, though as a matter of
fact his theses denied no proposition which had
ever been authoritatively established by the Church
as *de fide*.   And his acquaintance, Johann Eck, like
himself trained in the New Learning, vigorous,
able, with a prodigious memory and great dialectic
skill, denounced him in a pamphlet entitled "Obe-
lisks."

Then Luther dropped Latin, always a Saul's armor
to him, and came out in his sermon on "Indulgences
and Grace" in rough, virile German.   For he was
evidently of the opinion of his contemporary, the
Humanist Glarean, of Basle, who said that it was not
possible to describe Tiberius in Latin, but in German
it was easy to call him "ein abgefeimter, ehrloser,
znichtiger Bösewicht."   With this swinging weapon,
which he forged himself (he was the first German to
write great things in his native tongue), Luther smote
his enemies, hip and thigh, from the Baltic to the
Alps.   And when Charles was elected Emperor he

was become, by the testimony of friend and foe, the most noted man in Germany.

In particular the Humanists had rallied to his side, seeing in the assaults made on him a continuation of the battle against Reuchlin. Early in 1519 Christopher Scheurl, a common friend of Eck and Luther, wrote to remonstrate with Eck for attacking Luther: "Thou wilt draw upon thyself the disfavor and hatred of almost all Erasmians and Reuchlinists, all friends of classic studies, as well as the modern theologians. I have just been through several of the chief bishoprics, and find everywhere stately hosts of Martinists."

But had these been the only allies Luther found there can be no doubt that he would have perished at the stake like Huss and Savonarola. It was well for him that he found the support of the German people, rejoicing that at last they had a man after their own heart, who could speak their wrath at a system by which Italian prelates drained their gold for a luxurious court. To this support of the German people Luther soon began to make direct appeal. For slowly in these years he passed through the feeling of a prophet protesting against traditional abuses in a venerable institution, and became possessed by the idea that he was the defender of the truth of the Gospel and the liberty of a Christian people against the false tyranny of a foreign Antichrist. He thus united to the desire for reform that patriotic feeling, speaking to the people in their own tongue, which we have marked as one of the three tendencies observable among German men of letters for the last two generations.

There can be little doubt that progress in this direction was made easier to him by the example of Ulrich von Hutten. Before he left Italy, some months before the posting of Luther's theses, Hutten had arranged to receive a copy of the pamphlet of Laurentius Valla on the so-called Donation of Constantine. This was the first full exposition that the document on which the Dominium Temporale had long been canonically based was a forgery (a fact now universally recognized by all scholars, Roman Catholic and Protestant alike). Hutten printed the manuscript with an ironical dedication to the Pope, who would of course rejoice at the proof that the temporal power, which evil Popes had so frequently misused, was founded in error. He followed this by his "Address on the Turkish War" to the princes assembled at the Reichstag in Augsburg in 1518, in which appears the consciousness that Germany had been drained by Papal taxes for crusades which never marched, when the Germans, if they would, could defend themselves against the infidel. "Therefore," he ends, "if I may say boldly what I think, you must in this war be on your guard against Rome as much as against Asia." Luther was in Augsburg at this time, but Hutten gave little thought to him, regarding the discussion of his theses as only a monk's quarrel. But as the conflict deepened around Luther, Hutten, who cared nothing for the religious questions at issue, began to see in him a German oppressed by the great foe of Germany, and in two pamphlets of the spring of 1520 led the way in the path of an appeal to the nation.

"The Romish Triads" is a dialogue in the course of which one of the speakers repeats the triads of Vadiscus, a traveler returned from Rome. Three things, he says, are banished from Rome—simplicity, temperance, and piety. Three things are demanded by every one in Rome—short masses, old gold, and a licentious life. Of three things no one in Rome cares to hear—of a General Council, of the reformation of the clergy, and of the beginnings of common sense among the Germans. With three things the Romans can never be satisfied—money for bishops' palliums, Papal monthly taxes, and annates. Three things pilgrims are wont to bring from Rome—stained consciences, spoiled stomachs, and empty purses, etc. The hearer listens with applause and closes the dialogue thus: "See in Rome the great storehouse of the world, in which is heaped up what is robbed from all lands. In the middle of it is the great weevil, surrounded by his fellow-devourers, who destroy huge heaps of fruit. They have first sucked our blood, then gnawed off the flesh; now they have come to the marrow and are mashing up our very bones. Will not the Germans take themselves to their weapons and rush on with fire and sword? We give them our gold; we pay for their horses and dogs and mules and the instruments of their vices. With our money they nourish their wickedness, pass pleasant days, robe in purple, bridle their horses and mules with gold, build marble palaces. When shall we gain sense and revenge our shame and the universal ruin?"

The pamphlet entitled "The Spectators" was even stronger. It represents Phœbus and his driver Phaë-

thon halting the chariot of the sun at midday to look
down through the clouds on the earth. They see in
Germany a great gathering in a city. It is a procession bringing in the Papal Legate to the Reichstag at
Augsburg. Phœbus explains to Phaëthon what is hap-
pening, and describes the weakness and the strength
of the different orders of the German people as they
appear in the procession. He finds something to
blame in each, but thinks the priests worst of all.
They own half Germany, do nothing, and spend their
days in idleness. It is a shame for the nation, out
of mistaken piety, to tolerate them longer. Suddenly
they notice that some one is calling up to them
angrily out of the procession. It is the Papal Legate
scolding the sun for not having shone for ten days.
" Don't you know that, as the representative of the
Pope, I have power to bind and loose not only on
earth, but in heaven? " Phœbus answers that he
has heard some such thing, but does not believe it.
Whereupon the Legate calls him a bad Christian and
threatens to excommunicate him unless he makes
confession. Phœbus wants to know what would
happen then, and the Legate suggests several pen-
ances. Phœbus begins to laugh, and the Legate, in
a towering rage, excommunicates him. Phœbus tries
to soothe him by suggesting that he thought it kindness not to shine too brightly, because the Legate
might have things to do which he would not care to
have the Germans see. He answers that he cares
nothing for the Germans, and begs the sun to start
a pestilence among them, that there may be many
empty benefices, so that he and the cardinals can

make some money. Whereupon Phaëthon breaks in to call him a cursed scoundrel, and bids him tell the Pope that if he does not send better legates to Germany the sheep will rise against so unrighteous and bloodthirsty a shepherd. Whereupon the Legate answers with an excommunication. Phaëthon consigns him to the ridicule of the Germans, perhaps to something worse than their ridicule. Then Phœbus bids him drive on.

Hutten followed this modernized bit of Aristophanes by a collection of writings from the end of the fourteenth century, the time of the great schism: protests against Papal abuses, assertions of Conciliar Supremacy, and assertions of academic freedom. They were prefaced by a " Letter to all German Freemen," in which Hutten begged them not to let Luther suffer as other protesters had suffered. "The axe is laid at the foot of the tree. Therefore be of good courage, ye German men, and stand by one another. Do not be frightened, neither fail in the midst of the battle. For in the end we shall win through—we shall win through. Freedom forever! The die is cast."

Within a few weeks of these words appeared Luther's " Address to the Christian Nobility of the German Nation," a deeper note of the same tone, and in the heart of the people there was formed a fixed resolve that, come what might, Martin Luther should not be burned.

The Papal Nuntius to the Reichstag at Worms in 1521 wrote: "Nine tenths of Germany cries, 'Luther,' and the other, 'Death to the Roman Curia,' while

everybody calls, ' General Council.' Compared to
this, the trouble between Henry and Gregory [Ca-
nossa] was an affair of roses and violets." Luther's
journey to Worms, to answer before the Reichstag
on a charge of heresy, was a triumph. Cities threw
open their gates, universities crowned him with honor,
and he entered the hall the elected champion of
German freedom.

There was none of the pomp of Constance in the
crowded and noisy Reichstag, but the situation was
the same. To Luther, as to Huss, the word of the
Church was, " Retract or be burned," and, like Huss,
Luther chose death. Then, according to the agreement, the Emperor gave him a safe-conduct for
twenty-one days, and launched against him the ban
of the Empire. Luther started home, was taken out
of his wagon the second day by five men disguised
as robbers, who rode off with him, and for two years
not a hundred people knew where he was.

Meanwhile Ulrich Zwingli had also been slowly
drifting into revolt against the Papacy. In his case
the schism did not begin with any sudden accusation
of heresy. When he thundered from the pulpit of
Einsiedeln against a vender of indulgences, he had
the approval of his Bishop and the Papal Legate.
It was shortly after this successful protest that (in
the fall of 1518) his name was suggested as preacher
of the cathedral of Zürich. But the appointment
was opposed, as Zwingli's friends wrote him, because
he was accused of the seduction of the daughter of
a respectable man near Einsiedeln. Zwingli denies
the seduction of an honorable woman by acknow-

ledging with shame that he has not kept himself free
from the company of concubines; and this confession
of a fault common to all the clergy of the time was
considered so unimportant that he was elected cathedral preacher of Zürich, though in his penitent letter
he had begged his friend to withdraw his name if it
were thought that by his election "the cause of
Christ would suffer."

He began at once a style of preaching new to the
city. Instead of commenting on texts, he took up a
book of the Bible and expounded it in course from
beginning to end. In this way he went through the
whole New Testament in six years. He was a most
skilful speaker, and had carefully trained his weak
voice until it was flexible and penetrating. To the
logical exposition of the text he added practical
reflections upon the duties of the city at home and
abroad, and attacks upon the abuses of the times.
He had already protested against indulgences, and
when, early in 1519, a certain Samson brought the
traffic into the neighborhood, Zwingli attacked it
fiercely in the pulpit and by protest to the ecclesiastical authorities. The result was an inhibition against
the preaching of Samson by the Bishop of Constance,
an edict refusing him entrance to the country from
the Council of Zürich and the assembled deputies of
the Swiss Confederates, and the whole was crowned by
a Papal letter censuring him for misstatements of the
doctrines of absolution and ordering him to obey the
orders of the Pope's beloved sons, the Swiss Confederates. Such utterances brought to Zwingli the hatred
of the extreme conservatives, but the love of northern

Switzerland; and when the report of his death by the plague spread in the fall of 1519, he was mourned in Basle as "the hope of the whole Fatherland," "the trumpet of the gospel."

It was soon after his recovery from this illness that Zwingli received the writings of Luther which asserted that faith was not bound by any human authority. He was filled with joy to find another stating so bravely and clearly convictions to which he had himself arrived, and he wrote to Luther, calling him David and Hercules in a breath, and mixing up Cacus and Goliath in the approved fashion of an evangelical Humanist.

It was not long before the preacher of Zürich became involved in direct opposition to the will of Leo. When he first went to the city he had desired to surrender his small Papal pension, but the Legate had persuaded him to keep it, on the express condition that it was simply the present of the Pope, who loved learning, to a distinguished scholar, and bound him in no wise to the suppression of opinion. In view of the condemnation of Luther it seemed impossible to receive it, and Zwingli wrote to the Legate positively declining to accept another payment. The next year a Papal ambassador obtained from the Council of Zürich the hire of a legion of mercenaries. Zwingli instantly denounced this sale of lives, which ought to be risked only in defence of the Fatherland to "the wolves who eat men." "Well do these cardinals wear red hats and mantles," he said, "for if you shake them gold pieces fall out, but if you wring them there runs out the blood of your sons and brothers and fathers and friends." And the next year, horrified by a narrow escape from a conflict between their men and another body of Swiss in the army of France, and cheated out of their pay, the Council forbade foreign service to all inhabitants of the canton.

It was soon after this that Zwingli, having in vain sent in a petition to the Bishop, signed by ten priests, asking to be released from the priestly vow of celibacy, as not required by the gospels or practised by the early Church, married the widow of a dead noble-man who lived near him. In the middle of the year he published his first attack upon the principle of unlimited ecclesiastical authority. An attempt by the monks to forbid Zwingli from preaching on certain topics and disturbing the opinions which had the authority of approved theologians, resulted in a resolution of the City Council that the city pastor must preach only what was in the Bible and pay no attention to Duns Scotus or Thomas Aquinas. Five days later the assembled clergy of the canton passed unanimously a resolution to preach only what was in the Word of God. Then, in a pamphlet entitled "Beginning and End," addressed to his Bishop, Zwingli defended the liberty of preaching the Word against all traditional authority. And he closed with the hope that "we may unite as the bride of Christ, without spot or wrinkle, leaving the Church that is nothing else but spot and wrinkle, because the name of God is defamed by her." This was followed by a "Counsel concerning the Message of the Pope to the Princes of Germany," in which he besought them not to surrender Luther, with whose destruction the

Pope would fasten his power upon Germany and the whole world.

Meanwhile, at Paris, even the quiet Faber had fallen into trouble with the orthodox theologians. He published in 1518 a short treatise to prove that Mary, the sister of Lazarus, Mary Magdalene, and the woman who was a sinner were not one and the same person. But the lessons appointed to be read on fast-days implied that they were, and he was attacked for heresy. On the 9th of November, 1521, the theological faculty of Paris declared that any defender of Faber's proposition was a heretic. And a letter of that fall, from a monk of Annecy to a friend at Geneva, reported a conversation of Dominican monks, in which they concluded that there were four Antichrists in the Kingdom of Christ—Erasmus, Luther, Reuchlin, and Faber. Meantime Faber had been fortunately called out of the neighborhood of the heresy-hunters. Briçonnet invited him and several friends to reside at Meaux, the capital of his diocese, and aid in his pastoral labors for the reform of religion. Among those who went with him was Guillaume Farel, who resigned his position of professor of philosophy in order to go. Confident in the friendship and sympathy of the mother and sister of the King, and supported by these scholars, Briçonnet began a reform of the Church in miniature. The neglected pulpits of the city were regularly filled, and Faber began the translation of the Bible into French. The people flocked eagerly to the churches, but the conservatives were filled with wrath to hear the use of holy water for the dead denounced, and the doc-

trine of purgatory rejected as resting only on tradition and not found in the New Testament. Farel
recalled a dozen years later how, on one occasion,
Faber, pleased with the reception of his new commentary on the Gospels, prophesied in company that
the Gospel would spread through all France to repress
human tradition, and a certain monk named De Roma
answered him, " I and the other members of my order
will preach a crusade, and drive the King from his
kindgom by his own subjects, if he permits your
evangelical preaching." And scarcely had the work
begun at Meaux before the defenders of the faith at
Paris were taking steps to recall this erring bishop
from his dangerous paths.

Meantime, in England, a man of about the same
age as Luther and Zwingli was treading in spirit the
paths that led to revolt from the authority of the
Church and an appeal to the New Testament as the
final definition of religion. William Tyndale wrote of
having been educated at Oxford in the days when
" the old barking curs, Duns' disciples, and like draff
called Scotists, the children of darkness, raged in
every pulpit against Greek and Latin and Hebrew,
giving great sorrow to the schoolmasters who taught
true Latin; some, beating the pulpit with their fists
for madness, and roaring out with open and foaming
mouth that if there were but one Terence or Virgil
in the world, and that same in their sleeves, and a
fire before them, they would burn it, though it should
cost them their lives, affirming that all good learning
decayed and was utterly lost since men gave them
unto the Latin tongue." But through Colet and the

w

little knot of Grecians who had just left when Tyndale entered he somehow received the seed of the New Learning.   From Oxford he went to Cambridge, where he may have heard Erasmus, and probably fell in with a student named Bilney, who has recorded that he formed the views for which he died at the stake by reading the New Testament of Erasmus soon after its publication.   About 1521 Tyndale left the University an ordained priest, to act as chaplain to " Sir John Walsh, a knight of Gloucestershire."   The manor church of Little Foxbury was under an Italian bishop who had never been inside his diocese.   The clergy were therefore more given to comfortable orthodoxy than to work, and it is not surprising that at suppers in the hall of the manor this man of the New Learning became involved in debates with them. It being objected by Madam Walsh that those who differed with him were great beneficed clergy, spending from one to three hundred pounds a year, and that it did not stand to reason that a poor clerk like himself, however well he might argue, could really be right in opposing the authority of such dignitaries, Tyndale was put upon some other means of quieting the conscience of his worthy hostess.   And he bethought him of translating the " Enchiridion " of Erasmus, which he presented to her in English as the work of a man high in favor with the Archbishop and King of England.   This seems to have maintained his standing in the manor, and he was able to free himself from a charge of heresy brought against him by neighboring clergymen before the Chancellor of the diocese.

These troubles, which he perceived grew out of the ignorance of his accusers, suggested to him the idea of translating the Bible, not, as Wiclif had done, from the Vulgate, but from the original text. It is reported that when a certain disputant said to him, about this time, " It were better to be without God's laws than the Pope's," Tyndale answered, " I defy the Pope and all his laws." And then added, quoting Erasmus, " If God spare me, ere many years I will cause that the boy who driveth the plough shall know more of Scripture than thou." Such utterances soon made the country-side dangerous for him, and Tyndale went to London in the summer of 1523, hoping to obtain for his translation of the New Testament the patronage of Tunstal, the young Bishop, a friend of More and Erasmus. But Tunstal received him coldly, and despairing of obtaining the episcopal sanction, without which his translation could not be printed in England, he sailed in the spring of 1524 for Hamburg.

PERIOD III.

CHAPTER XXV.

ADRIAN VI., THE HONEST ORTHODOX ECCLESIAS-
TIC—THE OLDER HUMANISTS OF THE NORTH
STAND BY THE CHURCH—THE YOUNGER AP-
PEAL TO THE NEW TESTAMENT—CLEMENT
VII., THE HEIR OF THE MEDICI.

N the 1st of December, 1521, Leo died
suddenly, of malarial fever, in the midst
of the triumph of his politics, having just
received the news that of all Italy only
Genoa still held to France. The first
thought of the conclave of cardinals was for the
privileges of their order and the patronage of the
new pontificate. An agreement was drawn up, that
no cardinal might be arrested without a two-thirds
vote of his peers; that their property should be free
from tax; that every cardinal having less than six
thousand florins a year should receive two hundred
a month from a tax levied upon the cloisters; and
that the offices of the cities of the patrimonium
should be divided according to a detailed schedule
among the cardinals. All having signed the agreement, they proceeded to election.

It was difficult. England, France, and Spain had

their part in the struggle, the great nepots were working each for his own hand, the " younger " cardinals were united in common jealousy of the " older," and the better men were disgusted with the whole situation. When, for instance, Cardinals Farnese, Ancona, and Grassi offered the tiara to Zwingli's old friend, the Cardinal of Sion, he answered, " I do not want to be Pope, but I will vote for no Pope that has a wife "—a threat that silenced the three politicians. In the midst of a frightful wrangle, the Cardinal Medici, pointing out that after so many failures it was manifest that no one present could be elected, nominated the absent Cardinal of Tortosa, Hadrian Dedel. The conclave stampeded, and, to their own astonishment, unanimously elected the former tutor of Charles V. The world was filled with amazement that one with no hand in Roman politics, known for his theological learning of the old school and his ascetic life, should have been made Pope. Everywhere the election was hailed with joy by men who hoped for the conservative reform of the Church. But in Rome there was mourning. The people were enraged at the choice of a " barbarian," and the cardinals could not forgive themselves for electing one who had not signed the agreement concerning patronage and privileges. As they came from the conclave one by one, a howling mob led them to their palaces; and when he reached his door the Cardinal of Mantua bowed politely and thanked them for having used only words instead of stones against one who had been guilty of such a stupidity. A deep gloom settled upon the Papal court as the four thousand officials of Leo, who had paid big prices for their offices, looked forward to the coming of this strict churchman from the barbarous north.

When the Pope (Adrian VI.) arrived in the city, August 31, 1522, he found that he had a difficult task before him. The extravagance of Leo had left the treasury so empty that the cardinals had to pawn the tapestries of Raphael and the silver statues out of the Sistine Chapel to raise funds for the journey of the Legates who informed him of his election, and the mass of Leo's debts, at huge interest, was an almost ruinous burden upon the income of the Church. Rome was also in a frightful state of disorder. The Duke of Camerino had been murdered just outside the gates, and a few weeks before two bravos had been executed who were accounted guilty of one hundred and sixteen assassinations. To bring order out of this chaos Adrian depended on Spain. He came into the city guarded by Spanish troops and accompanied by Spaniards and Flemings to fill the household offices of the Vatican and be his counsellors. The luxurious life of Leo ceased instantly. Adrian's old housekeeper took charge of the cooking, and the Papal table expenses were at once cut down to a florin a day, which he took every night out of his own purse. The palefreniers (grooms to lead the horses) were reduced in number from one hundred to ten. Two French chamberlains and two Spanish pages completed the household. The Pope's first speech in conclave was ominous to the splendid cardinals of Leo. Its refrain was *reform* of the open and great scandals in the Curia, of which all the world spoke. Such economy made the Romans, whose trade had flourished on the luxury of Leo, hate the ascetic and taciturn foreigner; and his speech set every cardinal who loved the politics and patronage of the ecclesiastical machine entirely against the re-former.

Four things claimed Adrian's attention: the reform of the Curia, the heresy in Germany, the crusade against the Turks, and the rivalry of Francis and Charles, which threatened to fill Italy and the world with war. His papers were carried to the Nether-lands after his death and lost; but from what we know of his intentions he tried to manage all of these like an honest churchman, an old-school theologian, and a loyal Spaniard. He would gladly have taken up reform first, and he believed that the clergy ought to receive from the Church incomes only living ex-penses and clothes; but a short time convinced him that, with the debts of Leo to handle and a hostile College of Cardinals, he must go slowly. And the other matters pressed.

In Germany he was disposed to make every con-cession consistent with his ultra-orthodoxy. The abuses connected with the sale of indulgences were open, and admitted even by those who accepted the principle of them. Ximenes had limited the sale in Spain, and even the cardinals had agreed before the election that the privilege of selling should be taken from the Franciscan friars. No one recognized the abuses which had gathered round the Roman institu-tions better than Adrian. To the complaints which came from the German Reichstag at Nuremberg he sent an answer confessing the great sins of the Papacy, promising reform, and urging the princes to let Luther be dealt with according to the ban which had declared him guilty of death.   The Reichstag's answer hailed with joy the promises of the Pope to reform the Church and to unite Christendom against the Turk, regretted the discussions aroused by Luther, but said that nothing but civil war could enforce the ban of the Empire upon him.   It suggested that, under the circumstances, a General Council of the Church should be called in Germany, where every delegate might speak his opinion without fear or favor.   This answer meant a deadlock, for it seemed to Adrian that there remained nothing for a Council to adjudicate.

Scarcely had Adrian been inaugurated before Charles began to foreclose the mortgage on the Papacy which his ready support of his old tutor gave him, and his demands showed that there had been some reason in the thought of those who feared, before Adrian started for Rome, that the Church was threatened with a Spanish Babylonian Captivity. He demanded twenty-eight concessions.   They included the grant of large parts of the regular income of the Spanish Church, the use for the defence of his Moorish conquests of all the money raised in Spain for the crusade, the management of the three great Spanish orders of Spiritual Knights, and such other changes in patronage as made the crown absolute master of the Spanish Church.   In addition he asked that the Pope should censure all who went to the great fair at Lyons, because Julius and Leo had ordered it removed to Genoa with the purpose of weakening the trade of France. Finally he demanded that the Pope should join the league of England, Venice, and Spain against France. To be able to support these demands intelligently, his ambassador filled the Vatican with spies; and so successful was his bribery that every word spoken in the secret counsels of the Church was reported to him. Against this claim Adrian stood out long, in the vain hope that he might preserve the peace of Europe and unite France and Spain against the Turk. Sultan Selim in his will had left to his son the duty of taking first Belgrade and then the island of Rhodes, and from these points of departure on land and sea, of finishing the conquest of Europe. Belgrade fell in 1521, the first year of his reign. And after a heroic defence of eight months by the Knights Hospitallers, the Janizaries entered Rhodes on Christmas day, 1522. A few months later, despairing of making peace between the three young kings thirsty for glory, Adrian entered into the league to defend Italy against the invasion of Francis. Then, on the 14th of September, having seen the Turk capture the outer bulwarks of Christendom on land and sea, he died amid the clash of arms between the Defender of the Faith, the most Catholic King, and the most Christian King.

The cardinals pressed into his room as he lay dying and roughly demanded the key to his treasure-room. But they found only a few silver pieces, some rings of Leo's, and several hundred florins; for Adrian had been penurious, not for himself, but for the Church.

Rome rose in joy at the news of the death of a Pope who was too good, even as they had rejoiced before at the death of one who was too bad. The wits crowned the doors of the honest old man's physician with laurel and the inscription, " To the Liberator of the Fatherland, from the Senate and People of Rome."

But the election of Adrian, though it did not reform the Curia, was at least of service to the Church in hastening the break between the Older Humanists and the men of the radical reform. At his first protest the Humanists of Germany had stood by Luther almost to a man; but when Luther revolted entirely from the Papacy, and began to defend himself from the stake and his cause from extinction by war to the knife, one by one the Older Humanists—all the men whom we have mentioned in that class and many more—fell away from him. But their successors of the next generation were more unanimous in standing by the protest that grew to revolt than their fathers in abandoning it. Reuchlin died shortly after the election of Adrian, having tried in vain to prevent his nephew, Melancthon, from making close friends with Luther, but his younger brother became a firm Lutheran. None hailed the election of Adrian with more joy than Erasmus. " We have a theologian for Pope," he wrote to Zwingli, " and we shall soon see a turn in the Christian cause "; and soon afterward, in answer to Adrian's request, he was sending to Rome his counsel on the situation of the Church and the German schism. In February, 1523, he wrote one of his private letters, which became the property of the world, to explain that he had nothing to do with Luther. He had already broken with Zwingli, and within two years he was at sword's points with both the reformers.

But the men of the radical reform had by that time gone too far to care for lukewarm adherents. In France, in Germany, in Switzerland, even in England, the line had been drawn, and the world was asked to choose between the Christian institutions which had grown into authority by tradition and custom, and the record of the origins of Christianity as interpreted by reason and the conscience.

In January, 1523, Zwingli defended, in a public disputation before the great Council of Zürich, sixty-seven theses, of which the first was: "All who say that the Gospel is nothing without the authentication of the Church err and revile God." And at the conclusion the Council ordered that, "as no heresy had been proved, he and the other preachers of Zürich should continue to proclaim the true divine Scripture according to the Spirit of God."

Already Luther had issued the New Testament in a translation readable by North Germans and South Germans—the first great monument of their common speech and the foundation of a new literature. In the fall of the following year, 1523, the New Testament appeared in French from the pen of Faber Stapulensis, and in the fall of 1525 Tyndale printed at Worms six thousand copies of his English New Testament. Thus in the three chief transalpine tongues the appeal was made to the individual reason and conscience to test the Roman authority by the record of the origins of Christianity. The result among each of these three peoples was schism and revolt, leading to a century of religious war which convulsed all Europe.

In this great conflict Spain was to be the champion of the Papacy, ever striving to maintain or reëstablish its authority. But the able and pious youth of twenty-three who was King of Spain and Emperor of Germany at the death of Adrian did not realize at first the greatness of the spiritual force which was to destroy the power of the Papacy over half Europe. His attention was concentrated upon the prospects of a new and desperate struggle with his rival, the King of France, for the possession of North Italy. It seemed to him of the greatest importance, therefore, to have not only a good Pope, but a Pope friendly to Spain; and at the end of fifty days of conclave, when Giulio de Medici was elected and took the title of Clement VII., his ambassador wrote, "Medici is your creature."

The new Pope, though without any of Adrian's ascetic tendencies, led a very strict life. The Vatican was ruled by the utmost ecclesiastical decorum, and the Pope's musical taste was chiefly indulged in improving the ceremonies of the Church. He also listened gladly to learned discussions at table upon theology or philosophy. He kept himself from simony and was just and punctual in fulfilling his promises. His long experience in ecclesiastical affairs made all men who thought that diplomacy could save the Church expect great things of his pontificate. For it was only after he had obtained power that he displayed the curious mixture of obstinacy and lack of self-reliance which was in him. It was the misfortune of Clement to have been trained in an artificial school and then plunged into a field of action where primal passions of the soul were at work. The maxims of the politics of Machiavelli were made for a world where men were moved chiefly by appetites and the secondary considerations of a highly artificial system. Around Clement were moving the forces of national hatred and patriotic pride, the love of religious freedom, and the spirit of self-sacrifice for venerable institutions. What wonder, then, that his wisdom was worse than ignorance and his trained cleverness the most fatal blundering?

PERIOD III.

CHAPTER XXVI.

THE SACK OF ROME.

THE war between the League and France was pushed with vigor, and in May, 1524, the French General was driven across the Alps. To this victory the Pope, in spite of the pressure of the Spanish ambassador, contributed little, because he did not wish it to be too complete. The Papacy had erected the French kingdom of Sicily to prevent North and South Italy being in the hands of one power, which would then be too strong for it. By the same policy it had gladly seen the kingdom of Naples pass to Spain. If now Charles, Emperor and King of Spain, was to rule in Naples and Milan, would it not be at the cost of that political independence of the Papal States which for fifty years had been the chief aim of all Popes except the barbarian Adrian? So Clement gave but little aid, and secretly urged Venice to follow his example. Then, filled with fright at the triumph of the Emperor, he turned to him with expressions of loyalty and demands for a share in the conquests. But when Francis crossed the Alps the next year with the most powerful army of the generation, fifty thousand men, the Pope closed a secret treaty with him and Venice. All in vain; for in the frightful defeat of Pavia the army of France was destroyed and the King taken prisoner. A month later Clement entered again into alliance with the Emperor, agreeing to join in the defence of Milan against every assailant. But scarcely was the King of France back in his kingdom before Clement was active in favoring the League of Cognac, in which the Pope, England, Florence, and Venice joined to support Francis in breaking the oaths by which he had secured his release from prison.

The Emperor made every effort to withdraw the Pope from the League; offered to give up Milan if Clement and the Italian states would pay the costs of conquering it. He even offered to leave all questions which could not be agreed on by treaty to the decision of the Pope. But Clement was now bent on war, for he had heard that the position of the Spanish army was desperate. They were living in a wasted and hostile country without any line of communication, and serving a crown which, with all its wealth, was in a chronic state of bankruptcy. It seemed to the weak obstinacy of Clement a good time to bring pressure to bear on the Emperor. So the imperial ambassador left the Vatican with threats and sarcasms, and the Emperor fell back on the ancient plan of raising insurrection in the Papal States.

Cardinal Pompeo Colonna, with his brothers and relations, descendants of the old Ghibelline nobility, collected four thousand men and suddenly fell on Rome to seize the Pope. With them came the

Spanish ambassador.   The herald proclaimed, as they
rode without a shot into the heart of Rome, that no
one need fear, for the Colonna were only come to
free Rome from the tyranny of an avaricious Pope.
Clement proposed to meet them on the throne like
Boniface, but was persuaded without much difficulty
to take refuge in the castle of San Angelo.   Colonna's men plundered St. Peter's and the Vatican,
making a booty reckoned at three hundred thousand
florins.   The castle was unprovisioned for a siege,
and the Pope sent for the Spanish minister to make
terms.   He threw himself at Clement's feet, and, expressing his regret for the plundering, gave back the
staff and tiara.   There was nothing for Clement to
do but to grant all that was asked, which he promptly
did, but without the smallest intention of keeping his
word; and with full absolution the Colonna retreated.

Meantime Charles had slackened much in his efforts
to suppress the Lutheran heresy; for he was finding
out the wisdom of that ambassador who wrote from
Rome, in 1520, that he should show some favor
secretly to a certain monk Martin, for he might be
useful in case the Pope refused to join the anti-French
alliance or threatened to withdraw from it.   And
when the Reichstag at Speyer, in the summer of
1526, demanded a General Council of the Church,
and meanwhile left it to each prince and city "to act
in regard to the Edict of Worms [which ordered the
surrender of Luther and the suppression of heresy]
as he hoped and trusted to answer to God and the
Emperor," Charles probably did not mourn very
much at this disobedience to the sentence of the

Church and the ban of the Empire. At all events he had neither leisure nor means to divert from his contest with Francis and his ally, the Pope. And so the German Reformation gained time to develop the strength which enabled it a few years later to defend its life on the field of battle against Church and Empire.

Within a month the Pope had broken the forced convention, excommunicated Colonna and all his house, and put an army in the field against him. Meantime from two sides the Emperor was strengthening his force in Italy. A fleet landed seven thousand Spaniards on the coast of Tuscany, and in the north, Georg von Frundsberg, organizer of the German professional soldiers, was raising an army. These mercenaries, whose fame was now beginning to surpass that of the Swiss, were called the *pious* Landsknechts, though it is difficult to see why. The original members of these bands had been military retainers of the knights whose employment was lost by the decay of the feudal system. They had developed a loose organization, bound by unwritten laws, undisciplined, but with great powers of cohesion. However much they might quarrel among themselves, they stood in thick phalanx, bristling with eighteen-foot spears, against all outside interference. Their rough affection had nicknamed Frundsberg "the father of all Landsknechts," and he had little difficulty in raising among the mountains of Tyrol and South Germany thirty-five companies, amounting to twelve thousand men. The necessary funds he got by mortgaging his own estates for

x

thirty-eight thousand florins.   For future pay he
trusted to the Emperor or to plunder.   They were
a band of wild veterans, commanded by tried captains
of the lesser nobility who had won fame and skill in
the ceaseless wars of a lifetime, and, from the ranks
to the General, hatred of the Pope was almost as
strong as love of plunder.   With forced marches
Frundsberg hurried this army over the Alps by
untrodden paths, his men hauling the stout old
General up the rocks with their long spears, while
their comrades took turns in shoving behind.   He
had neither horses, provisions, artillery, nor money;
but he struck off boldly into the valley of the Po, and,
fighting his way through the Papal mercenaries,
scarcely touched by the inhabitants of the rich and
thickly populated states he traversed, safely formed
a junction with the garrison of Milan, which put the
Duke of Bourbon, its commander, at the head of
thirty thousand men.   He held the roads to Rome
and Florence, threatening to pour his army, maddened by lack of pay and long-whetted appetite for
plunder, now on one city, now on the other.

Then Clement tried to make peace.   It did not
seem a desperate situation.   The League had thirty
thousand men in the field.   The Spanish army was
penniless, cold, and starving.   Long stretches of
hostile country lay between them and the strong
walls of Rome; the burgher militia of the city was
fourteen thousand strong; it was still possible to
squeeze money out of the resources of the Church;
and Italy hated the Spaniard as she hated the
Frenchman.   If Clement had seen the real forces in
his own chosen game of politics he might at least

have lost with honor; but he was one of those politicians who always try to evade realities in the hope that something will turn up. Five days he remained undecided between the ambassador of France and Spain. Then he agreed to a truce.

The news was received in the army of Bourbon with indescribable wrath. The soldiers, cheated of the prospect of plunder which alone had made them bear their desperate hardships and total lack of pay, rose in mutiny. The Spaniards sacked the quarters of the Duke of Bourbon, and threw the golden tabard with his coat of arms into the ditch. Meantime he had taken refuge with Frundsberg and was hidden in a stall of the stable. Three days later it was the turn of the Landsknechts to mutiny. Frundsberg assembled them by beat of drum into a great ring, and stood in the centre to speak to them. He bade them have patience for a month. They answered with shouts of "Gold! Gold!" and lowered their spear-points against him. The insult broke the old soldier's heart. He staggered and would have fallen, but they caught him and helped him to a seat on a drum, while the wrath of the men quickly melted to pity. They laid him across the ass on which he rode during the march, and brought him to an inn near by, but Georg von Frundsberg was done. A year later they got the paralyzed veteran across the Alps to his mortgaged castle of Mindelheim, and he died in a week.

The wild mass of fighting men, as frightful in peace as in war, was left, half starved and unpaid, with no leader who could control them except in battle. Rome was their goal; for in Rome lay the enemy of

Germany, the insulter of the Spanish King, the Pope;
and in Rome were the wines and the women, the
gold and jewels, the silks and satins which would
make up for all hardships and replace their lost pay.
It was a force that was not to be played with for an
instant.   It must be bought off and turned back to
the north, or fought desperately like a herd of wild
beasts.   Poor Clement did neither.   Two hundred
and fifty thousand florins would have paid the first
instalment of the men's wages and halted them.   He
was unwilling to raise it; and having made a truce
with the Spanish Vice-King of Naples, he dismissed
four thousand mercenaries, and sent a message to
the army of Bourbon to offer sixty thousand florins
if they would retreat.   The generals ordered the
captains to ask the men if they were willing.   The
Spanish regiments made answer that they were deeply
laden with sins and must go to Rome to get absolution, and finally Germans and Spaniards bound
themselves by an oath not to intermit the march.
Bourbon sent word to the Pope and the Vice-King
that he was helpless in the hands of his men, and
came on toward Rome.   Then, too late, the Pope
found a desperate courage, entered once more into
league with France, England, and Venice, and made
efforts to arm the Romans and raise mercenaries.
He filled the city with tardy energy and Italy with
futile appeals for aid.

And that ragged and hungry host rolled steadily
along, eating unripe fruit by the wayside, plundering
and burning every city which did not feed them.
On the 4th of May Clement proclaimed a crusade

against them as Lutherans and heretics, and on the next day, forty thousand strong, they pitched their camp before Rome. Their situation was desperate. They had made the country behind a desert, they were in the direst want, the walls were strong, the city was capable of putting fourteen thousand fighting men in the field, and the army of the League was gathering to fall on their rear. It was with the mind of one who dared not fail that Bourbon marshalled the men at midnight. At daybreak, without artillery or proper scaling-ladders, they made the assault. The first rush failed, and the Landsknechts lost six banners. Then Bourbon sprang from his horse, and seizing a ladder made of vineyard staves, started to mount. A ball struck him, and with the cry, " Our Lady! I am dead," he fell. The news only roused the fury of his men. In another wild assault Spaniards and Germans planted their flags on top of the wall in two places at the same moment, and a desperate massacre began. A company of Roman militia lost nine hundred out of a thousand. The Swiss guard of the Pope perished almost to a man; and a maddened band of Spaniards even broke into the hospital of San Spirito and massacred the patients. The Pope was saying mass in St. Peter's when some fleeing Swiss rushed in at the great doors, with the killers hard after them. The attendants hurried him by the covered passage toward the castle of San Angelo, and the cries of his guardsmen cut down at the high altar pursued him. The portcullis of the castle fell upon the stream of fugitives, and two cardinals were afterward drawn up in baskets. Meanwhile Bourbon had died in the church of Campo Santo, crying in his last delirium, "To Rome! To Rome!" That frightful army was loose in the Eternal City, with no one who could hold it in check for a moment.

According to the laws of war which remained unquestioned for generations later, a city taken by assault belonged to the soldiers. They could hold every man, woman, and child in it to ransom, or, if they chose, put them to the sword. And when, the next day, the army, which with all its disorganization was still a frightful fighting-machine, passed from the Leonina over the walls of the city proper, a sack began more pitiless than that of Alaric and the Goths. At the end of three days the Prince of Orange, now ostensibly in command, ordered plundering to cease. But the order was unheeded, and when the soldiers were through it was said that no one over three years was left alive, unless their lives were bought by ransom. A certain bishop bought himself three times, and at last was murdered. The prisoners were dragged about with ropes to beg ransom from their friends, like Cardinal Cajetan, who was hauled and kicked through the streets until he had collected what his captors demanded. When the money was not to be had came torture. A Florentine, unable to endure longer, snatched a dagger from one of his tormentors, killed him and then himself. A Venetian threw himself backward out of a window to escape pain by death. Nothing was sacred to the crowd of Spaniards, Germans, and Italians, drunk with wine, lust, and blood. They stabled their horses in the chapels of St. Peter's, broke open and plundered the coffin of Julius II., played dice on the high altar, and got drunk out of the vessels of the mass. The relics were insulted. A Landsknecht fastened the holy lance-head on his own spear, and a captain carried the cord on which Judas hanged himself back to Germany, where he exhibited it in his village church. One cardinal was taken from his bed, laid out on a bier with wax candles in his hands, and carried to an open grave, where a funeral oration was delivered and the threat made to bury him alive unless he paid the demanded ransom. In one of the market-places drunken soldiers tried to force a poor priest to give the consecrated host to an ass, and he died under their torture. So the smoke of Rome's agony went up to heaven, and the long-hoarded riches of her luxurious palaces became the spoil of the cruel soldiers of Spain and Germany. The booty was reckoned conservatively at over eight million florins; some put it as high as twenty millions.

One month after the storm the Pope surrendered the castle of San Angelo, agreeing to pay as a ransom four hundred thousand florins in addition to the losses of the city. But it was the middle of June before the soldiers could be induced to leave the city, not by commands of their officers, but from fear of famine and the beginnings of the plague. Their new won wealth availed little. By the 1st of September half of the Landsknechts were dead of malarial fever, hunger, and debauchery.

The sack of Rome sent a thrill of horror through the world, for it shocked even that age, when war knew no mercy. But it appears from letters and pamphlets that everywhere earnest men, Protestants and orthodox alike, held it to be a judgment of God upon the sins of the Curia and that policy with which every Pope since Sixtus IV., except the short-lived Adrian, had used the power of the Vicar of Christ in the dangerous game of dynastic politics.

Radically revolutionary thoughts were not wanting to minds which had no connection with the movements of Luther or of Zwingli. From more than one side the counsel came to Charles to abolish the Papacy, to rule himself as Emperor in Rome, and to shape the unity of Christendom into a confederation of national hierarchies which should establish the reforms demanded by the laity under the direction of a General Council. It is not to be supposed that Charles seriously considered this plan. As a pupil of Adrian, who had said that "if by the Roman Church is understood its head, the Pope, it is certain that he can err even in matters of faith," [1] Charles did not believe in the doctrine of Papal Infallibility, which did not become a test of orthodoxy for two hundred and fifty years. But he was too much a man of institutions and too little a man of ideas to make it possible that his zeal for religion should turn toward a plan flattering to his pride, but destructive of so many venerable and sacred forms and sanctions of religious authority. And he was too much of a diplomat to try anything which would have met such powerful opposition from jealous interests. When he heard of the plundering of Rome he put on

[1] "Schaff Creeds," p. 177.

mourning, and wrote to princes and cardinals disclaiming all responsibility and laying the blame upon the treacherous Papal politics and the long curial corruption which had drawn down this judgment of God. But he made no move to free the Pope from the presence of the mutinous army constantly threatening to plunder the city again unless they received the promised pay. To the protests of England and France, fearing that a Council under the lead of Charles would make him too strong for their interests, he paid but little attention; and in November he closed a treaty by which Clement received back the States of the Church in return for a promise of neutrality in the wars of Spain and the League, secured by hostages and the payment of the wages of the army which had sacked Rome. In addition it was agreed that the reform of the Church in head and members should be undertaken by a General Council.

Before the sum agreed was fully paid the Pope escaped the power of the half-mutinous imperial soldiers by fleeing in disguise from the castle of San Angelo, and took up his residence in Orvieto, in want almost of the necessaries of life. Meanwhile Italy was wasted by war from the Alps to the sea, and her cities plundered by all the professional soldiers of the world. In this frightful duel between France and Spain for the possession of Italy the Emperor steadily won. His generals held the fastnesses of the north against every effort of the League, and the French army in the south perished by sword and pestilence before the walls of Naples.

Then, on the 6th of October, 1528, the Pope came
back to the city, escorted by a detachment of Spanish
soldiers.   The streets were burned, ruined, and empty,
for the population, which numbered eighty-five thousand under Leo X., counted now but thirty-two
thousand.   Many of these were beggars.   The minds
of all were filled with memories of loss or insult.   The
glory of the Eternal City was dimmed.   The whole
brilliant company of artists and litterateurs which had
made Rome the centre of the cultured world was
scattered in poverty through Italy, or had died
miserably of hunger, the plague, or the abuse of
avaricious captors.   Clement rode through the city
under a chill twilight rain, while the people watched
him in silence, broken only by reproaches or complaints.   He reached St. Peter's in tears.

One hundred and fifty years after Gregory had
entered the Eternal City on his return from Avignon,
the descendant of the typical family of the Italian
Renascence, the inheritor of Cosimo and Lorenzo de'
Medici, looked out of his plundered palace to see
Rome in ruins, Italy wasted by fire and sword, and
all transalpine Europe threatening revolt against the
Church.

A LIST OF THE POPES AND ANTIPOPES

FROM THE BEGINNING OF THE BABYLONIAN CAPTIVITY TO THE SACK OF ROME.

Avignon.

Clement V., 1305–14.
John XXII., 1316–34.
Benedict XII., 1334–42.
Clement VI., 1342–52.
Innocent VI., 1352–62.
Urban V., 1362–70.
Gregory XI., 1370–78.

The Schism.

Rome.

Urban VI., 1378–89.
Boniface IX., 1389–1404.

Avignon.

Clement VII., 1378–94.
Benedict XIII., 1394–1423.

Popes of the Councils.

Pisa.

Alexander V., 1409–10.
John XXIII., 1410–15.

Rome.

Innocent VII., 1404–06.
Gregory XII., 1406–15.

Paniscola.

Benedict XIII., 1394–1423.
Clement VIII., 1424–29.

Rome.	Constance.	Pisa.
Nicholas V., 1447–55.	Martin V., 1417–31.	Felix V., 1439–49.
Callistus III., 1455–58.	Eugenius IV., 1431–47.	
Pius II., 1458–64.		
Paul II., 1464–71.		
Sixtus IV., 1471–84.		
Innocent VIII., 1484–92.		
Alexander VI., 1492–1503.		
Pius III., 1503.		
Julius II., 1503–13.		
Leo X., 1513–21.		
Adrian VI., 1522–23.		Benedict XIII., 1394–1423.
Clement VII., 1523–34.		

A LIST OF THE HUMANISTS MENTIONED.

Italy.

Francesco Petrarca, 1304–74.

Giovanni Boccaccio, 1313–75.

Italy.

Coluccio Salutato, 1330–1406.
Luigi de' Marsigli, 1342–94.
Giovanni di Conversino.
Chrysoloras (died 1415).

Italy.

Cosimo de' Medici, 1389–1464.
Niccolo de' Niccoli, 1364–1437.
Lionardo Bruni, 1369–1444.
Ambrogio Traversari, 1386–1439.

Guarino da Verona, 1370–1460.
Vittorino da Feltre, 1377–1446.

Poggio Bracciolini, 1380–1459.
Francesco Filelfo, 1398–1481.

Laurentius Valla, 1407–57.

Antonio Beccadelli, 1394–1471.
Ciriaco de' Pizzicolli, 1391–1450.

France.

Jean de Montreuil, 1354–1418.

Nicholas de Clemanges, 1360–after 1435.

Germany.

The Forerunners of German Humanism.

Gregor von Heimburg, 1410–72.
Sigismund Gossembrot, flourished 1452.
Hermann Schedel, 1410–85.
Peter Luder, returned to Germany 1456.

Germany.

The Forerunners of German Humanism.

Alexander Hegius, 1433-98.
Ludwig Dringenberg at Schlettstadt, 1450-90.
Johann Wessel, 1420-81.
Johann of Wesel (died 1481).

Germany.

The Older Humanists.

Conrad Celtes, 1459-1509.
Johann Dalburg (Bishop of Worms, 1482).
Jacob Wimpheling, 1450-1528.
Geiler of Kaisersberg 1445-1510.
Sebastian Brant, 1457-1521.
Johann Reuchlin, 1455-1522.
Desiderius Erasmus, 1466-1536.

England.

William Grocyn, 1442-1522.
Thomas Linacre, 1460-1524.

John Colet, 1466-1519.

Thomas More, 1478-1535.

Italy.

Girolamo Agliotti (born 1412).
Alberto da Sarteano (died 1450).

Italy.

Lorenzo de' Medici, 1449-92.
Marsiglio Ficino, 1433-99.

G. Pico della Mirandola, 1463-94.

Pietro Bembo, 1470–1547.
Jacopo Sadoleto, 1477–1547.
Hadrian of Corneto (died 1522).

France.

Faber Stapulensis, 1455–1536.
Guillaume Farel, 1489–1565.
Guillaume Briçonnet, 1470–1534.

William Tyndale, 1484–1536.

The Younger Humanists.

Ulrich Zwingli, 1484–1531.
Martin Luther, 1483–1546.
Ulrich Hutten, 1488–1523.
Johann Eck, 1486–1543.
Melancthon, 1497–1560.

INDEX.

385